PHEBE ANN COFFIN HANAFORD

A Mighty Social Force

PHEBE ANN COFFIN HANAFORD

1829-1921

Loretta Cody

With

The Reverend Sarah Barber-Braun

Introduction By Alan Seaburg

Library of Congress Cataloging-in-Publication
Cody, Loretta

Phebe Ann Coffin Hanaford 1829 – 1921
Author, Feminist, Minister
Women in Ministry, United States
Women's Club Movement, United States
Woman Suffrage Movement, United States
Universalism, United States

ISBN: 1-4392-5849-X
ISBN-13: 9781439258491

Visit www.booksurge.com to order additional copies.

To
Women in Ministry

TABLE OF CONTENTS

INTRODUCTION

There can be no doubt that if Phebe Hanaford had been alive in January 2009 she would have gone to the inauguration of the first African American president of these United States. Who she would have supported in the primary race – the first serious woman candidate or the first serious African American candidate nobody can say for certain – but once a selection had been made by the voters she would have worked hard and written effectively for that person's election. And would have been proud to have stood on the mall facing the Lincoln Memorial with that great crowd who had gathered to witness this cause for justice and fairness finally realized.

The right of universal suffrage and universal civil rights had been twin themes of her writing and ministering – since the Seneca Falls Woman's Rights Convention of July 1848 and the Civil War. Indeed those causes were also at the center of the message of almost all the Universalist and Unitarian women who had become ministers during the nineteenth century. Their number might have been small and their ministries in some situations fragile – and not appreciated or fully endorsed by their male colleagues – but the women were a bold and determined group. As Hanaford had written in the late 1850s in her diary: "Ministers do not understand women have religious ambitions. When we share our common quest for growth in the love of God we give strength to each other. That becomes our common ground and we will grow from there."

Their story is a drama in three acts. It begins just after the close of the Civil War when our denominations started to ordain a few women – although previously some women – Maria Cook and Sally Barnes Dunn are examples – had done some preaching and other acts connected to ministry. Some of these first ministers – and my friend, the late Dorothy Tilden Spoerl, told me that the word "minister" is neither a male or female term and when using it one should not qualify it by gender – are now familiar to us all: Olympia Brown, Phebe Ann Hanaford, Augusta Jane Chapin, Celia Burleigh, Marion Murdock, Caroline Soule and Florence Buck to name some. An excellent presentation of the lives and work of a group of the women who served churches during these decades – and the challenges that occupied their attention as well as the accomplishments they achieved – can be found in Cynthia Grant Tucker's *Prophetic Sisterhood: Liberal Women Ministers of the Frontier, 1880-1930.* This present biography on Hanaford – while it focuses on one individual – really is a testimony to all of these pioneers in ministry.

One of the goals of Olympia Brown's ministry, she told Phebe Hanaford, was "to pave the way for other women" to be ordained and to serve as parish ministers. This was a goal shared by all her sisters in ministry during this first period and the result is the vibrant ministry now so characteristic of Unitarian Universalism.

When Hanaford was ordained to the Universalist ministry in 1868 – she was the third woman ordained by the Universalists. Julia Ward Howe wrote in the January 8, 1870 issue of *The Woman's Journal* congratulating her and the denomination but warning that "the success of women ministers is very problematical – an experiment, whose result is yet uncertain." This proved to be an accurate assessment of the situation – unfortunately – for after the first thrust of women into ministry there followed another period – the second act – when both the

Universalist and Unitarian denominations had very few women serving as colleagues to men in the ministry.

In 1870 one of the denomination's leading journals, the *Universalist*, flatly declared that it was "a waste of money and effort to engage in fitting young women for duty of pastors and preachers." Throughout the remainder of the nineteenth-century while some Universalist State Conventions welcomed women into the ministry there were still those who made it very difficult for candidates to receive fellowship. At the Universalist General Convention meetings for 1883 in Washington, D.C. Phebe Hanaford attended the lecture on "education" by Elmer Hewitt Capen, President of Tufts College, and noted in her diary that he mentioned "men as students only." Then she commented "Will such men ever learn to speak also of advantages for women?" Among the Unitarians the situation was no better.

Samuel Atkins Eliot, during his long service as President of the American Unitarian Association (1900-1927) was unequivocally opposed to women in the ministry. In the years from 1887 to1897 before he assumed the presidency – and he overhauled its responsibility and made it the strong leadership position that today still describes this office in the Unitarian Universalist Association – twenty-three women were ordained; during the first sixteen years of his regime only one woman was ordained. This led Clara Cook Helvie in her study "Unitarian Woman Ministers" to point out that "the churches of Congregational polity are neglecting their woman power." As for the women who were ordained even as late as 1935 Roger F. Etz, the Universalist General Superintendent, declared that he found in the churches "a tremendous prejudice against women ministers." So much so that he found it "practically impossible to get any woman minister a hearing at any salary whatever."

Among the women associated with this period were Hazel Kirk, Eleanor Bicknell Forbes, Hannah Jewett Powell, Ida Folsom, Edna Bruner, and Florence Buck. In all probability Alice Harrison (not ordained until near the end of her life) and Georgene Bowen – a Universalist missionary in Japan – would have sought ordination at the start of their religious work had that really been an option. Indeed, many who sought to be ordained even in the next period were women who had the inclination earlier in the their life but found that denominations and society were still not welcoming women into either professional, business, or religious careers

As we look at the third act of this drama for ministerial equality a word now needs to be said about statistics. Catherine F. Hitchings in her *Universalist and Unitarian Ministers* – a volume of short biographies of deceased ministers – stated when the first edition of her study appeared in 1975 that there were forty-eight living ordained women in the UUA ministry of which twenty-four had received their fellowship since 1960. In other words at the time of the creation of the new organization their parent ones – the American Unitarian Association and the Universalist Church of American – had but twenty-four living female ministers out of a total of 856. Yet both denominations over a period of one hundred-twelve years had ordained after Olympia Brown in 1863 and Celia Burleigh in 1871 close to two hundred women.

Clearly the initial support for women in ministry has declined over the decades. The decline seems to have taken during the time of the First World War and the Great Depression. It was not until the 1960s and early 1970s when America went through a dramatic change – for the better – in its key values that matters changed. That revolutionary decade and a half saw a basic improvement of the rights of African Americans, women, and gays. One of these was that finally women were admitted to ministry – in some denominations but especially in our Unitarian Universalist Association – in numbers that corresponded to their own decisions to serve as fully ordained ministers in churches and related religious occupations.

Today more than half of our Unitarian Universalist ministers are women; they serve at all levels of the denominational structure with the same or better pay as their male counterparts. At long last Unitarian Universalists have moved well beyond the old frontiers of ministry, which Hanaford and her sisters – with the help of some of their brothers – had to redefine and make more relevant. It's a struggle that never will have to be repeated in our "association" of churches and congregations.

Phebe Hanaford died in 1921. That was the year my mother married and the second year that she – as a woman – was eligible to vote. That she could vote then and that my wife, our daughters and granddaughters possessed the right to vote – is due to the hard work and advocacy of Hanaford and the minority of women as determined as she – who struggled so long and consistently in behalf of securing for woman – for all of us – the ability as human beings born with "certain unalienable Rights" – "to be or not to be." Hanaford's story, as presented in this fine biography, is a reminder of those who have made that choice possible.

ALAN SEABURG
Curator of Manuscripts, Emeritus
Andover-Harvard Theological Library
Harvard Divinity School

FOREWORD

I really didn't have a choice. Phebe Hanaford made it for me, on a warm July morning in 1982.

Just seven years earlier, in Dr. Maxine Van de Wettering's class at the University of Montana, I discovered that women in America are the missing part of our history. The life that caught my attention that day and changed the direction of my own life was the life of Anne Hutchinson. The next chapter of my own history began the following year as I left Montana in search of a profession where my historical curiosity could support me. I became a Unitarian Universalist and began seminary in Berkeley, California.

The summer of 1982 I received a research grant to look in our denominational archives housed at the Andover-Harvard Library at Harvard Divinity School in Cambridge, Massachusetts. I spent the summer working at a table in the corner of the office of Alan Seaburg, Curator of Manuscripts, looking for the XIX century lives of my newly acquired spiritual ancestors – America's first women ministers. I knew only one name, The Reverend Olympia Brown, the first woman ordained to the ministry in 1863 by a Universalist Convention of the Universalist Church in America. That July morning of 1982 I lifted down a small brown book from the library shelf. The top edge was covered with dust. (It had last been in circulation in 1902.) Olympia Brown was one of the book's authors. Its title: "Ordination of Rev. Phebe A. Hanaford." It is a slender seventy-one page volume containing the services of Phebe Hanaford's Ordination and Installation at The First Universalist Church of Hingham, Massachusetts on February 19, 1868.

As I opened the book it was as if The Reverend Phebe Ann Coffin Hanaford stepped behind me, placing the flat of her hands on my shoulder blades, saying to me in her clear Nantucket voice: "Trust me, I will show you how to find my life." There was more archival evidence across the Cambridge Common at The Arthur and Elisabeth Schlesinger Library at Radcliffe: Hanaford articles and papers, many of her fourteen published books and a formal photograph. Finding Phebe Hanaford's life has determined the map of my own life – and the location of my seven successive ministries.

I played hooky and spent a three year sojourn in the American Studies Program at Washington State University, feeling the urgent need to return to the Academy to see if anyone else had found Phebe. No one had! Then, by absolute chance, I was able to serve for two years as the Interim Minister at the descendant congregation of the Universalist Church in New Haven, Connecticut – the Church that had called Phebe Hanaford from Hingham and Waltham in 1870.

And it was in New Haven that Loretta Cody rang my doorbell, sent to me by Alan Seaburg. Our collaboration began as we met. We each knew a little. We did know that Phebe Hanaford had died in Rochester, New York in 1921. Through Loretta Cody's resourcefulness, Susan McNamara of the *Democrat and Chronicle* published an article "In search of Phebe Hanaford" inviting anyone with information to contact her. Loretta's answering machine soon carried the message: "Good Morning, Mrs. Cody. My name is Audrey Johnson. I am Phebe Hanaford's great-great-granddaughter."

In September 1995 Loretta Cody and I went together to Rochester to meet with Audrey Johnson. At our request she and her sister, Diane Dobberton, took us to Orleans, New York Cemetery where we were shown the grave of Florence Hanaford Warner, Phebe's only daughter. Beside it was Phebe Hanaford's unmarked grave. My response, as a founding member of the Unitarian Universalist Woman's Heritage Society, was to apply for a grant. With "Phebe-Good-Fortune," The New York State Universalist Convention funded a grave marker which was placed and dedicated in 1998.

Two summers earlier in 1996, when I was between ministries and "honestly unemployed," I was able to accept Loretta Cody's invitation to come with my Phebe Hanaford Files, gleaned from fourteen years of searching. Working together in the study of her home in Brick, New Jersey, we read everything; Loretta Cody's file of Phebe's two New Jersey ministries was all new to me. As we completed our archival assessment it became clear that Loretta Cody would write the biography.

I would continue as the Unitarian Universalist archivist, the spiritual excavator. Sorting what we had found chronologically, we have re-imagined Phebe's long and productive life. More than a dozen years of consistent collaboration bring before you now her life. Erasing silence and invisibility, this book honors her life. Searching for the evidence of Phebe Hanaford's life has become my spiritual practice.

THE REVEREND SARAH BARBER-BRAUN
Minneapolis, Minnesota

ACKNOWLEDGEMENTS

A chance encounter in a local antique book store triggered a life-altering event for me when the dealer, Arthur Weinberg, handed me *Daughters of America* by Phebe Hanaford. To him I owe my first expression of gratitude for the inspiration to write her biography. Over the years that my biography of Phebe Hanaford has been in progress, I have accumulated "Friends of Phebe," only a few of whom I am able to acknowledge by name, others by their profession. In search of Phebe Hanaford's untold story I met librarians and archivists in New Jersey, Massachusetts, Connecticut and New York to whom I express my gratitude for their gentle persistence. Among them, I owe a special thanks to Darrah Degnan who has been available with sound advice at every turn. Alan Seaburg's Introduction offers a window into his expertise. He is one of the earliest "Friends." He enabled me to gain access to Universalist archives at Andover-Harvard Theological Library. He educated me in Nineteenth Century Universalism and Phebe's years in ministry, 1868-1888. He encouraged me to travel to New Haven to meet Rev. Sarah Barber-Braun, founding member of Unitarian-Universalist Women's Heritage Society and the leading authority on Phebe Hanaford. Sarah led the way through each phase of the story of Phebe Hanaford and without her inspiration and skills; this book would not have been written. In sharing her love of women's history and her accumulated research on Phebe Hanaford, she shared her friendship.

Nineteenth century diaries transcribed by Marion Horne and Anne Mark personalized Phebe Hanaford with details of her relationships between 1857 and 1868. In search of information on her family life, at my request Susan McNamara of the *Rochester Democrat and Chronicle* wrote an article "In Search of Phebe Hanaford." In response to the article Audrey Johnson, Phebe's great-great granddaughter, made available the private Hanaford family archives preserved by Audrey's mother, Helen Feasel, an oral family history that opened a window onto Phebe's life as wife, mother and grandmother. Signed copies of her books, photos, and personal possessions brought Phebe out of archives into our world as Sarah and I read her story in her own handwriting. My husband drove us to Rochester for that memorable visit and over the years he drove miles and sat in libraries as I poured over microfilms in search of Phebe Hanaford. Finally our editor, Angela Bellacosa of Editing Lane, did a painstaking job of editing the manuscript and getting it ready for the publisher. A work such as this intrudes into the writer's family life in many ways. The innumerable contributions of my husband, Jim Cody, have earned him the title "St. James" among the many "Friends of Phebe."

Degory Priest, pilot of the Mayflower and signer of
the Mayflower Compact
-1620
|
Phineas Pratt m Mary Priest
|
Joseph Pratt m Dorcas **Folger**
|
Bethian Pratt m Sampson **Cartwright**
|
James Cartwright m Love **Macy**
|
Henry **Barnard** m Love Cartwright
|
Phebe Ann Barnard m George W. **Coffin**
1811-1829   1804-1889
|
Phebe Ann **Coffin**
1829-1921
|
Phebe Ann **Coffin** m Joseph H. **Hanaford**
1819-1900

Tristram **Coffin** m Dionis Stevens
1609 England   1609 England
-1681 N.I.   -1684 N.I.
|
James **Coffin** m Mary Severance
1640 England   -1645 Mass.
-1720 N.I.
|
Nathaniel **Coffin** m Demaris Gayer
-1671 N.H.   -1673 N.I.
-1720 N.I.   -1764 N.I.
|
Nathaniel **Coffin** m Pricilla Gardner
1739-1827   1745–1816
|
Robert **Coffin** m Mary **Coffin**
1774-?   1782 -1864
|
Phebe Ann Barnard m George W. **Coffin**
1811-1829   1804-1889
|
Phebe Ann **Coffin**
1829-1921
|
Phebe Ann **Coffin** m Joseph H. **Hanaford**
1819-1900

DESCENDANTS

Howard Alcott **Hanaford**
December 31, 1851

|

Howard A. **Hanaford** m Mary Landerkin
1851-1907   1855-1898

|

Maria Mitchell   Charles "Lennie"
August 10, 1875   November 24, 1881

|

Maria Mitchell Hanaford m Fred Feasel

|

Helen Mae   William Hanaford
1903-1997   1910-1985

|

Helen Mae Feasel m Bert G. Maxfield

|

Hazel Maxfield Knickerbocker
Diane Maxfield Dobbertson
Audrey Maxfield Johnson
Lynn Maxfield Domra

Florence Elizabeth **Hanaford**
March 19, 1854

|

Florence E. **Hanaford** m Thomas Warner
1854-1902

|

Dionis Coffin
July 10, 1880-April 29, 1959

|

Dionis Coffin Warner m Edward Santee

CHRONOLOGY

1829   Born May 6, in Nantucket Massachusetts to Capt. George Coffin and Phebe Ann Barnard Coffin. Death of her mother, Phebe Ann Barnard Coffin, on 3 June.

1830   Capt. George marries Emmeline Cartwright.

1841   Hears Frederick Douglass speak on Nantucket.

1846   Leaves school to care for Grandmother Coffin.

1849   Teaches school on Cape Cod.

1849   Marries Joseph H. Hanaford on 2 December and moves to the mainland.

1851   Returns to Nantucket Island for the birth of her son Howard Alcott, 31 December.

1853   Publishes *Lucretia the Quakeress.*

1854   Gives birth to Florence Elizabeth, 19 March.

1857   Founds the Female Union Praying Circle.

1857   Moves to Beverly, Massachusetts.

1861   Publishes *Chimes of Peace and Union* with Mary Trask Webber.

1863　Learns of the death of her half-brother Rowland at sea.

1864　Half-sister Mary Jane dies on 9 September.

1864　Moves to Reading, meets Emily Ruggles.
　　　Preaches her first sermons while visiting Nantucket
　　　Island.

1865　Publishes the first posthumous biography of Abraham
　　　Lincoln.

1866　Hired in April as editor of Universalist periodicals.
　　　Receives License to preach as a Universalist.

1868　Ordained a Universalist Minister and installed as
　　　pastor of the First Universalist Society in Hingham,
　　　Massachusetts.

1869　Called to serve the Waltham Universalist Church
　　　on alternate Sundays, meets Ellen Miles. Joins the
　　　American Woman Suffrage Association.

1870　Receives Letter of Call to the First Universalist Society
　　　in New Haven, Connecticut, moves with daughter
　　　Florence and Ellen Miles to New Haven, marking the
　　　beginning of her separation from Joseph Hanaford.
　　　Serves as Chaplain of the State Legislature, the first
　　　woman to hold that position. Publishes *Life of George
　　　Peabody*.

1871　Publishes *Life of Charles Dickens* and *Shore to Shore*.

1872　Joins Sorosis with Ellen Miles.

1873   Becomes a charter member of the Association for the
        Advancement of Women.

1874   Receives Letter of Transfer to the Church of the Good
        Shepherd, First Universalist Church in Jersey City.
        Becomes the first woman to participate in her son's
        ordination.

1876   Publishes *Women of the Century.*
        Becomes the first woman to perform the marriage of
        her daughter.

1877   Forms the Second Universalist Church in Jersey City,
        declared schismatic.

1878   Second Universalist Church not Schismatic, Rev.
        Hanaford reinstated to The Committee of Nomination
        for Fellowship, Ordination & Discipline.

1882   Publishes *Daughters of America.*

1884   Called to the Second Universalist Church in New
        Haven, Church of the Holy Spirit.

1887   Twenty years of active ministry ends with the death of
        benefactor, Mr. H.H. Olds and the sale of the Church of
        the Holy Spirit.

1888   Becomes a charter member of the Women's Press Club.

1889   Becomes a charter member of the Federation of
        Women's Clubs.

1890   Moves to the Warner home in Tonawanda, New York.

1891   Moves with Ellen Miles to New York City.
        Serves as Vice President of Sorosis. Publishes *Heart of Siasconset*.

1892   Assumes responsibility for Sorosis Folio for the Columbian Exposition.

1893   Presents Sorosis Club Folio at the Columbian Exposition in Chicago, Illinois.

1895   Contributes interpretations of the Old Testament in *The Woman's Bible* Vol.1.

1896   Organizes and serves as President of the Society for Political Study.

1898   Contributes interpretations of the Old and New Testaments in *The Woman's Bible* Vol. 2.

1900   Runs for president of the Woman's Press Club; defeated by Jane Croly 40 to 38.

1901   Becomes President of the Woman's Press Club following the death of Jane Croly, founder.

1905   Becomes Honorary President of the Woman's Press Club.

1909   Receives donation from the Woman's Press Club on her eightieth birthday.

1914   Buries Ellen Miles, her companion of forty-four years.

1915   Visits granddaughter Dionis Warner Santee in
       Tonawanda during which time Mr. Santee closes
       her New York apartment ending her active life as a
       reformer.

1918   Moves with the Santees to Basom in Genesee County,
       New York. Votes in the New York state elections.

1921   Dies in Rochester, New York on June 2.

CHAPTER ONE

A DAUGHTER OF NANTUCKET

Born on May 6, 1829
on Lower Hussey Street, Nantucket, Massachusetts[1]

The Coffin household surely hummed with activity in the early days of May 1829 as midwives busied themselves with preparations for the birth of Phebe Barnard Coffin's first child. As the days wore on, women in Quaker dress might have crossed Lower Hussey Street to bring oatmeal and tea made from snapdragon plants to nourish young Phebe. Here on Nantucket Island, midwives brought women through childbirth with the skill that comes with experience. Confidence gave way to anxiety as the exhausted mother struggled to give birth. On May 6, the long awaited cry brought the news that a healthy baby girl had been born into the world of Nantucket women.

As the days wore on into weeks, the young mother did not recover her strength. Accustomed to tending the sick, the women surely applied old remedies. With the removal of the infant from the room, the absence of the cries of a newborn must have added to the aura of awaited death, where days before they had awaited new life. Death came one month later on June 4.[2] The women prepared the body of the young mother and laid her to rest in an unmarked grave, according to Quaker custom.

----

1   1882 Coffin Family Genealogy
2   Coffin, 1962, p. 177

The fact that Phebe never knew the mother-daughter bond has not previously been noted in biographical sketches, which have stated only that she had a stepmother. Her mother's early death denies us information on the source of Phebe's personal traits – traits that seem remarkably different from those of her father's children born to his second wife Emmeline, widow of Joseph Cartwright. Phebe became the treasured granddaughter of Love Cartwright Barnard and Mary Coffin. "The little girl vibrated between the houses of her two Quaker grandmothers, finding in one the Bible and in the other Webster's dictionary."[3]

Both grandmothers were descendants of early settlers of the Island. Mary's father, Jonathan Coffin, and her husband's father, Nathaniel Coffin, were descendants of Tristram and Dionis Coffin. This husband and wife were among the original nine families on the mainland who wanted to isolate themselves from Puritanism. Their desire to do so increased after the Puritans made threats against Thomas Macy because he had taken Quakers into his home during a storm. This experience left Macy little stomach for bigotry and a deep distrust of any theocracy.

He and his friends made plans to escape the reactionary society of Puritanism that existed in the Massachusetts Bay Colony. Forever known as the original purchasers, Thomas Macy, Edward Starbuck, Chief Magistrate Tristram Coffin, Thomas Barnard, Christopher Hussey, Thomas Coleman, and the Swains arrived on Nantucket with the first group of white settlers in 1659. They were joined by Peter Folger, a Baptist translator who came from Martha's Vineyard to help the early settlers adjust to the rigors of Island life. This group of like-minded people came

---

3   McCleary, 1929, p. 2

to Nantucket Island in pursuit of economic prosperity as well as freedom from persecution.

Thomas Mayhew, who owned Nantucket, Martha's Vineyard, and the Elizabeth Islands, sold nine-tenths of Nantucket Island to the settlers for 80 pounds and two beaver hats. The settlers also paid the Indians for their share of the Island. Following Mayhew's example, they pursued the familiar work of raising sheep. The natural boundaries of the Island made it ideal for grazing, but lack of water for power forced the settlers to sell the wool as a raw material. The arrangement proved unprofitable and they turned to whaling, relying on the Indians to teach them the skill. Mayhew's converts, the Indians, were the only Christians on the Island. "The Nantucketers left their religion behind them ... they were decidedly against establishment religion and none existed on the Island for the first half of the century."[4]

Grandmother Love Cartwright Barnard's mother, Love Macy Cartwright, was descended from Thomas Macy. The Cartwrights traced their family back to Peter Folger and Degory Priest, the pilot of the Mayflower. Priest died in 1620 in Plymouth, leaving a wife and daughter, Mary. Mary Priest Pratt's son married Dorcas Folger. Mary Pratt's granddaughter married Samson Cartwright in the beginning of the eighteenth century[5]. Grandmother Love Cartwright's husband, Henry Barnard, a descendent of the original settler, claimed that Nathaniel Barnard brought the first pine boards to the Island. Their own home and many houses on the Island were built with these boards. For the descendants of the early settlers, the Island became their world and they referred to everyone else as "non-Islanders." Because

4   McCalley, 1981, p. 2
5   1882 Coffin Family Genealogy

of the frequency of intermarriage, it was a fact that "every noted person from the Island had the blood of one or both of these families in their veins"[6]. With Barnard and Coffin blood in her veins, Phebe Ann was a true daughter of Nantucket.

In the early eighteenth century, members of the Society of Friends on the mainland looked to Nantucket Island as a source of converts. They found a strong disciple in Mary Coffin Starbuck, daughter of Tristram and Dionis Coffin. Gifted at proselytizing, Mary assumed a central role in the religious community of the Island. Under her leadership in less than a decade, the Society of Friends became the Island's leading religion. They built their first Meetinghouse in 1711. The practices of the Society of Friends blended with the life of simplicity and frugality of the Islanders. As Quakers, they believed the atmosphere and climate of one's ordinary daily life molded the person. Quaker women wore their hair parted smoothly back from their forehead and covered with the traditional clear muslin cap. A white handkerchief worn across the bodice relieved the severity of the brown dress that was the mark of Quaker women at the turn of the century.

The Coffin Family: Records of Marriages lists the marriage of Capt. George Coffin to Emmeline Barnard Cartwright in October 1829.[7] Phebe would have been six months old when her father married the widowed cousin of Phebe's mother. Emmeline would be the only mother Phebe would ever know. At the time of the marriage, Emmeline had a son, Joseph, who was a year older than Phebe. The only written record of Emmeline comes from Helen Cartwright McCleary on the centenary of Phebe Coffin Hanaford's birth. "Capt. Coffin's second marriage

---

6   Hanaford, Phebe A., 1881, p. 427
7   Ibid, p. 179

with Mrs. Emmeline (Barnard) Cartwright, widow of Joseph B. Cartwright, gave the child a devoted elder step-brother, Joseph B. Cartwright Jr., and seven younger half-brothers and sisters." This paucity of records leaves us no clue as to Emmeline's feelings toward Phebe.

On New Years Day 1831 George and Emmeline's son Robert was born.[8] Phebe turned two in that year. During that year there grew some resistance to the oppressive rules of the Friends. A Quaker sect meeting in the back room of Thomas Macy's home in town attracted liberal minded Islanders who welcomed the reforms of Elias Hicks and his Liberal Separation Party. The resulting schism of the 1840's led to a marked decrease in Quaker membership. Hicksite Quakers numbered three hundred out of an Island population of 10,000. As distinct from the Guerneyites, the Hicksites relied heavily on the Holy Spirit to guide them in the reading of the Scriptures and in the interpretation of God's will for each individual. From an audiotape of Robert Leach, we learn that the Hicksites built their Meetinghouse on South Water Street.

The Friends' belief that the soul had no gender gave Quaker women a distinct role in religious matters. At weekly meetings women gathered in the women's section of the Meetinghouse to discuss the needs of the community. For example, women took responsibility for the widows and orphans of the men lost at sea. This work of caring for others had originated in Europe. "[P]raemuniring, which involved the government seizure of their land, livestock and houses, compelled the Friends to set up some structures in order to support the sufferings of their members."[9]

---

8   1882 Coffin Family Genealogy
9   Steere, 1948, p. 13

Washed by the ocean that gave it life and just as swiftly could take it away, Nantucket Island was the principal seat of the whaling industry. The oil was tryed out aboard, stowed in barrels and shipped to Nantucket in lighters, which made long voyages possible and lucrative. Ships frequently sailed to the Pacific in search of sperm whales. Whaling trips that extended from months to years brought wealth to the owners of the ships who took more than half of the profits. The balance went to the captain and the crew in different percentages. Captains could earn as much as 6% of the total profits. Nantucket's sources of income were the exported sperm oil and the candles manufactured on the Island and sold around the world.

The prolonged absence of the men from the Island resulted in strong, independent women whose contributions defined the Island just as truly as did the whalers. Women were left to deal with the birthing and care of the children. They reared their families while their men were at sea. Apart from raising food in their gardens, they wove baskets from rattan that seamen brought back from the Far East. Women traveled by ferry to the mainland to sell baskets, candles and other wares and returned with goods to sell in their shops. Businesses well run by women led folks in Nantucket to dub Center Street, Petticoat Row. This unique culture created a bond among the women and, with it, the freedom to engage in friendships.

Phebe's first female friendships began during her schooldays. Her earliest recollections can be found in her handwritten, unpublished *Old Time School Days in Nantucket*,[10] in which she wrote that she remembered her father carrying her at "twenty-two months old" to the kindergarten located on Chestnut Street,

10   Hanaford, Phebe A., 1902, p. 4

one block from home. Phebe describes the experience as more nursery care than education. Phebe's school teacher was Sarah Easton. Sarah's mother, Aunt Easton, as she was known to the children, took their youngest student to her apartment daily for her nap. "I slept till school hours were at an end, when I was taken home, refreshed if not enlightened."[11] Standing at the intersection of Chestnut and Hussey, one might wonder why Captain George considered school the appropriate place for Phebe rather than home? Was Phebe carried to school at two years of age because she was precocious, or because she was underfoot?

Schools were part of neighbors' households in the nineteenth century. Women who appreciated their minds and wanted to use them to earn their living opened up their homes to students. There were no educational standards, and a student was for-tunate if he or she found a teacher with the necessary skills. Sarah Easton, daughter of the widow Rachel Easton, and Mary Russell, her cousin, operated a school from the Easton home. Aunt Easton is on record as having kept a store where, as she got older, Phebe was "often mounted on the counter to recite poems. "I ... could read when so small that I had to stand on a chair for the light to fall on my book from the lamp on the mantel. When I was a child I used to sit on my father's knee, and recite to him the twenty-three stanzas, ninety-two lines written by Peter Folger in which the whale was mentioned."[12]

When old enough to be familiar with the kitchen stores, Phe-be took a bottle of coffee and a piece of gingerbread to school. In imitation of her classmates, who could sink beneath their desk to eat, towards noon she slipped down to the floor under the bench

---

11   Ibid, p. 5
12   Ibid, p. 13

she shared with other girls. Because she had her mouth full of gingerbread, she grew angry when she became aware that she was being watched. Believing it to be a classmate, she raised her hand to slap the intruder only to discover too late that she had struck Miss Easton. In shock and unable to apologize with her mouth full of cake, she came out to await her fate. Sarah Easton hustled her into the closet and closed the door.

In her account of this event, Phebe described the shame she felt at the thought that she had slapped this teacher whom she loved. Not wanting to be heard crying, Phebe choked back her tears and looked around the closet. A window at the top let in sufficient light for Phebe to realize the closet contained books. She understood she was in Miss Easton's new library. She managed to reach up and inch a yellow book to the edge of the shelf. It fell on her chest where she read the title *Swiss Family Robinson*. She wrote that she "soon forgot her punishment and read until she heard school being let out." She returned the book, knowing that she would ask Miss Easton for it when her turn came to borrow a book. The whole business ended very well. When she heard the steps outside the door, she took on a woeful face and apologized.[13]

Writing her account of her schooldays, Phebe credits Mary Russell, the orphan teacher, loved by all who ever knew her, with "teaching me my alphabet, and has ever been the dearest of my teachers, to all of whom my young heart was greatly attached."[14] In an age when educators applied more discipline than scholarship, Phebe found herself in a benevolent environment for learning. Her education at home included reading Macy's *History of Nantucket* and listening to Grandfather Coffin recite the

13   Ibid, p. 12
14   Ibid, p. 9

poems of Peter Folger. Mounted on the counter at Aunt Easton's store, Phebe recited these poems from memory. She showed no shyness and believed her performances to be worthy of reward. Although the store held many treats for children, she let it be known that she favored a penny primer.

At four years of age, with the birth of baby George, Phebe now had three brothers. The Easton's school grew into a District School with students of all ages. Phebe, studying *Brown's Grammar* and the *Speller and Definer,* learned the importance of good spelling and the meaning of words. Classes included *Colburn's Arithmetic, Parley's Geography* and *Olney's Geography and Atlas.*

At home she stood on a chair so the light fell on the page and read aloud to Grandmother Coffin from the Bible. She spoke very clearly and her talent did not go unnoticed. Those who heard her agreed she had inherited her Grandmother's voice. As a preacher, Grandmother Coffin projected her voice effortlessly. Coming from her lips, even a strong message had a mellowness that fell pleasantly on the ears of her listeners. Some thought Phebe might well follow in the footsteps of her grandmother.

"The Society of Friends has always had women among their preachers."[15] The stories of Quaker women preachers as well as of her ancestors became part of her story. On the Sabbath children shared in the close community life of the Meeting. On First Day Phebe entered the Meetinghouse through the women's door. Here she grew to identify prayer with silence and in that silence to hear the Inner Voice that would guide her through all the seasons of her long life.

Phebe finished her elementary education at the North Grammar School at age eleven and moved upstairs to the High School,

---

15   Hanaford, Phebe A., 1881, p. 417

where Mr. Morse served as principal. The Quaker belief in the importance of equal education for boys and girls allowed Phebe to attend classes with male teachers. The Nantucket system of education bore the influence of Horace Mann's philosophy, making their schools among the best in the State. Phebe's source for books remained Miss Easton's school. Judging from information given in Phebe's novelette *Lucretia, the Quakeress or Principle Triumphant,*[16] Quakers monitored the books their children read.

With his household growing, Capt. George extended his maritime pursuits. He added to his position as Chief Tidal Observer for the Coast Survey the duties of Captain of the packet that carried the mail between Nantucket and New Bedford. On a clear day when Phebe and her brother Joseph could see the mail packet, they would run like the wind to the wharf to greet their father. More often they peered through the thickening mist and heard the cry to throw the lines before they had a view of the packet. In time Capt. George would walk down the wharf onto the street where Joseph could press him for events of the voyage. Young boys of fourteen sailed as apprentices, and he longed for the day when he would go to sea.

Phebe would have been more interested in the newspapers and books her father had brought. Mainland Coffin relatives wrote to one family and the news spread quickly on the Island. From their news in 1840, Nantucket townsfolk learned that Lucretia Mott and other women had traveled to London for the World Anti-Slavery Conference. That year, Phebe's younger siblings, five-year-old Mary Jane and three-year-old Lydia, were joined by Sarah, born on March eighth. The youngest boy, Rowland Hussey, was born three years later on January 5, 1843.

---

16   Hanaford, Phebe A., 1853, p. 35

In her studies Phebe learned that the Friends had remained pacifists during the Revolution and how those who had gone to war had been disowned. Those times were difficult because England was the biggest market for sperm oil and many of the ships were owned by the British. The Island remained neutral, and after the war the first ship to fly an American flag in a British port left from Nantucket. Quakers survived the war without compromising their beliefs.

The years following the Revolution and into the nineteenth century "were the years of Nantucket's greatest prosperity."[17] Young Phebe promised never to favor war for any reason. Nothing, she believed, allowed the taking of life. That belief would be deeply tested during the Civil War. Phebe heard the story told of the seaman who came ashore years before, sick with fever. An Indian woman cared for him in the home of the family who offered him a place to stay. She went home each evening to her Indian community, and soon several Indians came down with the pox and died. Some white folks got smallpox, and many died, and those who survived were scarred. Nantucket history reports that almost all the Indians died in this epidemic.

From newspapers brought from the mainland in 1841, Islanders learned that Lucretia Mott and all the women who had traveled to London to participate in the World Anti-Slavery Conference had been refused their rightful position and relegated to the observation section. At the age of twelve, Phebe, along with her peers, would not have understood the consequences of the affront to the women. She did, however, understand slavery and knew the Friends had freed their slaves in 1720.

---

17   McCalley, 1981, p. 5

In mid August 1841, Anna Gardner, the secretary of the Nantucket Anti-Slavery Chapter, planned a meeting at the Athenium for the following week. Within days of the announcement, Mr. William Coffin sent word that he had heard Frederick Douglass, a freed slave, speak a few months earlier at the Zion Chapel in New Bedford and had invited him to come to Nantucket for the meeting. On the day of the meeting, the mail packet arrived in the late afternoon with the news that Mr. Coffin had asked the freed slave to speak.

People wishing to hear the freed slave speak gathered outside the Athenium and watched as a trustee emerged to speak to a small group of Friends. According to McFeeley, when "the trustees learned in addition that two hundred people from New Guinea had been invited, and that a black speaker was to be imported for the occasion, they withdrew their permission for the use of the hall."[18] New Guinea was the segregated section south of the town. Soon, the crowd began to disperse. The meeting moved to the Big Shop where, according to McFeeley, "The Quaker quiet of the room was cut through with an electricity of excitement that everyone from twelve-year-old Phebe Ann Coffin to her most somber senior relative would never forget."[19]

No black men whom Phebe had known on the Island had lived as a slave. Douglass' stories came from a different world. Perhaps it was here Phebe began to understand what the words she had heard as a child really meant. Until then words were tools of enjoyment, treasures to memorize and recite. Now they held a new power, and she soon took up her pen, an instrument that would become her lifelong friend. Her awakening echoed Douglass' awakening to his power of speech while addressing

---

18   1991, p. 87
19   Ibid, p. 88

a portion of the population that stretched back to the founding of America.

Ellen Miles wrote of Phebe Hanaford in *Shore to Shore*,[20] "At the early age of thirteen, she commenced writing for the press of her native town. That the child-poet was deeply sensitive to the blight upon our boasted freedom may be seen by the following stanzas, which close a short poem entitled *America* written at age thirteen."

> *Shame, shame the deepest, will be thine,*
> *Till Freedom's light on all shall shine:*
> *Till black and white alike are free,*
> *Blight will forever rest on thee.*
> *But change the scene, and let the sun*
> *No injured bondman shine upon,*
> *Then joy shall reign o'er all the land,*
> *And high 'midst nations thou shalt stand.*

In the preserved two pages of her undated *Anti Slavery Reminiscences*, Phebe wrote, "Born of Quaker ancestry, of course I grew up with a hatred of all forms of slavery, and an intense yearning that the colored people in our land might be freed."[21] In that essay she mentions her ancestral relative, Elihu Coleman, who a century before her birth bore testimony against slavery. Years later, writing her novelette *Lucretia, the Quakeress*, Phebe incorporated events of the lives of black men living on the Island. In the story of James Blossom, a slave who ran away from his master after his wife and children were taken from him, she described how Blossom found shelter among the Society of

----

20   1871, p. 13
21   p. 2 (n.d.)

Friends on the mainland. For his safety they sent him to Nantucket Island where he spoke of his dream of buying his wife and son from their new master. Townsfolk knew that no matter how long and hard Blossom worked, it would take years for him to save the money he needed to buy their freedom. Phebe had been taught that Obed Barnard returned one day from New Bedford with James Blossom's wife, Nellie, and their son.

The Blossom family would have taken up residence in New Guinea. Nantucket abolitionists were segregationists, and that too became part of Phebe's education. Not until 1846 when the daughter of Absalom Boston sued for the right to be admitted to the public high school and won, did the Island become one of the early Massachusetts districts to integrate its schools.[22] Absalom Boston was the only known black whaling captain, and his family members were leaders in their community.

Within the Quaker community, the Friends' way of life found expression in the simplicity of the Meetinghouse with its unpainted pine boards. The half hour of unbroken silence served to bring greater attention to one's Inner Voice. After the quiet period, the shutters were lowered to divide the room and to separate the women from the men. The women spoke of the needs of families without sufficient vegetables and asked members to contribute what they could from their own gardens. Women assumed the responsibilities of visiting these families. Phebe grew accustomed to women speaking in public.

From Helen McCleary's published talk given at a posthumous observance of "Phebe Hanaford's 100th birthday," we read,

From her father, Capt. Coffin, (who, to save a wreck, could out-roar the waves at Surfside!) and from his mother

---

22   "Landmark in Nantucket's Black History Restored," 2002

(a descendant of a long line of Quaker preachers) she inherited the clear, rich voice 'like a silver bell' which could reach to the farthest corner of an auditorium. To train her voice Phebe climbed up to Brant Point lighthouse to recite to the winds and waves as her audience, selections from Byron and Shakespeare, considered 'too worldly' for a Quaker household.[23]

Phebe left school at age sixteen to care for her Grandmother Coffin. In writing of her schools, she acknowledged that she "was never a graduate of any."[24] About this time her brother Joseph Cartwright left on a whaling ship. Phebe notes in her 1857 Diary,

> *His body found a grave beneath the waves of the far off Pacific when he was about 17 years old but I do hope, by the mercy of God, his soul is at rest in a better world. He was a kind brother and a dutiful son. Would that I had more evidence that he was a Christian.*

Nantucketers would soon learn they were vulnerable to more than the sea. The month of July 1846 was dry, and the night of the thirteenth foggy. Someone spotted smoke inside Mr. Geary's hat store on Main Street. Only later did the fire watchman see the flames from his position on the South Tower of the Congregationalist Church. The fire burned out of control throughout the night, enveloping a third of Nantucket Town. Known as the

---

23   p. 41
24   Hanaford, Phebe A., 1881, p. 427

Great Fire, the Island's history offers vivid descriptions of the bucket brigades that proved futile against the blaze.

At dawn the concrete building of the Pacific Bank provided the wall of resistance, bringing the fire to an end. The bank remained unharmed, but the houses destroyed on Lower Hussey Street included Phebe's birthplace. At town meetings in the days that followed, the commission appointed to investigate the fire reported that evidence showed wealthy families had paid men to save their property, thus reducing the numbers of those fighting to contain the fire. Without this intervention by a few, some of the town might have been saved and much of the damage avoided. Such loss brought hard times for many families. Phebe's Coffin grandparents owned several houses on Lower Hussey Street and suffered financial loss as did Grandmother Love, widowed ten years.

SIASCONSET

After the Great Fire, George Coffin moved his family to Siasconset, a vacationing site on the eastern coast of Nantucket affectionately called S'conset. Biographical sketches mistakenly report Phebe's place of birth as Siasconset. In her little known *Heart of Siasconset*, Phebe tells how the error originated in *Godfrey's Guide Book* and influenced future biographers.[25] Phebe wrote in *Old Time School Days in Nantucket* of attending school on Chestnut Street, "the next street to that in which I was born and lived until the Great Fire in 1846."[26] One had to be born on S'conset to be considered a native. Emma Coffin, the young-

---

25   1890, p. 93
26   Hanaford, Phebe A., 1902, p. 5

est in the family, born September 5, 1847, was the Coffins' only S'conset native.

According to Capt. George Coffin's obituary, "for twenty years and more he had charge of the life-boat belonging to the Massachusetts Humane Society." Phebe elaborated on this part of Capt. George's career as keeper of the Life Boat in *Heart of Siasconset:*

> *The Life Boat par excellence, for when he took charge of it there was no Life-Saving Service established on the island, or indeed on the coast of the United States anywhere......The old captain prided himself on taking good care of the boat, and regarded himself as sole custodian of the property which was in his hands, No coaxing could get the keys.*[27]

Today little remains of the S'conset Phebe knew as a young girl. *Heart of Siasconset* describes the delicate beauty of the flora and the mighty power of the sea, as well as the details of their house with the bedroom's sloping roof, unfinished laths and ridgepole. The cool sea breeze that came through the window filled the room at night as she lay listening to the sound of the surf and watching the darkness broken by the Sancoty light-house. One spoke to her of danger, the other of safety.

Their house was located on the main traffic path running west to east from town. In those days paths had no names because everybody knew where everybody lived. Phebe found amusement in the later naming of New Street since it had been there forever. From Helen McCreary we learn that at sixteen years of age, Phebe taught school. The room where she taught is now the S'conset firehouse. When S'conset later developed into

---

27   Hanaford, Phebe A., 1890, p. 126

a town of year-round residence, it still had no Meetinghouse or any churches. Phebe recalled in *Heart of Siasconset* that "every Quaker carried his church edifice within him."[28] Throughout her life she practiced her early instructions of always looking into her heart to listen to the Inner Voice.

This self-reliance served people well as they waited for news of their loved ones at sea. Crews trawled for months, even years, as they scanned the horizon for the movement that told of the passage of a whale. The long periods of waiting for news marked the life of the Islanders. They knew of the devastation and death tolls of shipwrecks in winter storms. Wreckage of foreign ships that washed ashore on S'conset reminded them again and again of their loved ones, perhaps in danger on faraway shores. People of S'conset knew that Capt. Coffin's voice could reach the ears of drowning men as he led rescue operations against the roar of the pounding sea. Young men like her brother Joseph Cartwright set sail unafraid of the ocean whose very strength apprised their elders of their vulnerability. Capt. George kept the rescue boats in good repair, and only he carried the key to the boathouse. The Coffin family would have appeared very fortunate to have Capt. George at home while other fathers were at sea for months.

CAPE COD

Many Nantucketers in search of better living standards left for Cape Cod. In an article that Helen Freeman Stevens of Chatham sent to the *Cape Codder* of Orleans, Massachusetts, which it published on February 5, 1948, Stevens enclosed a copy of a personal letter from Phebe to Grandmother Coffin, written

---

28   Ibid, p. 112

June 19, 1849 in Osterville on Cape Cod. It is the only archival evidence that Phebe had taken a position as a teacher on Cape Cod. Phebe's reference to Nantucket neighbors as her companions confirms what we know from the Island's history, that the failing economy on Nantucket drove Islanders to pursuit work elsewhere. In her letter, Phebe expresses gratitude at having been able to send her letter by hand.

> *Please ask Grandfather to put the enclosed letter in the Post Office. I received a farewell letter from him as he is going to California and felt as if I must answer it, but I did not wish to send it through this Post Office, for they are very apt to gossip in villages as thee knows, and I have no wish to cause any more than I have already.*

The letter includes the Friends' pronouns but leaves us curious regarding the gossip and the "him" who was going to California. She continues,

> *It cannot be said by anyone that I have neglected thee, for I have written thee more than to anyone else, and oftener. Knowing as I do that anything however trivial to others which relates to me is of interest to thee and is acceptable.*

The reader learns of the bond between these two daughters of Nantucket, separated by two generations. In her introduction to Phebe's letter, Helen Freeman Stevens states that "when Phebe was twenty she was married to Dr. Joseph H. Hanaford, a homeopathic physician of Cape Cod." Does this place Joseph and Phebe on Cape Cod at the same time? It is possible that is where they met. Also from Cape Cod, Phebe wrote that she "attended a Baptist Meeting."

CHAPTER TWO

A BAPTIST MARRIAGE

Marriage to Joseph Hanaford on December 2, 1849
in the Baptist Church on Summer Street
by Rev. Phineas Stowe of Boston[29]

Phebe "married out" of the Society of Friends. Four years into her marriage, in 1853, Phebe wrote in *Lucretia, the Quakeress*, of the freedom the Quaker parents afforded the heroine to marry outside the Society of Friends. In the same novelette, Phebe described in the bridegroom's words the Quaker wedding she never had.

Friends, he said, I take this my friend,… to be my wife, promising through Divine assistance, to be unto her an affectionate and faithful husband, until it shall please the Lord by death to separate us. The bride made a similar promise and both sat down again…when the ceremony was concluded, they were permitted to return to the home of her father, where a bountiful table was spread for the invited guests…. Should not the poor be oftener remembered by those whose board is amply supplied? The reflex influence of kindness is vast and incalculable, and they who seek to share their own joy with others, are but pursuing the very course which will double the joys, for as the poet wisely remarks, "Teaching we learn, and giving we retain."[30]

29   1882 Coffin Family Genealogy
30   pp. 73, 75

The Friends had become a minority as the Island opened up to a variety of churches. The North Congregational Church, built in 1711, was followed by the Presbyterian Old Vestry, built in 1725. The Universalist Church, begun in 1827, became Nantucket's first Athenium in 1836. The early nineteenth century brought the Methodist Church, the Unitarian Society, and the Second Congregational Church with the town's tower clock. The Baptist and Episcopal Churches also gathered members. Phebe's exposure to other faiths had prepared her to accept her husband's Baptist religion as part of her marriage agreement.

Phebe chose a non-Islander with a profession who removed her from the perils of the whaling industry and whet her intellectual appetite. "He taught school on Nantucket and Cape Cod earning enough money to study medicine at Bellevue Hospital, New York City, and became a homeopathic physician."[31] From the Hanaford Family Records of 1913, we read,

> Dr. Hibbard Hanaford …quite a writer on health and health foods; he lived in Reading, Mass. He married Phoebe Anna (sic) Coffin, born in Nantucket May 6, 1829. He was one of eight children born to Peter Hanaford and Polly Davis. Peter and Polly Davis were killed by lightening in a heavy shower in 1833.

According to the Nantucket Island Town Clerk's Office records, "Marriage took place in the Baptist Church on Nantucket Island on December 10, 1849. Joseph Hanaford of Newton, Upper Falls, MA."

---

31   1900, Obituary

NEWTON

Marrying a non-Islander brought an additional adjustment for Phebe and yielded more power to her husband, ten years her senior. As wives did, she accepted Joseph's decision to live on the mainland where he believed he had greater career opportunities. A biographical sketch of Phebe Hanaford by Ellen Miles in *Shore to Shore*[32] reads, "In 1849 she married and removed to Newton, Mass., where for a year she assisted her husband, Dr. J. H. Hanaford, in teaching, at the same time devoting her leisure time to literary pursuits." With the young doctor, Phebe experienced an intellectual compatibility she rarely found with the young men of Nantucket. Her marriage to the non-Islander, Baptist physician opened horizons for the curious young woman with only the limited experience of independent life on Cape Cod. From the pages of her 1857 diary, it is evident to the reader that they loved each other very much.

In the 1800's Christianity played a major role in society, and initially this served as a bond for the newlyweds. Embedded in Christian teachings lay the Biblical sanctioning of patriarchy with its capacity to deny women their full potential. This interpretation contradicted the Friends' belief that the soul had no sex. Over the years this difference became a crucial issue in their marriage as Phebe's Inner Voice clashed with the Baptist teachings of the day.

From her 1857 diary we learn that Joseph wrote poems for use at Sailors' Church in Boston where the Rev. Phineas Stowe, who had performed their marriage ceremony, served as pastor. Years later Phebe wrote to her grandson Lennie that at the time it was customary for women to publish under a masculine name,

---

32   1871

but that in truth she, not Joseph Hanaford, had written the still popular "Cast Thy Bread upon the Waters." This detail of proprietorship assumed by husbands characterized their marriage. Phebe initially published under the name Mrs. Joseph Hanaford and only in time as Phebe A. Hanaford. Phebe never hyphenated her name, a practice that was popular in the nineteenth century.

In October 1850 Horace Greeley's *The New York Tribune* told of the Woman's Rights Convention held in Worcester just forty miles from Newton, calling it the first national convention ever held for the cause of women's rights. The inclusion of William Lloyd Garrison, Wendell Philips, and Frederick Douglass indicated a strong anti-slavery force joining the women's movement. The paper reported that Lucy Stone's views on women's rights had grown out of the criticism she had faced as a woman speaking in public against slavery. She urged women to become more than appendages of Society.

The accounts in newspapers included the name of Phebe's cousin Lucretia Mott among the women who spoke in Worcester's Brinley Hall to an audience of over a thousand people and quoted Wendell Philips' description "as the first organized protest against the injustice which brooded over the character and destiny of one half the human race." Of Lucy Stone, Elizabeth Cady Stanton remarked, "She was the first speaker who really stirred the nation's heart on the subject of woman's wrongs. Young, magnetic, eloquent, her soul filled with the new idea, she drew immense audiences and was eulogized in the press. She spoke extemporaneously."[33]

The women's speeches from the Worcester Convention appeared in several newspapers where the mutual goals of women's rights and abolition received journalistic criticism.

33   Hanaford, Phebe A., 1881, p. 343

Phebe may not have recognized the names Mary Livermore or Julia Ward Howe in the newspaper accounts, but she would have believed these women spoke for all women struggling to control the basic terms of their existence. Elizabeth Cady Stanton acknowledged that to date the women's meetings had only been held on a local scale and that it was Lucy Stone who had brought women's issues to a new height.

Quotations from *The New York Herald* ridiculed the women's efforts as fanatical and worse because the issues went beyond temperance and abolition – they spoke of women's rights. Rev. Antoinette Brown, an ordained minister, spoke on the "Role of Women in the Church."

In the Baptist Church it seemed impossible that a woman would ever be recognized as a suitable candidate for the ministry. Women could only teach. As long as male ministers remained fundamental to the tenets of the Baptist Church, Phebe's contribution would be limited to her writing.

The Hanafords shared a common view on temperance. Phebe took the pledge to avoid alcohol at an early age. As he wrote in an undated article, "Alcoholic Stimulation," Joseph objected to the use of alcohol even for medicinal purposes:

When, therefore, alcohol, this active poison, comes in contact with any organ, muscle, nerve or fibre, resistance always results. As soon as it reaches the stomach, the absorbents immediately commence the work of ejection, arousing themselves to their greatest activity, removing the intruder. The remaining portion is almost rudely thrust out into the bowels, where it is as soon recognized as a foe to every function of the body, a part being absorbed, hurriedly sent to the various escritoires, soon escaping through various channels.[34]

Equally important to many was how the use and abuse of alcohol affected home and family. Women as wives and mothers suffered under the laws that protected the drunkard rather than the victims. On this topic, Phebe read Rev. Samuel May's *The Rights and Conditions of Women*, published in 1846, in which he states,

The people of this State were called, in their primary capacity, to decide whether the sale of intoxicating drinks should be licensed, a question of the highest personal, domestic and social consequence—and yet more than half of the people, the women, were not only not expected, but not allowed to influence directly a decision, in which they were so much interested. More than that, women should have a voice in all the decisions that affected their life. He believed women's physical weakness did not indicate any smallness of the brain and yet most men thought women inferior in both mental and physical strengths.[35]

As a homeopathic physician, Joseph imposed his strong views on foods to be served at home. He believed meat to be no friend to good digestion and referred to a paper he had written during his medical training where he referred to a sound stomach as a master builder of the body. Good foods were the materials needed, and he did not include meat in the category of good food. This was not a problem for Phebe. Raised on Nan-

---

34   p. 1
35   Reprinted in Kimmel & Mosmiller, p. 94

tucket's variety of lobster, cod, scallops, quahogs and oysters as well as bass and mackerel, meat had never seemed to her a requirement for good health.

Among his professional associates, Joseph found that Dr. William A. Alcott, a graduate of Yale Medical College, agreed with him on the requirements for good health. Dr. Alcott's opinions on ordinary daily living became part of Phebe's married life.

In his book *The Young Wife or Duties of Woman in the Marriage Relation,*[36] Dr. Alcott equated marriage with the happiness of domestic life. He wrote that the compromise and cheerfulness needed to create the atmosphere for a happy home life rested with the wife. "Women must go to the borders of self-sacrifice and self-denial in order to do everything for her husband."[37] He believed that this behavior on the part of the wife led the husband to do the same. In this convoluted way Alcott proffered that once educated by her husband's example, the wife would then accept the responsibility for restraining her husband's behavior as required. In Chapter Eleven, Dr. Alcott states that "every wife should remember the measure of a husband's respect will be graduated by the respect she manifests for herself." He goes on to write in Chapter Twenty, "I do not place too high an estimate on the domestic qualifications; her intellectual, social, and moral qualifications are of more consequence."[38] In her 1857 diary, Phebe writes, "I do love mental better than manual labor."[39] Alcott detailed the importance of hygiene, bathing, and neatness. He linked health with morals, emphasizing the wife's responsibility for her husband's health.[40]

---

36   1837
37   p. 76
38   p. 179
39   p. 11
40   p. 255

In *The Physiology of Marriage,* first published anonymously, Dr. Alcott wrote about the frequency of sexual intercourse, recommending once a month as a realistic expectation. He pro-scribed intercourse during pregnancy, believing it was injuri-ous to the fetus. He thought this danger increased if the mother experienced pleasure. "The nervous orgasm is too much for the young germ." He conceded that the prudent spacing of children might be necessary and that prolonged abstinence was in most cases an unrealistic goal. He offered the rhythm method or withdrawal as acceptable compromises.

As a physician there was no way he could escape the reality of sexual activity as a normal, if not indeed necessary, part of human physiology. His writings reflect his belief that the exis-tence of a function implied use; certainly this was the case with men. With regard to women, however, Alcott displayed "an am-bivalence characteristic of his generation."[41] He seemed pained to acknowledge that women did feel such desire. Much of his theory dealt with self-restraint in sexual matters in harmony with other aspects of life, self-preservation topping the list and ardency in sexual matters ranking second.

Dr. Alcott assured women that they as wives had to strive to keep their husbands happy. Keeping Joseph happy required a lack of candor with her husband that Phebe regretted. She could not bring up the topics that upset or angered him. She knew her interest in the news about women's rights would certainly anger him. Joseph Hanaford, as a Baptist, did not share her views on the right of women to speak in public or to preach. A woman had little preparation for marriage as Dr. Alcott defined it. In his abstract and impractical advice, Dr. Alcott wrote of the happy

41   Introduction to 1972 edition

atmosphere in the home, not of the happiness of the members of the household. He believed a wife should be content with her surroundings. Phebe, pregnant in 1851, became discontented with life on the mainland. She wanted her child to be born a "Nantucketer."

On Nantucket, Phebe would be among the people she knew. Joseph had reason to fear that meant Quakers, but he agreed to return to Nantucket Island. Before their plans were completed, Phebe received news that her grandmother, Love Barnard, had died. Love Barnard, who had contributed to the upbringing of the child whose birth led to the death of her own daughter, would never see the baby Phebe carried. Her grandmother's death confirmed her desire to return to the Island where she would enjoy the familiar customs of Nantucket family life. Some would be Quaker ways, no doubt. Phebe's preparations included the promise to be "a loving wife and a good Baptist." If they left soon, she would have the house settled by the time she had the baby. The surviving pages of her 1857 diary tell of the final months of her life on Nantucket Island where they lived from 1851 to 1857.

NANTUCKET

Joseph Hanaford leased Captain Ray's house located off Center Street, currently #6 Step Lane. Phebe now lived among Quakers and other women who were childhood friends, with opportunities to visit her grandparents during the day. Based on summaries of his *Plowman's Manual of Health,* Joseph encouraged Phebe to avoid tea as an unnecessary stimulant and encouraged her to rest, and nourished her with eggs and milk.

Folks on Nantucket soon requested Dr. Hanaford's professional services. His contact with the sick on the Island alerted
him to the false belief held by many there that alcohol could
relieve illness. Dr. Hanaford formulated his thoughts on this
subject in articles for the Massachusetts Total Abstinence Society
entitled *Intoxicants in Home Treatment of the Sick.* He applied for
the teaching position in the local school vacated by Miss Maria
Mitchell, a woman with a reputation as a strong believer in the
study of science for girls as well as the boys. Maria Mitchell is
remembered for bringing fame to the island upon establishing
the orbit of a new comet in 1847.

In the evenings, comforted by the other's presence, Phebe
and Joseph kept their desks close, spending hours writing under
the same lamp. On just such an evening in 1852, a poem poured
out from her heart. She entitled it *Love of Country.*

The land endeared by many tender ties,
When from afar it dawns on sailor's eyes,
A thrill of joy will send to every heart,
For "love of country" in each soul hath part.

With speed is done the work of every hour,
As each more nearly brings the wished for shore;
Each heart rejoices in the prospect bright,
For oh! the land they love is now in sight.

So with each Christian Sailor on life's sea;
All sadness, and all doubt forever flee,
As near, and nearer yet the scenes appear,
His heart so long hath held as very dear.

Oh, yes, who spread the white sail wide and free,
As voyagers on life's stormy, restless sea,
Seek ye a pilot, who will guide you right,
By heaven's own chart, until the land's in sight.

Seated at her desk, Phebe began writing a romantic novel. She used her family names of Love and Obed Barnard for the names of the parents of her heroine. The family would belong to the Society of Friends. The heroine becomes a preacher. In this novel, Phebe develops her assumption of the right of women to preach. Her vision of the role of women in ministry reveals her own unfulfilled desires. A storyline that included abolition reflected her Quaker concern for the abolition of slavery. Would she include her concern for temperance? Both issues could be linked with the need for women's rights. In the end, she chose abolition. The main character of *Lucretia, the Quakeress or Principle Triumphant*[42] takes shape as someone who would make great sacrifices for her convictions regarding abolition.

Phebe developed the character of Hannah, Lucretia's friend, to contrast with the docile Lucretia. Somewhat lacking in decorum and often rebellious regarding Quaker customs, Hannah will marry within the Society of Friends. Lucretia will not. As the story progresses, Phebe's heroine enjoys the loving attentions of young Morton Fitzroy, a southerner and slaveholder. Lucretia's mother tells her daughter she and Lucretia's father would never oppose her marrying the slave owner, nor could they ever condone it. The choice is hers. In spite of her love for the young, handsome, highly intellectual southerner, Lucretia follows the voice of the "Inward Monitor," telling her she could

---

42   Hanaford, Phebe A., 1853

not be mistress of a mansion staffed by slaves. Phebe vividly describes Lucretia's agony in her steadfast refusal of Fitzroy's offer of marriage unless he frees his slaves. His wealth and material possessions and his position in Southern society make it unthinkable for him to live without slaves. Years pass before the lovers meet again.

Phebe chooses New York City as the setting for their reunion. Fitzroy escorts his mother and sister to a Roman Catholic Church where the pomp displeases him and he leaves. He passes a Quaker Hall. Still haunted by the memory of Lucretia, he goes inside where he finds Lucretia to be the visiting preacher. She recognizes Fitzroy seated in the audience. Her topic is slavery. He leaves the Meeting without speaking to her. Lucretia sighs, "not to recall the words which banished Fitzroy from her presence, though she could not avoid, at times, the wish that there had been no occasion for their utterance."[43]

Phebe left her work on the story after the birth of their son on New Year's Eve, 1851. They agreed to name him Howard Alcott Hanaford. The weather and the care of her son kept Phebe confined to the house. Working on her novel, she developed Fitzroy's frame of mind as he leaves the Quaker Hall and returns to the fact that neither Lucretia nor her parents know how deeply Fitzroy has been affected by her sermon. She details his memories of faithful slaves, sometimes abused and never appreciated as full human beings. Fitzroy associates slavery with his family's extravagant lifestyle and its sharp contrast to all that he loves in Lucretia. Fitzroy faces down the objections of his family and the criticism of his neighbors and "he called his slaves together

---

43   Ibid, p. 115

as soon as the proper measures were taken, and secured to each and all their freedom."[44] His slaves, now free men and women in free America, remain on as paid servants. Ultimately, Fitzroy has won his own freedom. The reader senses Phebe's freedom as her pen flows easily over this topic dear to her heart.

The literary style of the day portrayed delicate, often sickly heroines. The author knew her novel had to appeal to the public. She compromised with a sickbed scene where Fitzroy returns to Nantucket to find Lucretia close to death. The romantic Phebe writes of Fitzroy's devotion to the dying Lucretia. The past is forgiven and the lovers accept the inevitable. Because of her vision of women's strength, Lucretia survives her illness. With her miraculous recovery, the novel continues on to their marriage. On Fitzroy's plantation the young bride becomes to their freed slaves all that any abolitionist would want to be.

Centered on the Fugitive Slave Law that had fired up the Quaker abolitionists since its passage two years earlier, the novel portrays how the husband and wife follow the path of the just and assist runaway slaves in defiance of the law. She portrays Lucretia not as a submissive wife but as a partner in a marriage of mutuality. Phebe's heroine exemplifies the role of women as a force for social change in the home, in society and in the church. The abolitionist paper, *The Independent Democrat* of Concord, New Hampshire, agreed to print her novel in the customary installments throughout the summer of 1852. That year Harriett Beecher Stowe's *Uncle Tom's Cabin* spread across the nation. Both authors addressed slavery through female characters. Lucretia, portrayed as a woman living on the cutting edge of reform, was

---

44   Ibid, p. 144

distinct from Eva, a child in delicate health who dies unable to free Uncle Tom, a symbol of the faithful slave.

Both authors acknowledge that women remain without political power. Both heroines depend to differing degrees on the rights and powers of their male counterparts. Stowe remained focused on abolition while Phebe wrote of a woman in ministry, an equal partner in marriage. In a significant portrayal of Phebe's attitude toward women's rights, she wrote, "If women had as much voice in the counsels of the nation as she has in Friends Meetings, this hideous evil would long ago have ceased to exist but since it is not woman's place, at present, to vote, she should prepare herself, and labor to influence rightly those who can vote."[45] The words "at present" speak of her political savvy in anticipating universal suffrage, which was six decades away. J. Buffum of Boston published her 172-page novel in 1853: *Lucretia the Quakeress or Principle Triumphant* by Mrs. Joseph Hanaford. In time Phebe sent a copy of the book to John Greenleaf Whittier. His response is found in Phebe Hanaford's article, "A Glimpse of Whittier" at the Phillips Library in the Peabody Museum.

Amesbury 3d 2d mo. 1853

My friend, dear,

I thank thee from my heart for thy very kind letter with the accompanying book and poem. My mother, sister, and myself have read "Lucretia" with a great deal of interest. It is very true to the Quaker character–as it should be always–and as it sometimes is. Hannah is a well-drawn picture from real life, I am sure.

---

45   Ibid, p. 162

I really feel grateful for thy lines, although jumbled by a sense of ill-deserving them.

It would give me great pleasure to visit your Island home, but my health is such that I seldom leave my residence. Should it improve, I should like to try the effect of your sea-air next summer.

Believe me, cordially thy friend,

John G. Whittier

In preparation for the birth of their second child, the Hanafords moved to Center Street, two doors from North Church where on March 19, 1854 Florence Elizabeth was born. The home in a photo of the Hanaford family standing on the porch is easily recognizable as the current home at 55 Center Street minus the front porch. Phebe's father and stepmother, Joseph and several children stand with Phebe, who regrettably shows evidence of having lost her teeth. Dressed in black with a white collar, she appears very thin with her hair pulled tight over her high forehead.

In the winter of 1855 members of St. Paul's Episcopal Church invited Rev. Charles Canfield to take pastoral oversight of the parish. Talk in town spread that a townswoman, Mrs. Chapin, had sources from his old parish that reported attendance had dropped during his time as pastor and that his former parishioners had asked him to leave. Rev. Canfield challenged the accusation and Mrs. Chapin publicly retracted her statements. The talk spread outside the parish where he now strove to increase attendance.

As Rev. Canfield pored over the registry to find the names of parishioners who no longer attended St. Paul's, he found Rev. Allen's entry of Phebe Coffin's Baptism and published this information in the press. Correspondence in the Hanaford Archives (Nantucket Historical Association) tells the story.

Mrs. Hanaford was baptized in the Protestant Episcopal Church, on this Island. One of my Wardens stood her God-father, and the doctrine of the church is "once a baptized member the obligation is forever." Admitting that I did say she was an Episcopalian what harm was that done her? None at all. With Mrs. H. I have but a slight acquaintance having been introduced to her in the house of a neighbor, then I saw her but a few moments, and between us kind words alone passed. I have always heard from members of my parish that she was held in the highest estimation, and until the reception of these letters, I have felt the same towards her. To the above letter, I took the advice of a friend and made no reply whatever and, from its reception to the present time, said nothing about the lady, because I did not consider it a matter of sufficient importance to talk about, and had supposed the matter dropped forever, when, to my surprise, I received the following letters from her pen, and that of her husband's. They will tell their own story and need no words of mine.

In defense of her position, Phebe wrote Mr. Canfield a letter.

Nantucket, March 22d, 1856

Mr. Canfield: — Learning that you have reported that I am an Episcopalian, I deem it a duty which I owe to myself, occupying a place in a Baptist Church, to state that such a report is erroneous.

Although there are some pleasant associations connected with that Church in the past, I have no wish to return to it, especially under existing circumstances.
Respectfully,
Phebe Hanaford

His insistence on her membership continued to be heard around town. Joseph suggested a rational approach to put an end to the matter. He advised Phebe to write again to Rev. Canfield, and he would also write under separate cover. She agreed to his suggestion and sat at her desk to write.

Mr. Canfield: — I deeply regret that the cause of Christ in this place has an enemy in one whose position and profession should make him its warmest friend. Yet, if you persist in declaring that I wish to re-connect myself with the Episcopal Church, but my husband will not allow it, I am compelled to believe you a true son of the "father of lies," especially after I have once denied it to you.

I am a Baptist from choice, not from necessity, and defy you to prove the contrary. My word to this effect is sufficient in this community, where I am too well known to be disbelieved. Unless you see fit to change your course, I shall feel obliged to report your conduct to my honored friend the Bishop of this Diocese, who is too good a Christian to suffer such conduct to pass unrebuked.

April 18, 1856.
P. A. HANAFORD

Joseph sat at his desk across from his wife and wrote to Rev. Canfield.

Mr. Canfield: — When a professed minister of the gospel descends from his high position to engage in petty tricks, deception and misrepresentation, he ceases to merit and receive respect from me. I unqualifiedly pronounce your statements in regard to myself and wife false! and may in the future feel called upon to demand your authority. And should you deem it expedient to call at our house with an "undocumented sheriff." I trust that you will not meet a frightened or a deluded woman. I shall feel myself at liberty to make any false statements as public as I please, (and I have some facilities for so doing that all do not possess) and shall not affix my name to any document that will restrain me. In closing, allow me to say that I have reasons to suppose that you may find enough in your own family to attend to, without intermeddling with those with whom you have not the most distant connection.

Yours pointedly,

J. H. HANAFORD

Nantucket, April 17th

P.S. You are at liberty to do with this as you may deem expedient.

J. H. H.

The Rev. Canfield went to the press with letters he received through the post office from people he described as "the opposition." His article appeared under the heading, An Appeal To The Public, and included the three letters from the Hanafords. The effect of this publication served to describe the Hanafords' united stand in defense of her choice to be a member of the Baptist Church without denying Phebe's baptism in the Episcopal Church. We know Phebe had studied higher mathematics with Rev. Allen, and this may have provided the occasion for her baptism in the Episcopal Church. She appears to have been in search of religious truths even when young.

In 1856 Joseph signed a five-year lease for the ground floor of a house on North Water Street for $100 a year. Flanked on both sides by residences, the wide road accommodated carriages and sleds. In their new home, Phebe placed their writing desks on the table where they shared the gas lamp. A woman named Nancy Coffin, who rented the top floor, welcomed the Hanafords and took a great liking to the children. Howard immediately called her Aunt Nancy. Nancy knew Mrs. Hanaford had obligations at her church and assured her she would be happy to mind the children. She introduced the Hanafords to Mr. and Mrs. Watson. When it became apparent the couple read good literature, Joseph invited them to see their collection of books, offering to make them available to them at any time.

Writing in the evenings, Phebe developed a children's book for Sunday school she titled *Leonette, a Sunday School Book*. About her book, she wrote in her diary that she took on the task at the suggestion of Rev. Alfred Colburn. He requested a historical account of different religions told as a novel with religious characters. In sharing the book, she commented, "L. G. S. almost but not entirely agreed with me against infant baptism but thought I gave the Presbyterians rather a bad character." The book, published in 1857, received favorable reviews. Phebe rejoiced at her success as a writer because she was able to contribute to the family income. Encouraged by her success, she wrote in her diary,

I wonder how many who read that book, and are strangers to my mode of life; imagine that the authoress ever bends over the wash tub, not pensively, but to work in good earnest. Well, am I ashamed of it? No, indeed! Yet if I had a market for all I could write, I would write myself and pay someone who needs the money to do the washing. But while my husband has to toil so hard to support us all, I must not shrink from work, even tho' I do love mental better than manual labor.

The twenty-five pages of the 1857 diary covering January through May reveal an active life for Phebe. Grandmother Coffin often kept the children, allowing Phebe a considerable amount of freedom. Phebe regretted she seldom saw her parents who still lived in S'conset with the rest of the family. Lower Hussey Street where the Coffins once owned their property was now seeded over for a park. She renewed friendships with Lydia Hussey, Sarah Easton and Mary Starbuck. Narcissus Coffin joined them in their visits to the Almshouse. The inmates, some of whom were seamen, greeted the visitors who brought them words of hope and salvation. Conversion of souls to Jesus stirred Phebe, and she felt called to this work. At times she became effusive in her praise and was cautioned against adulation.

On one such occasion, she said to an elderly seaman at work on a rattan basket, "Do you sell these?" Before he could answer, she ordered one to be ready next week when she came. He thanked her; his eyes brimmed with tears and Phebe moved toward him with her arms in the gesture of an embrace. Narcissus restrained her. In the hall she spoke to Phebe about her adulation, which the women considered inappropriate. On her walk home, she reflected on what had happened. She saw no inconsistency between her feelings and her behavior. Phebe wrote more than once about being corrected for her adulation, adding that she did not understand such restraint regarding those loved by God. In her diary she quotes Judge Storz who wrote that "flattery is not a vice if it relates to those we love with ardent sympathy." She believed what could be a vice becomes a radiant virtue when done with sincerity. Only suspicious minds consider expressions of esteem hypocrisy. "I am sincere when I praise those I love."

Among those she loved were Doctor and Narcissus Coffin who now shared the house with the Hanafords. Phebe wrote of visiting with them upstairs where with these devout Friends she shared her desire to spread the gospel, to be a missionary in foreign lands in imitation of Sybil Jones, a Quakeress who preached equality of the sexes to women in Muslim countries. She wrote of her daily responsibilities that they were an obstacle to her doing this type of mission work or other work outside her home.

The Lily, edited by Amelia Bloomer, told of a May meeting with Lucy Stone and Elizabeth Cady Stanton at Stanton's home in Seneca Falls, New York. The article listed Horace Greeley and Susan B. Anthony, described as longtime advocates of temperance. The logic of the union of the two causes, temperance and women's rights, seemed obvious to Miss Anthony. Phebe and Joseph discussed temperance; equally agreeable was everything that bound her to home and church. She records,

> *In my meditations, yesterday, over it, I came to the conclusion –*
> *not a new one – that* Religion *was the sovereign remedy for the*
> *social ills which mar the beauty and destroy the happiness of*
> *our world, and its inhabitants. The Gospel is the only antidote*

*for sin. Christ alone can overcome Satan. I told my dear hus-
band what I had been thinking about when he came home and
he agreed with me. How blessed this Christian agreement.*

At the Baptist services, Phebe listened attentively to the minister's words. She always looked for a practical application of the
scripture to her life. She wanted to be a good wife, and wrote that
she regretted the Baptist atmosphere found her ill at ease. On the
contrary, when she joined the women visiting the Almshouse,
she felt comfortable preaching to the men. She read aloud from
the Scriptures and saw to it that every room was visited. Privately
she embraced those she felt in need of additional comfort.

She tried to be home when Joseph returned from his tutor-
ing. There was love and agreement in their marriage as long as
she did not speak of her Quaker ideals. Alone, Phebe chided
herself for her inability to share her deepest aspirations with
her husband. She wanted to be a preacher. She admired his devotion to his faith and remembered her promise to embrace her
husband's religion when they married. Any discussion on differences of religious observances angered him. She wrote that
she felt dishonest because the religious practices she observed
did not harmonize with her Inner Voice.

Writing in a different light, she described the happy times
she and Joseph spent with the children. She repeatedly referred
to the appropriateness of raising her children in Nantucket,
speaking in the Quaker tongue to those who remembered her
when she was carried in her father's arms. She recalled memories of her happy childhood. Phebe told Howard of the hours
she spent at Brant Point. She recited her poems to him to amuse
him during their hours together. From *Shore to Shore,*

There have I gamboled oft in childhood's glee,
Climbing each sandy hill,
Gathering fair shells and wave-worn pebbles bright,
Watching each snowy sail.
And there I saw, in pebble and in shell,
In wave and fish and weed,
Those tokens of God's presence which I crave
To meet my spirit's need.

Dr. Hanaford's homeopathic practice flourished and the herb garden became his favorite project. Her husband's health, never good in the winter, improved visibly in the warmer weather. Food for the table came from the garden. Phebe enjoyed tending it more than the housecleaning that the change of season demanded.

She saw the Sabbath as a day of rest as well as a time to glean a message from the scriptures and Rev. Bartlett's sermons. She prepared carefully for the morning and evening services, avoiding the usual round of visits. Joseph made every effort to settle his obligations to his patients during the week. Teaching classes at the Sabbath school provided a delightful change for Phebe. She rejoiced at the faith the children expressed as they read the Bible stories. She told Joseph she did not always agree with the material in the books provided by the minister.

Phebe writes that she loved being with Joseph, but that they continued to disagree on many things relating to her Quaker ways. He disagreed with her stand against war. Phebe dreaded the thought of her or anyone she loved killing another human being for any reason. She admitted he argued his point better than she hers, but she remained steadfast in her thinking. When Joseph spoke at the church, she often did not have anyone to stay with the children and she regretted not hearing him. During the week she visited friends, talking with those of like mind, and she prayed that these conversations would bring them to a closer union with God. She described these exchanges as sweet conversations, noting in her diary that for herself "she enjoyed the power as well as the form of godliness."

While paying one of her visits to the sick, Phebe noticed a number of people gathered at the Unitarian Church. She learned they were waiting for Lucy Stone, their guest speaker. Phebe wrote in her diary that she remained outside to listen to Lucy Stone's talk because she knew Joseph would not approve of her going into the church. She and Joseph did not discuss Lucy Stone's public life because they could not come to an agreement on her work. Lucy did not appear to Phebe to be the average wife, and she could not deny that the social convention of the day disapproved of any woman speaking in public. Quakers limited this right of women to preach to the work of God's Spirit. Phebe believed Lucy used her God-given talent for a worthy, even a religious, cause when she spoke in support of the abolition of slavery. Dr. Hanaford agreed with Lucy's views on slavery, but he thought her continuing to speak her political opinion in public as a married woman to be an embarrassment.

Drawing from his knowledge and practice of homeopathic medicine, Dr. Hanaford wrote *Intoxicants in Home Treatment of the Sick*. Joseph served on the editorial staff of both *The Weekly Mirror* and *The Nantucket Inquirer*, and taught school. Phebe understood that her husband's positions increased his standing in the community. When the town agreed to build a new school on Academy Hill to house both the North Grammar and High Schools, Joseph, in his position as the principal of the Grammar School and a member of the Board, offered Dr. William Alcott's published opinions in *Confessions of a Schoolmaster* on good ventilation, lighting, seating arrangements and facilities for exercise. The project required months of negotiations. The committee ordered pine for stairs and black walnut for railings. Separate entrances for boys and girls admitted one hundred and seventy five students to classrooms fitted with inlaid blackboards and oak desks. The townsfolk watched as the two-storied edifice rose from the ground.

Joseph's meetings kept him late after school, and Phebe frequently wandered into the weekday gatherings at the Meetinghouse. On one occasion she stayed late, and Joseph reached home to find her out. The evening spent in uncomfortable silence carried a sense of foreboding. Even when she responded to his request that she read from the Bible, the mood did not change. It was not a prayerful experience. She agonized over their differences and wrote in her diary, "Came home today and Doctor H. here displeased. I felt very sorry I had done so and resolved that I would not do so again. He is afraid I shall be a Quaker. I do not wish to be, if I can stay conscientiously where I am, for I would rather be with him I love so well."

On the completion of the construction of the new school, Islanders gathered to hear the speeches and enjoy the ceremony. Seated on the raised platform, members of the Board accepted the expressions of appreciation for their work. According to newspapers of the day, the main announcements included the names of A. P. Whipple, principal of the High School and Doctor Joseph Hanaford, principal of the Grammar School. In his speech Mr. Whipple announced that, warmed by two Stimpson furnaces, there would be no more cold days for the Nantucket students. Phebe's heart filled with pride for the town and for her husband. His position as principal, along with his practice, gave his family a sense of security. Joseph spoke about buying land out west for future income in the event of his death. They never talked about death as a reality for either of them. Phebe wanted to be sensible about it and appreciated her husband's concern. She indicated that she would agree to any plans he made. That night she wrote in her diary, "May we live long together."

In spite of her resolve, she continued to feel discomfort during the Baptist services and her sense of disunion grew. In the evenings she read Haynes' *Baptist Denomination* to increase her understanding of the religious practices and looked for opportunities to discuss her discomfort with many of the practices. She believed the singers more interested in the tune than the words and the organist more interested in the choir than the service. She frequently refused to stand and join in the singing she believed unessential to public worship. She wrote in her diary, "It seems to me as if water baptism and the Lord's supper as we simply celebrate it are right, but if not, I desire to be taught otherwise."

Mary Farnum was among those Phebe sought for spiritual guidance. In her diary she recalls having seen Mary years earlier aboard the steamboat for New Bedford. She knew her as Mary Allen then, whom she had heard preach many years ago, and she recalled the eyes that shone when she spoke of God's goodness. Now in her eighties, she still possessed a keen mind under her frail appearance. Phebe made a habit of visiting Mary, and she listened to her words and sometimes challenged her on different issues. She loved their discussions and often, after more reflection at home, she would write a note to Mary acknowledging that she had been right on one of their matters of discussion. She considered Mary a Quaker saint full of Gospel love, possessing the wisdom that comes with a life lived following one's Inner Light. She loved Mary Farnum in Jesus and "enjoyed a kiss from a disciple of her Blessed Master." In time she shared with Mary her desire for spiritual growth.

At home, Phebe prepared topics appropriate for her children during their study time and read to them for recreation. The fire burned all day, consuming the wood brought weekly by the cart man. Phebe wrote that she offered him religious tracts, believing him ready for God's word. She also continued her Sabbath school classes. When her students requested entrance into the church, she knew them to be children of God, already baptized in the Spirit, which she believed to be the true baptism.

In an attempt to learn what was right in the sight of God, she occasionally ventured inside the Gurneyite Meetinghouse. She remembered Joseph Gurney's visit to the Island when she was nine years old. The English Quaker had written unfavorably about his American experience. Along with his disapproval of the abstinence from tea and meat, he was critical of the American Woman's Rights Movement.

Some of the talented women in this country are making a grand effort to obtain the same political rights and privileges as the man. They are aiming to be voters, orators... etc. What shall we all come to? I do not approve of ladies speaking in public, even in the Antislavery case, except under the immediate influences of the Holy Spirit.[46]

Mainland newspapers carried the news of the death of Hugh Miller, the Scottish geologist who died by his own hand in 1857. His suicide disturbed Phebe due to the opinion of many that Miller's insanity was due to his having overtaxed his brain. The

46   Leach

Hanafords had read several of his books including *Footprints of the Creator* and *The Old Red Sandstone*. Phebe wrote that she feared her own inclination to overtax her brain. In the same mail Joseph received a letter from Dr. Alcott asking him to give his opinion on his new book *Laws of Health*. Another letter told of Joseph's election as a corresponding member of the Iowa State Medical Society. Phebe believed Joseph deserved such recognition. Islanders considered her husband upright and an intelligent, gifted educator. They sought his opinion on church and civil matters, but his being recognized on the mainland meant more to both of them.

In the evening when they were not at church or attending lectures at the Athenium, Phebe read to Joseph from the *Essays of Tuckerman*, the American botanist. Their habit of reading often extended to the time before rising. The Sabbath began with reading the Bible followed by the first of two church services and Sabbath school. Phebe listened carefully to the sermons by Brother Gorham and judged them for their practicality. Together she and Joseph read the *Memoirs of Martha Whiting*, a Baptist teacher and the founder of the Charleston Female Seminary. The story of this woman, who died in Hingham, Massachusetts, not far from Newton, inspired Phebe with a desire to do good for Christ's cause. To fulfill this desire, she continued her work on a *History of the English Bible*. Along with their churchgoing, their relationship seemed best expressed in the pleasure they took in the quiet evenings, writing together. Phebe attributed this to their intellectual compatibility.

As a parent Joseph delighted in the children. To his great pleasure, Howard learned to read and do his numbers with remarkable speed. Phebe supervised the children's hours of play and hours of study and work. Both parents took careful note of how the children spent their time. On the Sabbath Phebe allowed the children to play with their toys because she believed it appropriate until they could read without supervision. As part of Howard's education, he accompanied his mother to the Almshouse. Along with her Quaker friends, Lydia Hussey and Mary Starbuck, they sang hymns and read the scriptures. Very often Phebe felt a duty to speak on a practical application of the readings. Any words she spoke to them she applied to herself. The response from the residents was her reward. Before she left, she visited the rooms of the sick. She often wrote that these refreshing seasons gave her peace and satisfaction. She enjoyed her companions at the Quaker Meetings that she now attended regularly. She truly desired to keep herself unspotted from the world. Her personal journey included a search of the truth. She read constantly and listened carefully and sorted through the inconsistencies she found in religions.

Phebe found great pleasure in visits from her parents. One evening they arrived with the news Governor Gordon had appointed Capt. George Coffin Commissioner of Wrecks. George asked Joseph to serve as one of his bondsmen and he willingly agreed. It is clear from her diary Joseph's relationship with her family mattered greatly to Phebe. In the closing pages of the surviving diary, Phebe wrote that she and Joseph took walks together after weeks of winter weather. From her diary we learn that on such a walk it was Phebe who spoke first of leaving the Island. She told Joseph that at times she felt she would like to leave the Island. He answered that he felt that way all the time. His words confirmed her suspicions. She knew living in the cold aggravated Joseph's lung problems. She also knew Joseph never liked living on the Island and he stayed these six years for her sake. In her diary she wrote, "Where thou goest

I will go for I love him too well not to be willing to go wherever is best for him."

Bitter winds and snowdrifts of March confirmed their decision. On days when school closed, Phebe read *Roles at Play* to the children for entertainment and *Marmeduke Multiply* and *The Worcester Primer* to prepare them for school. After Howard's spelling lessons she spent time with Florence who would be three years old that month. When her children were settled for the night and Joseph wrote at his desk, Phebe concluded her latest work entitled *Best of Books*. The inclement weather curtailed the visitors that Phebe sometimes felt frittered away her time. She saw all this visiting as an evil consequence of social intercourse. Even knowing some good came of it for those who did not need the quiet, the interruptions bothered her. She preferred their time together and she wrote in her diary, "We try to live in harmony and seem to be successful for the most part. At any rate we love each other and differences are only of opinion on a few important points." Their marital differences centered on the important point of her renewed attraction to Quakerism.

Her friends in Christ with whom she found spiritual comfort as they attended meetings and visited the sick caused constant irritation to Joseph. She did not intend to offend him and prayed for guidance, but she could find no reason why she should abandon all that gave her the same spiritual comfort she tried to bring to others. When Joseph expressed disapproval, she prayed for forgiveness. She understood her commitments outside the home angered him and she made special efforts to make his evenings at home comfortable, preparing packs for his chafing skin and reading to him. She picked topics where they had agreement. Her willingness to go with Joseph could not hold back the tears when she visited her grandparents. Knowing how they would grieve when they went away, she told them they would not be with them the following spring.

The presidential election of James Buchanan disappointed both of them. They preferred the more radical Republican candidate, John Charles Fremont, because of his views on the plight of the Negro. Young men like Thomas Borton, who came to say good-bye before leaving for Boston where he had the promise of a job, heightened her awareness of the injustices colored men suffered when looking for work. That night she wrote in her diary, "Would that his entire race were free." The ferry that carried young Thomas to his new life brought mail and a book from Dr. Alcott. Howard claimed the privilege of carrying the book since he knew the meaning of namesake. Phebe continued her work on the *History of the English Bible*.

Phebe's reputation as one who could help others frequently brought troubled souls to her door. One evening a neighbor arrived claiming to be locked out of her house and had nowhere to go. Joseph agreed she could stay with them as long as necessary. Phebe took her to the evening prayer meeting believing it would bring her some peace. In the morning she found the woman reading her Bible. That afternoon she announced she would return home. Phebe believed these incidences provided opportunities to bring people closer to salvation.

At the close of winter a young woman named Sarah Patterson joined the group visiting the Almshouse. Phebe knew the young convert from the Baptist prayer meetings and judged her to be a devoted Christian, talented and willing to labor for Jesus. In time her growing attraction for Sarah made it impossible to take her eyes off her at services. Convinced God had given her this young girl to love and to do her good, Phebe signaled Sarah to sit next to her. After the service they walked home where she gave Sarah Todd's *Student Manual*. She offered to instruct Sarah in her studies and suggested her husband could also help her with her lessons. That night Phebe prayed God would sanctify their friendship. In her diary she wrote, "She is 19 and I 28, but that is nothing. I loved Eliza intensely, tho' I was younger than she."

The next morning Phebe could not settle her mind on anything; she could only think of Sarah. She sent her a message expressing her feelings and received a note in return. Sarah's words of love for Phebe served to increase her preoccupation with her. She attempted to work on her *History of the English Bible* but could not concentrate. It vexed her she had so little self control. In an effort to keep busy she went out to make calls and to ask women to make a joint purchase of a twenty-five dollar sewing machine. She ended her calls at the Patterson home to visit Sarah's mother. She and Sarah could not talk privately. Mrs. Patterson agreed Sarah would benefit from lessons in Latin and Geometry from Dr. Hanaford.

Phebe knew Joseph never denied her anything that kept her at home. She spoke of Sarah and Joseph agreed to tutor her. The evenings spent with Sarah became part of their routine. She believed loving one very much, as she did Sarah, did not cause her to love others less. Watching Joseph with Sarah intensified her sense that because she loved Sarah, she loved her family, the whole world and God better. She remembered the words of Whittier, "God was loved through love of man." Recalling their evening hours spent together helped Phebe get through her morning chores. In the afternoon Sarah called on Phebe.

On Communion Sundays, Phebe took communion with less pleasure than usual. In her heart the idea of communion with Jesus had little to do with the form it took. Her Quaker convictions were not strong enough for her to give up her Baptist practices. She thanked God for Sarah's love that made the Sabbath hours more joyful. Their time together served to convince them both that their love brought them into true communion with Jesus. Phebe returned home only to look forward to the evening when Sarah came for lessons.

Sarah and Phebe often met accidentally or as Phebe preferred, providentially. They always sat together at Services. Joseph frequently called on patients on Sunday and on those occasions she and Sarah walked together after Sunday school. They found excuses to be together and left messages for each other in an oak tree arranging to be together after the Almshouse meetings. If through some misunderstanding they did not meet, Phebe visited Sarah's parents and even though Sarah did not speak, just seeing her brought a comfort to Phebe who wanted to be with her.

She also thought of Sarah when working in her garden with the children. Florence held the gate open for Howard who pushed his own wheelbarrow. She enjoyed their company and took them for daily visits to their grandparents. One evening Joseph showed Phebe his letter of resignation he intended to give to the School Committee. Joseph experienced failing eyes and some weakness in his lungs. His health, he wrote in the letter, would not permit him to continue but he would remain until they found a replacement. He also told Phebe he was tired of Nantucket.

Sitting alone she knew Joseph had never enjoyed the people of the Island. She went to talk to Aunt Nancy who was like a mother to her. Now that the letter of resignation had made their departure seem imminent, the tears came in spite of her effort to choke them back. She sought consolation in prayer and the belief this change meant better days for them. She prayed, "My trust, oh God, is in Thee."

When Joseph took a trip to Hyannis, Phebe prepared everything for him but showed her displeasure at being left alone. She took the children to see their grandparents and then went to invite Sarah to spend the night with her. She got caught in a heavy rain and a passerby carried Florence. Phebe's long dress was soaked by the time they got home. When Sarah arrived late afternoon wet from the rain, Phebe gave her a gown to wear. The rain continued the next day and a gentleman came in a cart to take Sarah home. She promised to return again that evening. Although Sarah eased the loneliness, Phebe wrote in her diary that she missed her dear husband.

The next day the weather forced her to stay home. Her cousin, George Coffin, stopped by to see her and the children and he lightened up the dark day. He bid them good-bye after supper and she put the children to bed and waited for Sarah. She delighted in her company as Sarah talked of her work at school and her studies. They planned a program for the Almshouse, prayed together and prepared for bed. Of their time together Phebe wrote in her diary, "Sister Sarah came again and spent the night. She is an apt scholar in kissing, which is something I like with those I love as I do her."

The weather cleared on Wednesday and Phebe called on her friends. She visited Mary Farnum and then went to see her grandparents. In the evening Aunt Nancy stayed with the children while Phebe went to the prayer meeting. Brother Graham, Sarah, and other members of their group came back to her house for their usual visit. When they left, Sarah and Phebe prayed together and read from the Bible. They slept together through the night.

At the customary Friday meeting at the Almshouse, Phebe and Sarah met Sarah Easton and her sister, Emily Jane. Phebe prayed they might become sisters in Jesus. George Coleworthy read from the Gospel of John and the guests joined in the singing. At the close of the meeting they gathered around, shaking hands and expressing their gratitude for the visit. Phebe and Sarah Easton made the rounds of the sick rooms. Phebe remained with Aunt Wright while the others distributed tracts to those unable to attend the meeting. She records the dying Negress' words, "I'se going home." Phebe praised the sincerity of the woman's words and believed them to be true. She sat with her offering words of comfort. Phebe had witnessed death from a distance as seamen's bodies washed ashore on S'conset amidst the roar of the ocean. This was very different. Not only feeling close to the dying woman whom she had come to know and love, she rejoiced in the beauty of the silence. Aunt Wright dozed off to sleep and Phebe left her.

As she turned into the foyer Phebe saw Joseph. He obviously had come directly from the boat. He looked pleased to see her. Phebe knew he loved her very much and it lifted the sadness she had felt while he was away. They left to pick up the children, delighted to be together again. The hours were filled with talk of his trip and how she had kept busy while he was away. Phebe sat thinking of how Sarah helped her through her separation from Joseph. She wrote in her diary, "I was sorry for Sarah, for we were both disappointed in not being able to sleep together one more night as we had expected, since we may never again have the privilege."

Phebe helped the children with their reading at home as the cold day foretold of a storm. A messenger came to the door with an envelope saying no answer was needed. Phebe opened it and read a love note telling her Charlotte H. was in love with her. Her first reaction was to wonder that in spite of her faults she could merit so much love. Phebe welcomed new friends as added blessings sent by God as tokens of his goodness. The letter suggested they meet the following day at the Athenium. Phebe, Sarah, and other women friends met there for their regular prayer meeting. She prayed, "if God designs our acquaintance may he sanctify it to our good." Charlotte joined the group and Phebe welcomed her with a warm embrace and they exchanged their first kiss of friendship.

Later a message of a very different nature brought word to her that a Mrs. Gross had proved false to her marriage vows. The unsigned note referred to Phebe's concern for the spiritual well being of others. The information saddened her and disturbed her usual Sabbath enjoyment. She found it hard to believe this woman guilty of such a sin. Self-respect, she thought, would prevent such a crime. She remained at home praying for direction. On Monday she walked slowly to the address given, resolved not to speak harshly or to condemn in any way. She would take her cues from the accused woman the moment she opened the door to her. In response to her knock a well-groomed middle-aged woman answered and looked at her through eyes that betrayed hours of crying. She recognized Phebe and gestured for her to come in. Phebe followed Mrs. Gross into a tastefully decorated parlor where she joined her on a settee. She took her hand and kissed her. She spoke to her of Jesus, friend of sinners. Phebe believed her to be deeply repentant. In writing of her visit in her diary she concluded that she felt the woman "more sinned against than sinning." She prayed that no such evil should befall her family and thanked God for his mercy in keeping her from such sin. Where, she wondered, could Mrs. Gross turn for assurance of God's forgiveness and love? She wrote in her diary that this experience renewed her desire to use her remaining days on the Island,

> *...to start a Union Female Praying Circle an association where women of different religious affiliations could freely speak of their spiritual needs. I felt a call of duty to the work on Fast day while praying at noon. Women need time to pray with women and a place to address their personal needs, spiritual or otherwise. Ministers do not understand women have religious ambitions. When we share our common quest for growth in the love of God we give strength to each other. That becomes our common ground and we will grow from there.*

On May 5, Phebe wrote,

> *....met with a number of ladies at the Methodist (Center street) Church, where I was requested to propose Mrs. Fish as moderator and she then read a Constitution which I had previously prepared. We discussed, modified and adopted it, chose our officers.*

Sensing the importance of this historic event, Phebe added,

> *Perhaps in after years, it may be interesting to me to know who the first officers of the Nantucket Female Union Praying Circle were. Mrs. Fish Presiding Sister-Assistants — Mrs. Elisha Smith, Mrs. Derrick, Mrs. Dunham, Mrs. Cathcart. At Mrs. Fish's request I closed the meeting with prayer. Thus was organized this Union Circle which I believe to have been divinely suggested.*

On May 11 Phebe concluded,

...the band of sisters of the Union Prayer Meeting met in the vestry of North Church upper room. 77 were present, 32 signed the Constitution. Mrs. Fish presided admirably. I had a few words to say on Grieve not the holy Spirit of God for thereby we are sealed unto the day of redemption. I dare not be dumb when my Master calls.

It may be time here to reflect on the strength of Phebe's conviction that she was called by God to fill this void in women's lives. This ecumenical gathering of women may have been the first of its kind. With no model to follow, no one affirmed her but her Inner Voice. Here Phebe entered into the world of her cousin Lucretia Mott, Sybil Jones and Mary Farmer, preachers whom she admired and wanted to emulate. This fulfilled what may have appeared to the reader of her diary until this time to be the romantic dream of a pious soul.

Phebe told her Sunday school students she would soon be leaving the Island. Over time she had grown very fond of her pupils and they of her. Turning her class over to Sarah Patterson offered some consolation. On dark stormy days when Phebe appeared unable to hide her sadness, "joy and peace were again restored through the kind words of my noble and generous husband. I do dearly love him. Oh may nothing interrupt the course of our confidence and affection! Above all may we be united in Christ."

Walking along the beach, Howard and Florence spoke of their love for their parents. She wrote in her diary that she shared in their innocence and prayed she would always be as pure as the angels. In the evenings she wrote dialogue for Joseph's book.

Friends stopped by to say good-bye. On another evening she sent Howard with a note to Sarah to invite her to come and recite for them. It gave her pleasure to watch Joseph's enjoyment as he listened to Sarah read. Phebe wrote, "How pleasant it is! My own darling husband, here enjoying my dear sister's gentle ministry, and I enjoying both. God be praised!"

On May 24, Phebe wrote, "Sabbath beauty has clothed the earth today." She wrote of visitors and visiting and of Howard running errands for her. "Sun very hot. Vegetation advances rapidly." In the evening Howard joined his parents at a meeting and then they took a walk "to enjoy the stillness and the sunshine."

The loss of the remaining pages of her 1857 diary casts a stillness over her final days on Nantucket. Unlike the young woman who years ago left her family behind to sail to the mainland, in 1857 she took her family with her. With Joseph, Howard and Florence at her side, they were a family like other families leaving the Island with no plans to return. In time aboard the ferry, Phebe would watch her beloved Nantucket fade from view.

CHAPTER THREE

LITERARY WOMAN

I write for every kind of paper
that will pay me since the burden of
supporting my family is laid upon me.[47]

In the decade, 1860-1870, Phebe A. Hanaford published seven books,

...which have met with encouraging sale. The Best of Books and its History, published in 1860, having previously been delivered, chapter by chapter, as lectures given in the Baptist Sunday school of Nantucket; The Young Captain, a memorial of Capt. Richard C. Darby, who fell at Antietam, published in 1865; Frank Nelson, or the Runaway Boy a juvenile, published in 1865; Life of Abraham Lincoln, published in 1865 by B. B. Russell of Boston, the sale of which reached twenty thousand, five thousand of which being also published in German; Field, Gunboat, Hospital and Prison, being records of the war, published in 1866; and The Soldier's Daughter, a prize story, also in 1866; The Life of George Peabody in 1870 (which reached a sale of sixteen thousand).[48]

47   Letter to Sister Martha Jane, 1866
48   Hanaford, Phebe A., 1881, p. 222

BEVERLY

During the early years of the Civil War, the Hanaford family lived in the maritime city of Beverly, Massachusetts and attended the local Baptist church where they were assigned "109, wall pew." To reconstruct this period of her life, we depend on her publications and the surviving pages of her unpublished "Sabbath Journal," where she wrote weekly entries between August and November 1860. Phebe opens her Journal,

> *I am convinced by past experience in journalizing that I shall more fully fix the sermons I hear upon my memory, and so deeply upon my heart, if I keep some sort of record of them. I have resolved upon commencing this Sabbath Journal, hoping it will be found useful as well as pleasant to me now and in years to come – if years to come be mine.*[49]

Her Nantucket experience of hearing women preachers confirmed her belief that women had the right to preach. Her hours of voice training at Brant Point and keeping her "Sabbath Journal" provided her personal learning tools. These entries witness to her spiritual journey in search for truth. Her critique of sermons and detailed descriptions of preachers serve as a manual for good preaching. Of their first Sabbath, Phebe noted that Pastor Rev. Foster conducted the familiar service, and his delivery and the content of the sermon were very well done. She appreciated his logical and practical style and signs of scholarship that influenced her faith. She particularly appreciated a sermon she described as pungent exhortation to back sliders. She gave her pastor good grades for one in which he described a

49   Nantucket Historical Association

good Christian as sociable as distinct from a recluse … and his description of household duties as requiring household piety.

Writing of a visiting clergyman to the Baptist church, she described Rev. Thatcher's fine forehead, adding, "He has an unpleasant voice … contortions of the face when speaking, and speaks rather low at times, but sometimes his voice has a rich ring as he uttered some eloquent sentences, and then his face was smooth with an open, pleasing expression."

Phebe heard Rev. Dr. Hamlin preach at the South Church in Salem. He spoke of the fate of missionaries in Turkey and the threat of death that hung over them. It moved Phebe to write her poem "No Turning Back."[50] In her "Sabbath Journal" she wrote of her view of women as missionaries no less than men,

…disseminating the truth that maketh wise unto salvation, by labors as teachers among the heathen, and, by their pens and voices in nominally Christian lands, stimulating those who were in the foreign field. Of all the many Christian sects, none have so fully acknowledged the equality of woman, and her consequent right to engage in all church work and missionary service, as that branch of Zion known as the Society of Friends.

The city of Beverly claimed the site of the first Sabbath school in the country, established in 1810 by Hannah Hill and Joanna Prince. When Phebe agreed to teach in the Sabbath school, she offered Mrs. Abby Foster a copy of *Leonette*, inscribed, "To my dear friend, Abby." In her "Sabbath Journal," she evaluated her performance in the Sabbath school sessions. If she did not think she had done well, often due to a headache, she remarked, "The

---

50   Hanaford, Phebe A., 1871, p. 187

children did not change a poor season into a good season." Phebe spoke out at prayer meetings held after the weekly sermon with the result that when asked, she agreed to give Bible Classes on Saturday evenings. Her "Sabbath Journal" contains descriptions of Sunday services – two, sometimes three – plus teaching the children in the Sabbath school when weather permitted.

Phebe found the intellectual environment that she relished at the weekly meetings of the Woman's Poetry Society. Although she considered all the women her friends, she was particularly fond of Mary Trask Webber, a poet of considerable talent who published under the name "Mary Webb." In 1861 Phebe and Mary collaborated on an anthology of poetry entitled *Chimes of Freedom and Union*.

It was during this time that Phebe met Lucy Larcom. From *The Rushlight: Special Edition of Papers at Wheaton* (1894), the reader learns that Lucy taught at Wheaton Seminary in Norton, Massachusetts. She left her position because she never had time for the solitude and silence she needed. She returned to her hometown of Beverly to spend a year with her sister, Mrs. Baker. There, free from her responsibilities, she hoped to recover her health. She explained to Phebe that much of her need for rest stemmed from a mind tortured with unorthodox thoughts regarding the "Articles of Faith." Lucy could not join any church because she was unable to make the required profession of faith. The teaching of eternal damnation for unrepentant sinners was abhorrent to her. She did not believe "there is any corner of God's creation where hope never comes" (Letter to Miss Homiston, August 2, 1858).

Five years older than Phebe, Lucy came from a seafaring family; her father served as master of a merchant vessel. Both women had spent their childhood by the sea. Like Phebe, much of Lucy's learning came from outside the classroom. While Phebe's learning came from books, Lucy learned from the natural beauty around her. Their friendship included questions regarding faith. Lucy's search harmonized with Phebe's restless soul. Phebe admired Lucy's intellect and shared her search for freedom of spirit. Phebe talked to Lucy as she could to no one else and found comfort in their visits. After a discussion on anyone's ability to love God unselfishly, Phebe wrote to Lucy,

> *...love for the Saviour can never be any other than the love of* <u>*reciprocation*</u>*. To* <u>*everyone*</u> *of His children doth the Father say,* *"*<u>*I have loved thee*</u> *with an everlasting love, therefore with loving kindness have I drawn thee," and the response from every candid spirit must be "we love Him* <u>*because He first loved us*</u>*."* *Yet we are commanded to be like God, and how, in this respect, can we imitate Him? By loving man as God loves him with the love of benevolence, I think; — loving on, even when the pure flame of our Christian love (Christian because like Christ) shall fail to kindle a spark in the bosom of those whom we love. And so we shall grow into the image of our Master, in whose likeness, when we wake, we shall be satisfied. May the Divine Spirit lead us in this heavenly path!*

Continuing with her view of poetry, she wrote, agreeing in part with Lucy:

> *Your remarks on writing poetry met my concurrence as I told you. We do mistake enthusiasm for inspiration, and write too much, doubtless while. But I agree with you that the touches of Art are needed for a real poem, I am constrained to say that one ought not to repress utterance because he cannot speak the language of angels. We are not yet fully companions of angels. There are many on earth, whose souls are blessed*

by lyrics simple, but heaven-born, who could not comprehend and be blest by a grand epic—or any perfect poem. If all the flowers grew on the tree tops, nearest the sun, where would the children find any "buttercups and daisies"? I arrive at the conclusion that while we are bound to cry "Excelsior"! we are also bound to scatter seeds as we climb the mountain. Its summit will be bright, but barren, full enough of "angels food," but not laden with sustenance for those of earth. The poet's mission is like that of his Master –"who went about doing good." As there are readers of all grades of intellect, so there needs to be writers of all shades of ability; the humblest of which though he may lovingly aspire to reach the top of Parnassus, should yet be content to toil long on the slope, cheering himself with the thought, "They also serve who only stand and wait." So there is comfort in the idea that tho' we have outgrown some of our writings that they seem puerile to us now, they may yet be a blessing to some who stand where we stood when we wrote them. We shall not be ashamed of anything we have written, when we are in heaven, for unless the motive which prompted the words was unworthy, for we shall be better able to weigh our deeds in God's balances then.[51]

A letter from William A. Folger, husband of Phebe's sister Mary Jane, resonates with Phebe's 1857 diary notations regarding her visits to dressmakers on Nantucket.

> Ship Massachusetts lying at Philos
> November, 19, 1857
> Owyhee Sandwich Is.

51   Beverly Historical Society

...have obtained 1000 Bbls of Oil and 14000 lbs of Bone and if wee (sic) can get as much another season wee shall come Home I think the prospect is good for us to do it. Wee are about ready for sea now and shall probily (sic) get Mewee to see if wee canot (sic) get a chance to Ship our Bone if wee canot Ship Oil. I want you to put on two or three extra Hoops and hoop Florence well anything to keep bone up for it never was worth as much as it now is and I say it is oweing (sic) to the Laydie's (sic) Hoops do all you can to keep the Fashion good as I am <u>aware that you always follows Fashions</u> ever loving brother Wm. A. Folger[52]

Phebe's apparent interest in fashions did not prevent her from developing a deep admiration for Joanna Quiner, whom she described as "an unprepossessing person...a rather repelling outward appearance and blunt manners and speech full of remorseless truth."[53] Joanna Quiner was sixty-one when the two women attended meetings of the Essex County Good Templars Union where Joanna held official positions in the Order of Good Templars. Phebe read her poem "God Reigns"[54] at the Essex County Good Templars Union in Beverly, May 3, 1865. Her letter written as a Universalist in 1867 to "Dear CoWorker & Pioneer" gives evidence of her continued temperance work. Phebe wrote of herself in *Daughters of America:*

...she signed the pledge when eight years of age, was chaplain and treasurer of the Daughters of Temperance when eighteen;

52   Hanaford Family Archives
53   Hanaford, Phebe A., 1874, p. 42
54   Hanaford, Phebe A., 1871, p. 254

Worthy Chief several times and Grand Worthy several times in subordinate Lodges of Good Templars, Chaplain of the Grand Worthy Lodge of Massachusetts, and a member of the Right Worthy Lodge in 1867.[55]

Phebe visited Joanna Quiner's one-room home on Cabot Street that also served as her studio. She noticed that Joanna's lack of material things appeared to be of no concern to her. Townspeople who practiced a formal religion spoke of Joanna as an infidel because she had no outward connection with the Church of Christ. The intuitive Phebe realized Joanna lived by an inner reality that transcended her life experiences. At a time when Phebe was searching for unity of soul, she saw Joanna's spirituality as liberating and uncomplicated with a trust in the Spirit that acknowledged an Inner Voice.

Joanna spoke to Phebe of the weeks she spent in Boston doing upholstery work in the home of Rev. Theodore Parker. With her salt-of-the-earth wisdom, she came to recognize the famous preacher and social reformer as "my ideas of a good man." She offered Phebe two articles that he had given her. Theodore Parker's writings on the restrictions in formal religions described the discomfort Phebe felt. These visits provided as pleasant a season as Phebe had described her hours spent with Mary Farnum on Nantucket, a very different companion in her search for truth. In her time with Joanna, they shared their mutual love of the arts.

Poor in spite of hard work, few folks in Beverly took the trouble to look beyond appearances, as Phebe did, to find a talented sculptor in Joanna Quiner. Joanna told Phebe how in her

---

55   Hanaford, Phebe A., 1881, pp. 407-08

forties, while working for Doctor Bass at the Boston Athenaeum, she had seen Shobal Clevenger teaching a sculpture class. "Miss Quiner declared she could do better than that, and Clevenger encouraged her to try. The first attempt showed a remarkable aptitude for the art. Joanna's first sculpture, a head of Doctor Bass was declared life-like."[56] Her work elicited an article in the *Boston Transcript* on January 19, 1843 claiming that her work "will compare well with those which have been executed by experienced artists in Boston." Miss Quiner shared an article from the July 1843 *North American Review* that reviewed an edition of the *History of Beverly.*

One omission we notice with surprise. In a town more remarkable for the sober good sense and unostentatious manners of its inhabitants than for their taste in the fine arts, the discovery of an undoubted genius is a remarkable event, and deserving of record. Miss Quiner, of Beverly, with proper patronage and advantages, would take no mean rank among American artists. Without instruction or cultivation of any sort, her talent for modeling in clay has already attracted much notice.[57]

We glean these details from Phebe's biographical sketch of Joanna Quiner.[58] The request for the sketch came from the Officers of the Essex Institute who knew the Hanafords from their enrollment in the Institute. Mr. George Peabody, living in London, had endowed this band of scholars in his hometown of Salem to research the history of the local area. It grew into the Historic Society of New England.

---

56   Hanaford, Phebe A., 1874, pp. 39-40
57   Ibid, p. 35
58   Ibid, pp. 35-42

Joseph and Phebe joined in their trips to historic sites, known as Field Meetings. Phebe's detailed accounts of these trips published in *The Beverly Citizen* include their trip to the quarries of Rockport with Rev. Barden, pastor of the Rockport Universalist Church and an expert in mineralogy. He shared items from his collection with Phebe, including ferruginous limestone from Mount Zion. Phebe's published accounts of these trips provide a window into the family life of the Hanafords. Phebe took the children to Salem when Joseph preached before the Young Men's Christian Association at the Central Baptist Church on St. Peter's Street. He inspired young men to true manliness through religion and piety. Phebe and Joseph agreed on moral matters. She remarked in her Sabbath Journal on the joy she felt when they went to church united as a family. Only her expressed religious differences caused disharmony in their relationship.

Tensions facing the nation included the breakup of the Union over the expansion of slavery through self-determination in States where slavery did not exist. In 1860 Abraham Lincoln received the nomination for the presidency on the Republican ticket. His election in March 1861 brought fear to the South that, as president, he would destroy their economic security and lifestyle, which depended on slave labor. On April 12 of that year, the first shot was fired at Fort Sumter. When Sumter fell to the Rebels, President Lincoln's call for unity became a call to arms.

Chaos and despair filled the city of Boston as volunteers lined up in Faneuil Hall, vowing to avenge those who had disgraced the flag. The men of New England organized into the Massachusetts Sixth Regiment. War as a solution to the plight of the slaves appeared abhorrent to the Quakers and other pioneers in the Abolition Movement. Newspapers printed stories of the angry mob that attacked the soldiers as they marched through the city of Baltimore towards Washington. Clara Barton, working in the Patent Office, treated the wounded. Those who survived without serious wounds boarded trains heading south.

The war changed the course of the lives of women in the North and the South. For many women it was the first time they had faced life without the protection of men at their side. The familiar domestic scene yielded to the demands of war as women laid aside their personal needs and plunged into the war effort under The Woman's Central Association of Relief. Initially organized in New York, the women's efforts grew and soon came under the direction of Rev. Dr. Henry Whitney Bellows, a Unitarian clergyman. Rev. Bellows presented the plan for the United States Sanitary Commission to Washington on June 9, 1861. He was named president of what Abraham Lincoln dubbed "a fifth wheel to the coach."

In Chapter VI of *Daughters of America,* "Women During the Civil War," Phebe quotes from Rev. Bellow's Introduction to *Woman's Work in the Civil War,* which detailed Mary Livermore's work for the Sanitary Commission. Of these times, Phebe wrote in her 1880 genealogy, "My own part in the War was that of writing patriotic songs and poems, knitting and sewing in connection with Sanitary Commission Work." Her preoccupation with the war can be seen in her extensive poems, twenty-four of which she contributed to *Shore to Shore* under "Poems of Patriotism." She used her poetry to ease her pain and to bear witness to her conviction that God was on the side of those who fought for freedom for all. In poems for the dead, known and unknown to her, she expressed her concern for their youth and her admiration for their valor. Her poems, published in the local papers, brought letters to her from families of the enlisted men. A mother wrote to her asking for something to fill her void.

When I watched his baby face with streaming tears, painting sad pictures in the far off yet to be, I little thought how alleviating such precious gifts, in actual sorrow and suffering, would be. I gather them up to fill the vacancy. Even the touching letters of some of his comrades, so full of soul, I hug to my heart. Still, *you* know, the mother, in a moment of anguish, will ask of all the world, '*Where is he*'?

Phebe wrote to the mother and attempted to answer her question: "Where is he?"

Where Is He?

They say that his body is laid in the grave;
They say for his country he died;
But the mother-heart in its loneliness throbs,
And has still in its anguish sighed,
"Oh where is he now, — my generous boy!
My precious one! where is he?
Will he never return, in the battle who fell
As he fought 'neath the flag of the free?

Where is he? I tended his baby form;
I watched him in childhood's glee;
I cheered his young manhood, and hoped his strength
Would be prop in old age for me.
But I gave him up when his country called;
I laid him on Freedom's shrine:
Oh! why should I murmur if God, who asked
for the offering, accepted mine?

I murmur not, though the far-off West
Is the grave for such as he,
While I must miss him forevermore
From my home by the sounding sea:
For my country needs in this peril-hour
The costliest gift I know;
Then I'll murmur not, but I still must weep.
I'm his mother, and loved him so!

I am cheered by the shout of the victor-host;
I rejoice in the triumph of Right;
And I look on the flag with a loving eye
Beneath which my son could fight;
And comforting words which pitying friends
Are speaking so oft to me, —
They are welcome, — I'm thankful; but midst them all,
I whisper, "Where is he?"

His merry laugh and his graceful form,
His words full of kindness and love,
Shall I know them no more, save by Memory's power,
Til I meet my young soldier above?
I will try to be patient, O land of my birth!
I'm willing to suffer for thee;
And the patriot's fire in my heart still burns,
Though I'm asking "Where is he?"

O God of the mother whose holy trust
Is placed on thy promise sure!
Give strength to the torn and bleeding hearts
Counted worthy to endure,

And answer the cry, "Oh! where is he?"
With the whisper to each sad heart,
"Though he comes no more, thou shalt go to him:
Ye shall meet no more to part."[59]

President Lincoln declared the last Thursday in September 1861 a day of fast and prayer. Phebe's love of her country demanded that all men be free and she was willing to sacrifice her Quaker pacifism to help accomplish that end. Reluctantly she accepted the war as the legitimate means of gaining liberty for all men and women, something she believed in passionately. Phebe records that her abhorrence of slavery outweighed her hatred of war. When some of the best blood of Essex County had been shed for liberty, she rose at a Baptist Prayer Meeting and relinquished her pacifism – probably her most important act in this period of her life. She recorded the event in *Heart of Siasconset:*

Child of a peaceful sect though I was born
Taught the brave warrior and his deeds to scorn
Yet, if I must, my birthright I resign,
And henceforth own my country's cause is mine![60]

Phebe completed thirty-seven essays on "moral imperatives for exemplary men in various professions and walks of life to imitate." In 1862 she published this volume of prose and verse, *My Brother,* under the name Mrs. Joseph Hanaford. At home with their desks once more facing each other, they studied and wrote under a shared lamp. Before retiring they engaged in their

59   Hanaford, Phebe A., 1871, *From shore to shore and other poems,* p. 107
60   Hanaford, Phebe A., 1890, p. 147

customary readings from the Bible. Phebe described Joseph and herself in these exchanges in her Sabbath Journal as "united in a common expression of faith." In their exchanges, Joseph showed that his faith never wavered. Phebe admired that quality in her husband as she continued to search for greater truth. Phebe repeatedly wrote that his Sundays were spent in Salem visiting patients, adding "the children and I had to do without him." On these Sundays Phebe and Mary Trask Webber went to church, where Phebe prayed Mary would participate in the communion service.

After the Confederate iron clad frigate, the Merrimac, was destroyed in March 1862, Phebe wrote with some glee, "No more the Merrimac defies our little Monitor." Her poems of patriotism reflect her conviction in the justification for this war. In September the School Ship "Massachusetts" docked in Beverly Harbor. Rev. Foster, along with Dr. Joseph Abbott, planned a Sabbath afternoon service aboard the ship. The Hanafords were on hand to hear the seamen sing "Rock of Ages." This poem, written in 1776 by Augustus Montague and put to music by Thomas Hastings in 1830, was one of Phebe's favorites. While she found fault with singing during religious services, she obviously enjoyed religious music at other times. The combination of the sea and song left Phebe reluctant to leave. During the trip back to shore in the evening, she bathed in the rising moon and serene current. She remembered the sailors in her poem, "The Boys' Hymn." In her Sabbath Journal, she wrote that she prayed nightly for President Lincoln.

Phebe saved press releases concerning President Lincoln, of whom she later wrote in the preface of her biography of him "that the course of human events was such during his earthly existence and his relation to them so peculiar in the providence of God, as to indicate that he was specially commissioned for his day and work...." Like many, she viewed him as a Moses born to lead the slaves to the promised land of freedom. In April, Phebe's faith in the president was justified when he abolished slavery in the nation's capital.

Rev. Arthur Fuller's letters from the front kept her informed of his spiritual care of the soldiers of the Sixteenth Regiment Massachusetts Volunteers. He sent her an acorn from Fortress Monroe, which she planted. She wrote her poem "The Live Oak Tree" as a prayer for the Union "that it will endure and for the black man's freedom." In August 1862, news came of the death of Harvey Dix of Malden. Her poem "The Young Soldier," written that same month, honors his bravery in the battle near Kirksville, Missouri. When Rev. Fuller wrote from Virginia, he told of death and sadness and he enclosed a flower as the only sign of life remaining at battle's end. Rev. Fuller was killed in the Battle of Fredericksburg.

The promise of the Emancipation Proclamation remained uppermost in the minds of the Abolitionists as they pressured the president to free the slaves in the rebel states. On September 22, President Lincoln agreed that on January 1 he would free the slaves in rebellion states. The war dragged on far beyond anyone's expectations. News of battles and young lives lost darkened the close of the year. The President issued the Emancipation Proclamation on New Year's Day, 1863. He had long ago declared himself as an enemy of slavery, saying: "If slavery is not wrong, nothing is wrong." He had resisted efforts to free these slaves earlier, as he steadfastly maintained his goal was the preservation of the Union.

On hearing Rev. Foster preach, Phebe wrote the poem "O River of God Roll On." As her pastor, he was aware of

Phebe's restless soul in search of truth. He guided her as she studied scriptures. She wrote in her Sabbath Journal "the children accompanied her to church and were sometimes a great distraction to their mother." She allowed Howard to go home after the service. Florence remained with her mother while she taught Sunday school. Florence was confirmed in June 1863. Rev. Thatcher of the Congregationalist Church occasionally preached at the Baptist Church. When not at her Baptist church, she went to his church on Washington Street in search of an inspiring sermon. She talked with advocates of other creeds and listened to their sermons. Fidelity to religious obligations made great demands on her, and she regretted having to visit the sick on the Sabbath but wrote that she could not find the time during her busy week. At day's end, she closed the Sabbath with pious reading.

The war heightened Phebe's search for truth as she came to believe that only the freedom of all the slaves could justify this massacre. She viewed the President as being as wise as a serpent and harmless as a dove. Her poem "Emancipation" claims the right to victory.

> *Break each accursed chain,*
> *Let the enslaved go free,*
> *Or never hope a righteous God*
> *Again will prosper thee.*[61]

During the war Joseph continued his medical practice, the children were safe and the family suffered few hardships. Phebe's brothers did not enlist. Rowland went whaling in the

---

61   Hanaford, Phebe A., 1871, *From shore to shore and other poems*, p. 102

Pacific. At night when she prayed for family and friends, she prayed for wisdom for the President. She believed he was the nation's only choice and prayed he would see peace during his time in office and that he would not be led by political gain. She taught the children to pray: "Deliver us from slavery and ring out Freedom's chime."

Phebe's days were filled with the care of the children, Florence now twelve and Howard fifteen years old. She took Howard on an Essex Institute trip to Newburyport, the smallest town in the Commonwealth. Phebe left the group long enough to visit the aged Hannah Gould, whose poetry she recalled from her childhood. The visit proved a disappointment because although Hannah Gould's mind was clear, she was no longer the vibrant woman Phebe looked forward to meeting. The next attraction was the tomb of Rev. George Whitefield an, evangelist and orator It was Phebe's first encounter with a tomb. She descended the steps beneath the pulpit with religious awe. A friend went so far as to open the coffin, and Phebe viewed the remains of the famed preacher. She had a sense of satisfaction looking at the receptacle that once contained the brain of that flaming evangelistic orator. As the other members rested, Phebe and Howard climbed the tower to take in the view of Plum Island, with its lighthouse and the rolling sea she loved. Of her account of events, published in *The Beverly Citizen*, she wrote that her trip to Newburyport had been worthwhile.

News of the victory at the battle of Gettysburg in July 1863 also told of the terrible price young men had paid to win it. People agonized over a war that had claimed so many lives. With news of the victory at Vicksburg and the defeat of the Confederate armies in Louisiana and Tennessee, people believed the war would soon end. With autumn came the rain. In a melancholy mood, Phebe wrote of the "Cold and sad, forlorn and dreary sounds, once more the autumn rain is falling." As the women knitted and packed warm clothing, they hoped the soldiers would not have to fight through another winter.

Of winter, Phebe wrote,

> *I do not love the snow: it softly falls*
> *Like an angelic footstep on our paths,*
> *But it divideth me*
> *From those I love; and though its starry flakes*
> *Of geometric beauty charm my eye,*
> *I wish it soon away.*[62]

After the depressing era of military uncertainty, the tide of war changed in favor of the Union. Phebe saw this as a sign of God's blessings on the side of justice because of the Emancipation Proclamation. The following year the Hanafords had their turning point when they moved to Reading, Massachusetts in 1864. Phebe bid good-bye to her friends and accepted Joanna's gift of the bust she had done of Phebe. The bust, seen today in the Beverly Historical Society and Museum, proved to be Joanna's last. Rev. Foster continued counseling Phebe through their correspondence.

READING

In Reading, Massachusetts, the Hanafords took up residence in an old house on the corner of Spring and Orange, currently #19 Spring Street. In August Phebe learned of the death of her grandmother, Mary Coffin. During the early days of September,

---

62   Ibid, p. 217

she received the numbing news that her sister Mary Jane was dead at age twenty-nine. Her marriage to William Folger had lasted only a few years, and much of that time he had been at sea. The sea again claimed a Coffin life in 1863. News arrived detailing the death of her youngest brother, Rowland. Aboard the Adeline Gibbs, Rowland Coffin died while fighting against a powerful whale. She later wrote of it to her grandson, Lennie Hanaford.

He threw it just right and it lodged in the whale, but the long line attached to it got round Rowland's leg and he was drawn down into the water and carried down, and fast away and his body was never seen again. The rest of the whalers returned at once to the ship. They loved Rowland so well but they could not do any more at that time.[63]

In grief, words always flowed easier for Phebe than tears.

Not by his Grave I stand, — loved long ago, —
My playmate sleeping "Death's long, dream-less sleep."
He on the tossing billow met Life's foe;
And he, alas! was buried in the deep.

No marble cenotaph, his tomb to mark,
Can rise above those waves afar;
But while remains unquenched in me Life's spark,
Still bright for me shall beam his natal star

His birthday! it is here, and bids me turn

63   Hanaford Family Archives

To vanished hours of childhood's careless joy,
When Love's sweet lessons oft my heart could learn
From that dear brother, that kind sailor-boy!

Now far from that loved early home I dwell;
No more those paths our childhood knew we tread;
Nor can we meet till I have said "Farewell
To earthly scenes," and o'er Death's river sped.

Yet Memory ever true, with magic wand
Oft gilds each hour of our glad life anew;
And Faith reveals a better land beyond,
Than e'en our island-home 'mid waters blue.

I hope to meet him on the shining shore,
Where none of friends bereft shall lonely weep,
Where rolls new watery waste forevermore,
Where no loved forms are buried in the deep.[64]

On learning of the death of her beloved friend Abby Foster, Phebe poured out her grief in poems honoring her "sweet sister of my soul" and "cherished friend." Phebe said good-bye to the desolate year of 1864 in a lengthy poem.

Thou hast taken away, O passing year!
The loved of long ago;
Thou hast left the lips that my love hath pressed
In the casket lying low.
And the noble youth, our household pet,

---

[64]   Hanaford, Phebe A.,1871, *From shore to shore and other poems*, p. 155

Our brother young and brave,
Thou hast hid him, too, from our loving sight,
Far under the distant wave.
My fair young sister! the evening breeze,
Through the pine-trees sighing now,
Seems whispering "Mary." O heart of mine!
Be still, and humbly bow;
For the dear God dealt with that sister fair
So tenderly the while,
That the tearful eyes which above her watched
Could upward look and smile.[65]

In search of solace, Phebe read the views of learned men on the human search for the Divine and found them full of contradictions. She studied the scriptures but found no rest in others' interpretations when applying them to her life. The one redeeming factor of 1864 was the reelection of President Lincoln. Every loyal state except Kentucky, New Jersey and Delaware swept him into office in triumph on November eighth. Phebe described the event in her journal as a rare moment in their family life. She and Joseph prayed that evening with the children, who understood who Mr. Lincoln was and what he had done to end slavery. She believed Mr. Lincoln would lead a united nation to the end of the dreadful war and to the freedom of the slaves.

General Robert E. Lee surrendered at Appomattox on April 9, 1865. Celebrations spread throughout Reading and music filled the churches in thanksgiving for the Union victories. Lincoln promised a humane reconstruction of the war torn country in his call for peace "with malice toward none, with charity for all." His words were met with the ultimate retaliation. The impos-

65   Ibid, p. 166

sible happened. President Lincoln was assassinated. He died on April fifteenth.

Phebe prepared a poem for the local memorial service held in the Old South Congregational Church. Congregational, Universalist and Baptist choirs sang her Funeral Hymn to the tune of "Mount Vernon" at public funeral services. She wrote an eleven-page poem, "Our Martyred President." B. B. Russell published the poem under that title and included her Funeral Hymn. She determined that she would publish Abraham Lincoln's biography using the facts of his life that she had accumulated over the years.

Phebe wanted to present a truthful picture of the character of the great and good man whom she believed had been a man of and for the times. She did not want this book to be a history of the War or a record of all the acts of the President, but rather stereoscopic views to show that Lincoln was commissioned by God. Phebe also wanted the biography to be "within the limits of any person who ever bought a volume."

To achieve a quick publication, she quoted accounts of his early life from *The Pioneer Boy* by Rev. William Thayer, and events of his political career came from Henry J. Raymond's *Life of Lincoln*. She quoted Lincoln's speeches in their entirety. She used newspaper accounts by C. C. Coffin in the *Boston Journal* and magazine articles from the *North American Review, Harpers*, the *Atlantic Monthly, North American Review* and *National Republican*. She quoted accounts of the battles from Abbott's *History of the Civil War*, Horace Greeley's *History of the American Conflict* and the writings of H. C. Deming. Phebe edited the articles, putting together a profile of the President Lincoln as the nation saw him titled *Abraham Lincoln: His Life and Public Services*. Spending hours at her desk, she described the war as a necessity that Lincoln accepted.

It swept on. No man guided it; no man could foretell its dura-
tion or its issues. So tumultuous and perplexed were the move-
ments that the avowed and wise policy of the President was to
have no policy, but simply an end sought as wisdom might be
given moment by moment.[66]

The President is described,

Not by nature a leader, neither was he by nature a follower;
and by force of his rare union and balance of certain qualities,
both intellectual and moral, he was enabled to rise to the dignity
of master of his own position in a place exacting and difficult
almost beyond the precedents of history.[67]

B. B. Russell & Company of Boston, Massachusetts agreed
to publish the first posthumous biography of Abraham
Lincoln. In the preface, Phebe dedicated her tribute to Abraham
Lincoln to...

All men and Women, North and South, East and West, to The
Union Army and Navy and especially to the long-oppressed
race for whom President Lincoln wrote the Emancipation Proc-
lamation, this record of his stainless life and martyr's death is
now inscribed.[68]

Once published, *Abraham Lincoln: His Life and Public Services*
sold rapidly. Phebe accepted invitations to lecture in the cities
of New England. At age thirty-six, recognized as a writer and

---

66   Hanaford, Phebe A., 1865
67   Hanaford, Phebe A., 1865
68   Ibid

lecturer, Phebe Hanaford became financially independent. The primary source of her words regarding her literary career has been lost, but she writes of it:

All my books have been prepared among pressing duties of a domestic, editorial or pastoral character, and I have never had leisure to do justice to any powers God may have bestowed upon me. But I have done the best I could under the circumstances, and have attained some measure of success far beyond any expectations. Some of my books were made to order, and such are never the best which a writer might prepare. If the coming years afford me the leisure, I do hope to do something more worthy of our church, and of the Woman's Cause. I claim to have been industrious and conscientious in my work, and if I have often written for money, it was because I had children who needed bread and education, and I therefore preferred the means of helping them rather than literary fame for myself. I am no poet; I am a preacher, and God called me to preach.[69]

---

69   Hanson, 1882, p. 454

CHAPTER FOUR

BECOMING A PREACHER

I did not intend to be a preacher when I began to preach.
I was caring for my children still, and using my pen.[70]

Emily Ruggles' friendship filled Phebe's years in Reading, Massachusetts. Emily's 1866 diary mentions Phebe at least once on almost every page. Preserved on microfilm in the Reading Public Library and transcribed and forwarded by Anne Mark, the diaries provide the archival material for this crucial period of Phebe's life. Both Phebe and Emily were descendants of early settlers. Family archives of Emily Ruggles' great grandniece, Ruth Ruggles White, provide an account of their ancestor Peregrine White. The infant Peregrine White, safely delivered on the Mayflower as she lay anchored off Cape Cod, was the first child born in New England to English parents.

Evidence of her early friendship with Emily comes from Phebe's poem "The Palace and the Angel." Phebe read her tribute to Emily at a meeting of the Social Readers in November 1864 on the occasion of Emily's move into her new house. Phebe Hanaford and Emily Ruggles worked for the Sanitary Commission during the Civil War, though Emily would have preferred to serve in a more active role. Emily volunteered as a soldier to fight in the Union Army but was refused admission. She paid a hundred and twenty five dollars to the State for a representative recruit

70   Hanaford, Phebe A., 1890

to serve in her place. Eventually Emily learned his name, Private Matt Briggs of the 5th U.S. Company, a heavy artillery unit.

Emily, a successful businesswoman and one of Reading's foremost merchants in the Lyceum Hall Block, owned a Dry Goods Bazar (sic).

Miss Emily was a Smart Trader

In Emily's alluring notion store, children bought marbles, rubber for slingshots, toy soldiers, air guns, and paper dolls as well as school supplies. Emily Ruggles changed the contents of her glass counters with the seasons and the children never understood how at each season Miss Ruggles always had the kind of marbles and toys they wanted to buy. The door to the store opened with the sound of the bell that brought the tall, strong-looking owner to her feet with the familiar admonition, "Shut the door young man and do not slam." The deep voice and the familiar command terrified young customers. When the heavy door closed silently, the young customer awaited the standard question, "Which side young man?" before moving to the designated counter. After the selection was made the savings the child placed on the counter always appeared enough for the purchase. The wrapped package included an extra marble.[71]

From undated reminiscences of Emily's fiftieth birthday on July 16, 1871, we learn that "Emily served as a leading member of Christian Union Society of this town and the possession by them of the site upon which stands the church building is due

71   *The Reading Chronicle,* May 26, 1944, p. B-3

to her foresight and generosity." Her donation is confirmed by the following statement: "Emily Ruggles...buys land on Main street and transfers it to the congregation."[72] The history of the Reading Association of Liberal Ladies for Benevolent Purposes recounts the days when there was no place of worship and people rode to Woburn to hear Rev. Theodore Parker or Rev. Ralph Waldo Emerson preach. The members of the Universalist Society eventually had the money to rent the top floor of the Lyceum Hall, where the Liberal Ladies Benevolent Society provided the melodeon. When the church prospered, they paid the preachers very well and always managed the music.

The greatest number of women enrolled in the Reading Universalist Society occurred in 1856 with sixty-seven members. These ladies kept the group united, while remaining financially autonomous. Emily's mother, Almira Ruggles, held the position of president of the Liberal Ladies Association for fourteen years and remained active in the Association. Her obituary describes her as "consistent Universalist."[73]

In a poem Clara Gowing reports that Emily served as director of the Reading Association of Liberal Ladies for Benevolent and Useful Work, whose purpose was to "add to the benevolent and useful enterprises around us." The annual report commencing May 4, 1865 lists Phebe and her daughter, Florence, as members. In the annual reports for the following three years, Phebe, but not Florence, appears as a member. In lieu of benevolent works, members could pay an additional $1.25 toward the

---

72 Rzepka, p. 10
73 *The Reading Chronicle*, "A Mother in Israel," 1865

general work of the society. The 1866-67 record lists Mrs. P. A. Hanaford as paying $1.50.

At the Silver Anniversary of the Association of Liberal Ladies, celebrated on June 8, 1865, Emily Ruggles opened the program with a reading of one of Phebe's poems, which was then sung by the members to *Auld Lang Sine*. Officers made several toasts followed by a response from a member. In her response to Emily's toast, Phebe compared the Association of Liberal Ladies to a mighty oak:

...sprung from an acorn that has survived and flourished till it stands to-day, after the lapse of a quarter century, with a strong foundation, and spreads abroad its branches of sympathy and friendly feeling far up into the serene atmosphere of faith and hope, while the deeds of usefulness and benevolence which it has wrought are the birds singing sweetly in the leafy shade.... While they cherish the dear memories of the Past, and look with bright anticipations to the Future, may they faithfully, hopefully, lovingly act in the living Present, heart within and God o'erhead!

In this environment Phebe began her study of the history of Universalism.

She learned that the founder of Universalism in America, John Murray, became a Universalist in England after studying the writings of James Relly. He then sailed from England, arriving in America in 1770. Shipwrecked off the southern coast of New Jersey near Barnegat Bay, Murray went ashore in a small craft. With the other survivors, he landed on the banks of Cedar Creek. Murray and the boatmen headed for the tavern, but Murray soon left them there. Eventually he found a man cleaning fish and asked to buy some for his crew. Since the fisherman had not paid for the fish, he would not sell them to Murray but sent the gift of the fish to the boatmen at the tavern. Here began the friendship between John Murray and the fisherman, Thomas Potter. Potter offered Murray the use of a chapel, which Potter had built on his property for itinerant preachers. It was here that John Murray brought Universalism to America. Within months, he received repeated requests from New York to preach. He traveled to New York and eventually to Philadelphia before settling in Gloucester, Massachusetts.

Among John Murray's first converts in Gloucester was the Sargent family, including their daughter Judith, whom John later married. In 1790 Judith Sargent, a woman of great talent, wrote an essay on the "Equality of Women," saying, "Ye haughty sex, our souls are by nature equal to yours." She challenged the domestic role imposed on women, calling for "broader educational opportunities for women." Judith had a career as a playwright, and was the first woman born in America to have her plays dramatized by professionals.

Phebe also learned that by 1838 women outnumbered men in the Universalist Church and that many women held offices in Universalist Societies. She studied the writings of Thomas Starr King, American Unitarian Minister, and found his teachings to be in harmony with her personal reflections on the Scriptures. Instead of the contradictions she had noted in other church teachings, she rested in the comfort of Starr King's integration of holiness and happiness, the teaching of one God, whose nature is love as revealed in one Lord, Jesus Christ. In search of confirmation of these beliefs, she read the early fathers of the Christian Church, where she repeatedly found in the apostolic teachings, "We love him because he first loved us."

This belief in universal salvation released Phebe from the oppressive dogmatic teachings of the Calvinist religions relating to damnation and election. In contrast, Joseph Hanaford was a member in good standing at the Calvinist Baptist Church on Ash Street in Reading, where his family attended services. Here Phebe heard nothing of the Universalist belief that all souls would eventually find salvation in the Grace of God. John Murray's departure from the Methodist teachings of George Whitefield would have offended Joseph Hanaford. As a father he wanted to protect his children from the teaching of universal salvation.

As Phebe grieved the deaths of her Quaker grandmother and her siblings, Rowland and Mary Jane, she found comfort in the Universalist teachings. At her father's request, she visited Nantucket. From her position on the ferry, the South Tower of the Congregational Church, once a symbol of stability, would have served to announce the changing times. At the pier, the familiar routine of docking would have held but a shadow of its former vitality. Capt. George Coffin and his wife Emmeline had aged with the passing years as well as their personal grief. Phebe's sister, Emma, now lived alone with her parents. It was here that Phebe first preached. We glean the circumstances of her first sermons from her article in *The Woman's Journal,* "Twenty Years in the Pulpit."

Being on a visit to my Island birthplace, at the request of my father I prepared and delivered two sermons in the little school-house at Siasconset, where when I was sixteen years of age I had been the public school teacher. They were sermons right out of my own heart experiences. In the midst of sorrows and trials I had found consolation, and that comfort I strove to impart to others. My first audience was composed of my nearest relatives and others, many of whom had known me from a babe. The little school-room was crowded. It was summer time and men stood outside leaning in at the open windows to hear my gospel message. Though tears were on many faces, yet I believe the sunlight of truth entered their souls. The storm-beaten, sea-worn veterans of many perilous voyages were not unwilling to hear of an everlasting love and a port of rest. Twice I preached on that Sunday.[74]

Phebe believed she was preaching the truth of God's everlasting love for all people. She heard echoes of her Quaker Inner Voice in the Universalist teachings. Here on her beloved Island, where her calling to preach had begun at the Friends Meeting, Phebe acknowledged the desire that had always been with her and now had come to life in the schoolhouse on S'conset. The details of this event, remembered twenty-five years later, speak of an integrating moment in the life of Phebe Ann Coffin Hanaford.

At home in Reading, Phebe wrote to Rev. Foster, her friend and counselor in Beverly, to tell him what preaching in Siasconset had meant to her. She explained that she was currently attending a Friends Meeting as well as the Universalist Church. She told him that in the teachings of Universalism she had freed herself of the conflicts that troubled her in the Baptist Church where she was still a member. She concluded her letter with her feelings of gratitude for his friendship.

In his letter of February 8, 1866, Rev. Foster asked,

Do you go regularly to the Universalist meeting, leaving the Baptist meeting as a general thing, Sabbath afternoons in order to go to the Universalist meeting? Do you use your influence to induce others to leave Baptist meeting

74   Hanaford, Phebe A., 1890, p. 1

and go to the Universalist Meeting? Do you have a class, as teacher in the Universalist Sabbath School? Do you teach Universalism in your class in the Baptist Sabbath School? Have you written an article for a Universalist newspaper which would justify any candid reader to the conclusion you are a Universalist? Are you a Universalist, and not a Baptist?[75]

Phebe knew that, as her pastor, Rev. Foster was hoping for negative replies to his questions, but he had asked her for the truth. His kind words reflected all she shared with him in her search for truth. His friendship, he assured her, would remain unchanged whatever she decided. Phebe would have understood Rev. Foster was asking her to make a choice. From "Twenty Years in the Pulpit," we read,

> *I read the Bible from Genesis to Revelation, both included, carefully and prayerfully. I studied books; I heard sermons. It is interpretation of them that has caused me unrest in the Baptist Church. I talked with advocates of various creeds. Finally, I came out into the light and joy of liberal Christianity. I became a Universalist.*[76]

This light cast a shadow over the Hanaford family. Learning that his wife had united with the Universalist Church, Joseph Hanaford remained firm in his rejection of the teachings of John Murray. The doctrine of universal salvation, with no fear of punishment for sins, was anathema for a Calvinist Baptist. The Universalist belief in the Old and New Testaments as the

75   Nantucket Historical Association
76   Hanaford, Phebe A., 1890

revelation of a God of love revealed through Jesus found harmony with Phebe's Quaker belief in a God who directs souls individually. Phebe's convictions and her ability to hold her own in an argument with her husband led to a mutual loss of respect.

Men of this age had little understanding of the difficulty a wife had in adopting her husbands' religious beliefs. A husband expected his wife to attend his church. With his wife no longer seated next to him in his church, Joseph Hanaford appeared weak as a husband. What did Joseph Hanaford know of Florence's membership in the Ladies Benevolent Association that met in the same Hall the Universalists used as a place of worship? Florence, now twelve, had memories of her mother as the faithful Sunday school teacher. The children witnessed the division within the family over the religious observances that for years had united them. For years Phebe had cherished these observances as a wife and mother in a church-going family and wrote in her Sabbath Journal of her sadness on the Sundays when she and the children "did without him."

As she became active in the Universalist church she appears to have had no more regard for Joseph's situation than he for hers. In the Minutes of a meeting held on March 1, 1866, Article 9 notes that S. E. Gleason chose a committee to consider the building of a church, and Mrs. P.A. Hanaford is listed as a member of this committee.[77] The 1866 entries in the Ruggles diary show Emily and Phebe canvassing for the building fund for the Reading Universalist Society.

In addition to their differences in matters of faith, there was the fact that Joseph's wife's income as a writer provided for the children's needs. Joseph no longer headed his household.

---

77   Unitarian Universalist Church of Reading, Reading Archives, pp. 52-53

Phebe's biography of Abraham Lincoln reached a sale of 10,000 copies. Julia Wuzberger translated the biography into German to meet the demands of the local German population. In a letter addressed to "Dear Sister Mary Jane" written to a friend on February 8, 1866, Phebe told of a tempting offer she had received from her publisher to go to California. She was considering the offer and added that Miss Ruggles has agreed to go with her, "but I cannot bear to be so long without my children." A more interesting offer helped Phebe forget about any plans to go to California. Russell Miller, in *The Larger Hope: The First Century of the Universalist Church in America 1770-1870,* reports,

> In 1866 Mrs. Hanaford, the third woman ordained in the Universalist ministry and one of the most prolific writers in the denomination, admitted that much of her writing was inferior, sandwiched as it was between pastoral, domestic, and other duties...In 1866 Mrs. Hanaford was employed by the Universalist Publishing House as Editor of the Universalist monthly periodical, *The Ladies' Repository* and at the same time editing the *Myrtle,* a Sunday School paper. If that were not enough, she had charge of the children's department of the *Universalist Quarterly.*[78]

Phebe gives evidence of her humor in her first editorial as she offers a description of an Editor as "wonderfully wise, usually peculiar...Our readers may rest assured that if we fail mentally we shall not morally; if we may not be so profound and brilliant as they would like, we shall be at least sincere and outspoken." First published in 1834 by Daniel Smith, *The Ladies' Repository*

---

78   1979, p. 560

had established a tradition of articles encouraging women to write about women's rights. Initially Phebe noted the paper's lack of news of the woman's suffrage movement. Lucy Stone's lectures on equal rights for women were not quoted, but article after article promoted Stone's ideas on the dignity of women.

Phebe's position as the editor provided an opportunity for her to report news of the Woman's Rights Movement. Clergymen across the nation quoted from Genesis to Paul to reinforce the sectarian view of male dominance. The Universalist Society's practice of sound reason expressed in social reform affirmed Phebe's personal belief in the dignity of all people regardless of gender or race. Under her editorship, the number of articles and news bites relating to women's rights went up sharply. Mrs. Hanaford's hand, anonymously or not, was visible during the three years she edited *The Ladies' Repository*.

As a businesswoman Phebe understood that the financial success of the paper depended on subscribers from outside the Universalist Church. Phebe believed the teachings of the Universalist Church echoed the spirit of American democracy. As evidenced from copies of *The Ladies' Repository* held at the Andover Harvard Theological Library, she worked to maintain broad content. She also believed the paper could diffuse mis-understandings about Universalist beliefs about the Bible. She wrote an extensive editorial on Universalism for the October issue, quoting from Universalist tracts and outlining the Profes-sion of Faith adopted by the 1803 General Convention in New Hampshire. Her articles caught the attention of Universalist minister Rev. Olympia Brown, who recognized Phebe's passion for women's rights.

Knowledge of Rev. Olympia Brown's reputation as a preacher spread amongst the Universalists. Her Church in Weymouth flourished partially because she invited speakers such as William Lloyd Garrison, Rev. Ralph Waldo Emerson and Maria Chapman, pioneers in the cause of human rights. Phebe saw Olympia's work for women's rights as an essential part of her ministry. In "Twenty Years in the Pulpit" Phebe describes how she received her first invitation to preach in a Universalist Church.

> *In the fall of 1866 when I was editor of the <u>Universalist</u> maga-*
> *zine, <u>The Ladies' Repository</u>, then published in Boston, I was*
> *about to leave the city for my home one Saturday afternoon,*
> *when a gentleman rushed up to me in the Boston & Maine*
> *depot, and asked for an immediate response to a letter he had*
> *brought from Rev. Olympia Brown. She begged me therein to*
> *go in her stead to preach in South Canton, Mass. I had only the*
> *two sermons I had delivered in the (Nantucket) schoolhouse.*
> *I doubted if they were suitable but I dared not refuse to go.*
> *It seemed to be the Lord's call. I went.[79]*

Rev. Olympia Brown, learning of Phebe's successful preaching in South Canton, offered her opportunities to preach in the Universalist churches of Hingham and Waltham as well as her church in Weymouth. Phebe resolved to ask for a license to preach.

> *Becoming a member of a Church, with no women in its ministe-*
> *rial ranks and having various family cares, the thought of a*
> *preacher's or missionary's vocation was necessarily relinquished,*
> *over the years I buried any hope or thought of a preacher's or*
> *missionary's vocation. That's all changed now. During a visit*

---

79   Hanaford, Phebe A., 1890

to Nantucket my father asked me to speak to the community of my faith in a compassionate God. I had no books to refer to but I spoke of the faith I found in Universalism. I preached of God's universal love and explained that I was now free of the fear of a just God who punishes His children for their failings.[80]

In November 1866 Mrs. Hanaford received her license to preach from the Committee of Fellowship, Ordination and Discipline for the Massachusetts Universalist Convention. The License to Preach was a disallowance of Joseph's right to determine Phebe's religious observances. As a Baptist in good standing, it was the ultimate rejection of his religious beliefs. Phebe knew Rev. Olympia Brown had encouraged the committee in Hingham to hear her preach before making any decision regarding the appointment of their new preacher. Joseph Hanaford could not have been pleased to learn that his wife was preaching. It is for us to wonder just how Phebe explained that she had received a Letter of License from the Committee of Fellowship, Ordination and Discipline of the Massachusetts Universalist Convention; but we do know her ministry added to the strain on her relationship with Joseph.

On the last Saturday of November, Phebe dressed in her gray traveling suit and boarded the train to Boston, where she would begin the twenty-mile ride to Hingham. She carried a black pulpit dress free of excess material for easy packing. On arriving in the charming waterfront town, the trolley stopped at the Old Ordinary Station. She walked toward North Street to the two-story building at 196 North Street. The cornerstone read May 18, 1829, the month and year of her birth. Her tour of the church and the Sabbath school indicated she would be

---

80   Ibid

expected to conduct classes between the morning and evening services. The Church held sixty-four pews on the ground floor and twenty-eight in the gallery. Phebe knew that Rev. Hosea Ballou, renowned as the "Ultra Universalist," had preached the first sermon in this church.

Seeing that Phebe showed interest, residents of Hingham informed her that since the end of the war, immigrants had moved into town. The immigrant women, considered unskilled, worked as cooks or nursemaids. Local women rarely worked outside the home. Sunday morning Phebe would have observed people entering the church while others walked on past. A new preacher always brought a larger than usual attendance, and word of a lady preacher brought a mix of approving and disapproving listeners. Emily Ruggles' entry that she waited for Phebe at the station with faithful "Kittie Lucas," the most beloved horse in Reading, provides the last record of Phebe's first day in Hingham.

Phebe's activities outside the home went beyond her preaching ministry. She continued to attend Temperance meetings at the Mystic Lodge in Reading. In her poetic tribute to the temperance flag, she praised the youth who joined their ranks and saw them as the future of the Temperance Movement. Their present work required example "in word and deed, in heart and soul, to temperance ever true, let our appetites control, and win companions true." Though temperance was one thing that Joseph and Phebe agreed on, Phebe believed his restrictions on food went beyond common sense and endangered the children's health. She provided for the family's additional food from her salary, again weakening Joseph's position as head of the household. It may be remembered that by law a wife's income belonged to her husband; a right Joseph seems never to have claimed.

Phebe paid regular visits to Emily Ruggles at her home, and on some occasions remained overnight. Together, they put on programs for the Literary and Dramatic Association. When the season ended, the two friends went on holiday to Nantucket the first week of June. In an article for Nantucket's *Inquirer and Mirror,* Phebe wrote about the vacation highlight, entitled "Ladies Off Sharking." The excerpts from the story of Emily's prowess bring out a lighter side of their relationship often buried in the business of their busy days. In good humor Phebe begins reading her article to the Social Readers.

Let me take you with us sharking, if I can. We are about to embark on a new and untried experience. No women have ever dared to seek those monsters of the deep on the side of the island where we tarried, where the shoals are ever tossing their white caps, and the wild waves always break in foamy surf upon the beach with their reverberating music, in winter the solemn dirge of the ship-wrecked seaman, awakening in many anxious hearts the cry 'God save the mariner.' Here is the boat, it has seen service already. It has breasted the billows of the Arctic seas... But now look at the crew of the little barque. The men three in number Capt. George Coffin and sons...They, then seem native and to the manor born, are attired in nondescript apparel. Would you recognize your president and secretary in such costume?...Look at your president's face and see there the expression of satisfaction at the near prospect of pursuing a cherished plan, and of hope that all desired ends will be gained...Will you spare a moment for a glance at your secretary? She has a large, flapping, old fashioned lady's hat, which has been under the surf too often to look as if it were just from the milliner's but it is gaily trimmed with red ribbons and tied in usual fashion, with a red bow, under the chin. The shawl is there too-but it is of red plaid...There is the clumsy life preserver over the gray shirt and the strong pants are turned up and tied round the waist with a rope yarn....On they go to sharking ground. There is no need to describe the deathly horror that stands like a mocking phantom telling her she cannot escape the Demon of sea sickness...She bears up as long as possible, but she talks less, and you can see that her eye prefers to rest...She is shelved on the bow of the boat, her head ingloriously lying on her arm and her cold, numb body enveloped in her brother's coat. Now see your President! Overboard may go her breakfast, but inboard must come a shark and in he does... It lies athwart the little draft and though curled over is a pretty good cargo...How it makes your Secretary long to get once more to beach...

Once back in Reading, Emily records she and Phebe canvassed for the building fund for the Reading Universalist Society.

Every Saturday during the winter months of 1866, Mrs. Hanaford could be seen making her way through the snow to the Reading Station. On Sunday she preached at the morning and evening services in Hingham, returning home later that evening. After three months she settled into the First Universalist Society of Hingham as their supply preacher. Each weekend her involvement in the parish grew, and soon her duties appeared to be that of pastor rather than supply preacher. In March the members held a "presentation party" at which they gave their preacher a gold watch and an invitation to serve as their pastor.

Evidence of her ability to integrate the two roles of preacher and editor appears in her editorial for May 5, 1866 entitled "Woman in the Ministry."

...a few words in regard to the preaching of females, and their right and ability to occupy the place of an ambassador of Christ. We confess to a belief in the right of all — men and women — to proclaim the Gospel. ....None are called into the Lord's vineyard to be idlers there. All have the right to labor in His cause.

While pursuing her right to preach, Phebe failed to integrate her family life and her career. Her personal success only distanced her from Joseph. In her 1857 diary she had written that love overcame their differences. What Phebe saw at that time appears to have been her bride's perception of her husband's domain as the vineyard where she was to labor. In that vineyard Phebe's compliance with Joseph's beliefs maintained the familial harmony she wanted for her children. Although she shared her beliefs with her children, there is no evidence that Howard or Florence attended religious services with either their father or their mother.

As a preacher Phebe Hanaford's voice continued to be heard through the spring and fall of 1866. She sent forth "an earnest appeal from an earnest heart to sinners to be reconciled to God in thought, in purpose, in spirit and in life."[81] She fostered the Sabbath school and lectured from the pulpit on temperance and women's rights. Ever the businesswoman and journalist responsible for the support of her family, Phebe had her sermons printed and made available for sale. In June she announced "a new volume of *The Ladies' Repository* would commence with the July number, and in accordance with a promise made last summer, it will be enlarged, so as to have 80 pages instead of 64.... We hope our readers and patrons share this feeling with

81   Hart & Hart, p. 157

us, and we earnestly bespeak their favor and co-operation in making our magazine what our friends of our cause most desire, to see it one of the very best."

In the first 1867 edition of *The Ladies' Repository*, the Editor reiterated her promise of improvements, including engravings and additional pages in the coming year. The articles she selected covered a broad range of interests from around the nation. Along with news from national newspapers, Phebe requested specific articles from friends. Her editorial, "Equal Suffrage," included quotes from the New York *Independent* on the meetings of the Equal Rights Association and the letter from Theodore Tilton to Susan B. Anthony dated December 4, 1866, in which he wrote, "One woman whose rights I am most bound to respect is an American citizen who wants the American citizen's ballot."

Traveling to Universalist Societies in and around Boston, Phebe read poetry to earn money for the new Reading Universalist Society's building fund. Her poetry earned a ten-dollar donation to their building fund. She also recited for the benefit of The Freedman's Aid Society. These appearances brought fine reviews from the *Salem Register*, the *Beverly Citizen*, and the *Lynn Reporter*, where she had advertised.

"Sunbeams and Shadows!"
Mrs. P. A. Hanaford

OF BOSTON

Well known to the literary world, as the
Quaker Poetess

City Hall Monday Evening
January 14th, 1867

In this same generous spirit, Phebe wrote the story of her distant relative, Thomas Coffin, the sole white survivor of the *Manchester* for *The Inquirer and Mirror.*

Capt. Alexander H. Coffin, his wife, and son Thomas sailed April 1854 from New York for the Chincha Islands. Passing round the Cape of Good Hope in August, the ship was destroyed when it struck rocks. Capt. Coffin and Thomas, along with the second mate, David Evans, and George, a black deckhand, were the only ones to survive. They managed to reach the island of Tierra del Fuego, where Evans died. Capt. Coffin drowned during an attempted escape from an attack by the natives.

Marking the dates on a stick, Thomas and George made it to Wreck Island and stayed there until December 1854. Then they headed for San Carlos where friendly natives accepted them into the group as servants. There they met other sailors suffering the same fate. The first ship they spied, the *Liberty*, never came close enough to reach Chile. Thomas transferred to the *Meteoro* on May 24, 1855. In June he arrived at Valparaiso, Chile. Living in a boarding house, he remained under the protection of the American Consul. Thomas was sixteen years old when he returned home to Nantucket, still suffering from his ordeal. In 1867, Carlton and Porter Publishers in New York published

Phebe's account of his story, *The Captive Boy in Tierra del Fuego*. It was rumored that Phebe offered the money earned from the book to Thomas Coffin.

On March 10, 1867, standing in the pulpit, Phebe surveyed a full house of regular worshipers and welcomed visitors in her familiar style. With careful enunciation and a voice full and clear, she explained in her sermon "Reciprocal Duties of Pastor and People" her vision of her role as their pastor. She left them no doubt of her fitness for the task. "I am satisfied that this is the portion of His vineyard wherein He would have me labor at present." Phebe's satisfaction in her ministry coupled with her achievements as an editor presents to the reader a picture of a woman riding the crest of success.

On a more carefree side, Phebe enjoyed the company of Emily Ruggles on a trip to Niagara Falls. The two women left on September fifth, boarding the *Boston and Maine* at ten o'clock for the first leg of the trip. Phebe sent notes of the trip to the *Universalist*. In Boston, where they transferred to the Fitchburg road, Phebe described "the best depot in Boston."

In Fitchburg they took a carriage to Mrs. Sheridan's modern mansion on the side of "Rollstone" where she welcomed them to her elegant home. After tea the travelers returned to the station at seven and took a berth in a sleeping car destined for Rutland. Adjusting to this novel kind of "camping out," the two adventurers called frequently on the services of the conductor, explaining the train felt like a rolling tenement. The accounts of their trip afford us a fresh look at these otherwise serious adults. Looking at Phebe's articles and Emily's diary, we get different perspectives on the same events and, more importantly, an insight into their friendship. Phebe writes,

I cannot soon forget how strange it seemed to lie there looking up first at Cassiopia's chair, and then Ursa Major, while the wheels rumbled, the cars jolted, the bells rang, and the steam whistle gave forth its demon yell, as we drew near quiet villages whose inmates were wrapped in the unconsciousness of slumber, and had not a thought for fellow mortals whirling by them at the mercy of an axle tree or a switch—or rather the hand of God.

Even a sleepless night could not lessen their appreciation of the beauty of the Vermont hills as the dawn broke. At six in the morning the train left for Saratoga where, on arrival, Phebe and Emily settled in the Clarendon Hotel. Accounts of a given day include a visit to Capt. Judson at the office of *The Saratogian* and a visit to High Rock Spring for the healing water. Armed with as many bottles of water as they could carry, they toured the city until six in the evening.

The tourists returned to the train for another night spent listening to whistles and locomotive bells from their hard bed as they passed Schenectady. Riding the remaining 289 miles on the New York Central with scarcely a pause until, "drawing rein," they boarded an omnibus for Cataract House. Somewhat deaf from the din of bells and wheels, they were escorted to their room where they viewed the Rapids from their open window. Phebe wrote, "Standing together we suddenly realized we could hear and said in harmony, "It is the Falls." Phebe recited, "'Tis the voice of the great Creator that dwells in that mighty tone." They walked to Bath and visited the Biddle Stairs and Terrapin Tower. Emily adds that after dinner they went to Prospect Point. They returned to the hotel where they attended a "hop" in the hall before closing their first day in Niagara Falls with a prayer of gratitude.

Once fortified with a Sabbath breakfast of beefsteak and armed with good guidebooks, they agreed to walk to the Falls. Both women reported that they repeatedly refused carriage service and assistance from coachmen, who expected to see women with bandboxes. Walking briskly, they agreed their arrangement to be better by far for their health and their pockets. They agreed to pass by the churches and "worshipped in the grand and ever open temple whose mightiest anthem sounds in our ears." They then bought tickets for the ride on the Ferry Railway with its cable three hundred feet long, fully assured that if the cable broke they would end up in the Niagara River. The Ferry Railway took them to the bottom of the Falls where Phebe shouted above the roar, reading from the guidebook, "It is nine hundred feet wide and one hundred sixty feet high." Of the experience, Phebe wrote,

I awoke our first morning in Niagara dreading the boat trip to the Canadian side. If it had not been for my lion-hearted fellow-traveler who was desirous of rocking on that mighty tide, the little cockle-shell of a boat would never have danced about on those rushing waters with me on board.

In Canada the travelers stayed at the Clifton Hotel, and after a short rest were conducted to Horseshoe Falls. Skipping the opportunity to risk one's life by climbing the famed Table Rock, Phebe and Emily gathered flowers as they walked to the foot of the Falls. The beauty of their surroundings called to them but the suggestion was that they should start the return climb up. They took refreshments at the Prospect House. Realizing the Canadians were not observing the Sabbath any more than they were, Phebe and Emily walked down Lundy's Lane to an English

Church. The preaching over, they remained for the Benediction. Once back in the Cataract Hotel, they bedded down, lulled to sleep by the rushing sounds of the Falls. Emily's diary described their morning toiletries as brief. They then had breakfast and left for the day. Most evenings they arrived back at the hotel in time to bathe off dusty hands and brows and smooth rumpled locks. The women at the hotel dressed for dinner and Emily referred to them as "the Feejeean warriors in full dress."

These days spent with Emily reveal a lighthearted Phebe Hanaford. Phebe writes, "I would give ten years of ordinary, hum drum, tread-mill life for one day in Niagara." Phebe's hum-drum days ended soon after their return, when "Miss Brown asked me to her own pulpit while she went to Waltham. There she so far opened the way for me that I was soon preaching in Hingham, then at Abington."[82] Phebe saw her position as editor as an adjunct of her ministry. She used both the press and the pulpit to promulgate suffrage, a basic right of citizens, and preaching, a basic right of believers, with neither denied to women.

The November editorial in *The Ladies' Repository,* "Woman at the Polls," enumerated the success of several women by name. When criticism of women in bloomers overshadowed the good works women were doing, Phebe wrote, "Whatever woman wishes to do and can do—we say—in God's name hinder her not, so long as she can lift a calm, pure brow to the searching eye of God." Phebe reprinted articles from out of town newspapers written by women who lived on the forward edge of reform. Phebe stood shoulder to shoulder with the women who spoke out fearlessly for support of what they believed. In her editorials Phebe quoted accounts from the *Star of the West* of Olympia Brown's suffrage campaign in Kansas.

---

82   Hanaford, Phebe A., 1890

The business manager of *The Ladies' Repository*, Mr. Benton Smith, wrote asking Phebe to meet with him at the Publishing House at 37 Cornhill in Boston. When they met he told her that over the last few weeks he had received requests from readers for the name of the person responsible for the improvement of *The Ladies' Repository*. Although it was the policy of the Universalist Publishing Company not to reveal the name of the Editor, Mr. Benton Smith said that since readers had requested it, he saw no reason not to grant their request. Perhaps encouraged by this approval from her readers, the February issue featured the story of Lily Maxwell of Manchester, England entitled "The Cause of Woman." As a taxpayer, Lily Maxwell had registered to vote, and once registered, she could not be denied the vote. She reported, "And with it all the throne of Victoria did not topple."

Mary Livermore, organizer of the Sanitary Fairs during the Civil War and a convert to the suffrage movement, wrote articles for *The Ladies' Repository* on the work of Elizabeth Cady Stanton and Susan B. Anthony in order to dispel the negative image of the founding suffragists. Of the suffrage debates held in the nation's capital, Mary Livermore wrote, "Mr. Cowan of Pennsylvania advised his colleagues to read the proceedings of the Woman's Rights Convention before they concluded that women were suitably represented by their husbands. Mr. Wade of Ohio spoke in favor of woman's right to vote, as did Mr. Anthony of Rhode Island." Both Houses of Congress had passed the bill for Impartial Suffrage in the District of Columbia, inserting the word "male" into the law that granted black residents of the District of Columbia the right to vote. Phebe reminded her readers that this bill called for an honest and impartial administration of the law in the District. Her concern for justice for the freed slave remained strong but did not overshadow her zeal for women's rights.

In the April 1867 edition of *The Ladies' Repository*, "Mr. Smith acknowledged Mrs. Phebe Hanaford as the sole Editor since April '66. Letters could be directed to her at the Publishing House, 37 Cornhill, Boston." In the same issue Phebe Hanaford addressed her editorial, "Help for Fallen Women," to the benevolent and philanthropic ladies among the thousands of readers. She urged them to read prayerfully and with sympathy the statement from the *Independent*, including the First Annual Report of the "Home in West Houston street, and its work in which it estimated sixty percent success rate with the inmates of the home for women." Phebe's concern for women living questionable lifestyles and the need for moral reform remained an essential part of her ministry as a Universalist preacher.

Each Saturday Phebe traveled to Hingham from Boston. In "Not All Is Changed: A Life History of Hingham," Lorena and Francis Hart report in *The Hingham Journal*, September 20, 1867, "Mrs. Hanaford was in her mid-thirties, neatly molded, with dark eyes set in an amiable face." Phebe Hanaford recalled one weekend in which express man Eli Kenerson made a desperate forty-five-mile drive to and from Boston via Hull to find her misplaced baggage. It contained not only her black pulpit dress but, of more consequence, "the sermon over which I had spent some long and weary hours." Phebe gently preached the early feminist gospel, anticipating "the day when the ballot is given to woman and her place as a citizen is fully acknowledged."

The Hingham Society showed their appreciation to their pastor, by purchasing one of the first "life memberships in the convention"[83] with a donation of $20 to the fund that served as a relief fund for clergy. As their pastor, Mrs. Hanaford applied the new morality to children, fostering Sabbath school outings and entertainments. She believed "the desire to give pleasure to children is ever an indication of a noble and benevolent nature, and parents and guardians cannot but feel grateful as they see their children happy." As an expression of her philosophy, Phebe introduced the idea of a special day for children with the church filled with flowers and canary cages hanging from the gallery. The event known as Floral Sunday would be open to children from the area's churches. This contact brought an opportunity for her to host the South Shore School Union meetings at the Universalist Church. The success of Floral Sunday also propelled plans for a Sabbath school anniversary celebration at the end the month. Phebe Hanaford accepted an invitation from the captain of the steamer *William Harrison* for a trip around the Boston Harbor Islands for the students of the Sabbath school and the members of the Hingham Universalist Church.

The summer brought little relief from her duties as preacher. In August the *Hingham Journal* carried her schedule. "At the Universalist Church on Sunday next, Mrs. P. A. Hanaford will preach in the morning at 10 o'clock. In the afternoon she will exchange with Prof. Orello Cone of the Canton Theological Seminary. In the evening Mrs. Hanaford will preach at North Weymouth." The affirmation she received from the congregations she served as a preacher convinced Phebe the time had come to seek ordination.

In the winter of 1867 Olympia Brown suffered a great personal disappointment with the defeat of the suffrage referendum in Kansas where she had labored for months. On

---

83   Miller, p. 648

her return to the Weymouth Church, the reception accorded her as their pastor brought her great comfort. In a letter to Phebe Hanaford, Rev. Brown wrote, "I have made a decision to remain in the ministry rather than continue campaigning as Miss Anthony wants me to do. It is a difficult choice but one of my goals in life is to pave the way for other women in the ministry." Phebe Hanaford would have understood this, as she was one of the first women Olympia had encouraged to be a minister.[84]

Recalling Rev. Brown's account of her sad seminary experience, Phebe continued her private studies with the goal of meeting the requirements for ordination. Conscious of the fact that she had never graduated from any school, Phebe wondered how her request to continue to study privately for ordination would be received. The negative reaction came not from the Universalist Society but from the Universalist Publishing House. The Publishing Company fired their popular Editor in January 1868, believing they had evidence that while being paid as Editor she had used writers and articles from other papers. Rumors spread about the owners of the Publishing House's criticism of Mrs. Hanaford's performance as Editor of *The Ladies' Repository*. In Boston Benton Smith confirmed he had received complaints about Mrs. Hanaford's work. The belief among Universalist editors was that Mrs. Hanaford had been fired because the Publishing House did not approve of her plans for ordination. *"The New Covenant* (Chicago) raised a hue and cry and alleged the real reason was that the Publishing House did not believe in women ministers."[85]

The Publishing House reminded their readers of their liberal stand on women's rights and printed a denial of a policy against

---

84   Cote, p. 122
85   Miller, 1979, p. 561

women ministers in the weekly *Universalist.* They further added that Mr. Smith had warned Mrs. Hanaford prior to her studying for the ministry that her new responsibilities would interfere with her editorial duties. On learning Mrs. Hanaford had been forced to resign, other denominational papers, including *The Star of the West,* objected to the fact that Mrs. Hanaford had been denied an editor's privilege of a "valedictory."[86] Mr. Benton Smith pointed out that it was the policy of the Publishing House to edit their periodicals without publishing the editors' names. While he credited Mrs. Hanaford with increasing subscriptions by thousands, Mr. Smith affirmed that her work with Temperance Lectures, Suffrage Meetings and personal writing, along with her family responsibilities and that of the ministry had proved too much even for her boundless energy. Russell Miller writes in his chapter on Women and Literature, "Only one had to be removed from her position by the publisher for failure to perform satisfactorily. The reason was simple…she (Mrs. Hanaford) had, by any standards, attempted to take on too much."[87]

Letters appeared in Universalist publications acknowledging the fact that in her three years as Editor of *The Ladies' Repository,* Mrs. Hanaford had provided nationwide news on political issues and treated her readers to credible editorial comments. Supporters of women's rights acknowledged that every topic relating to women, professional to political, had received full coverage. These acknowledgements may have softened the personal affront to Phebe Hanaford, but she believed the position taken by the Publishing House did an injustice to all women who desired to enter the ministry.

---

86   Ibid
87   Ibid, p. 560

Phebe turned her hand to preparations for her ordination. Traveling to Boston on January 23, 1868, Phebe appeared before the Universalist Examining Ecclesiastical Council. At the conclusion of their meeting, Mrs. Hanaford received official word that the approval for her ordination had been unanimous. Phebe asked Rev. Brown, as her mentor, to extend the Hand of Fellowship at her ordination. "I owe my entrance upon the work of the ministry in the Universalist denomination...to Rev. Olympia Brown."[88] Being only the third woman in the Universalist Church to be ordained, Mrs. Hanaford understood that men would necessarily play a large part in her ordination service, but all the music would be written and performed by women.

In Hingham, the Committee agreed that her ordination would be held on Wednesday, February nineteenth. The Committee prepared a statement for publication in *The Star in the West.*

Educated in the good old fashioned way, she had the Bible from Genesis to Revelations at her tongue's end; having common sense and a good heart she understood our faith. And when the question about pastoral labor was put (in examination for ordination), the chairman of the Committee of the Hingham Society, where she had been preaching for a year, stated that she had done it more effectually than any man they had for the last twenty years.

The entry in Emily Ruggles' diary on February 18, 1868 reads, "In the afternoon went to Boston and met Mrs. Hanaford at the Old Colony depot and went with her to Hingham to attend her ordination." There is no record of the reaction to her ordination on the part of Dr. Hanaford or the children. Emily

88   Hanaford, Phebe A., 1890

Ruggles records Phebe's sisters, Lydia Cressy and Emma Coffin, were in the group traveling from Boston to Hingham.

Wednesday, the nineteenth of February dawned crisp and cold in Hingham. Friends entered the Universalist Church to witness the ordination of Phebe Ann Coffin Hanaford. Eighty-four pews were filled before the services began at half past ten. Ten Universalist preachers and ministers officiated at the ceremony that opened with an invocation by Rev. H. R. Nye of Springfield. Rev. J. Marsden of Abington read a hymn written by Mrs. Mason. Scripture readings by Rev. Eben Francis of Cambridge were followed by a hymn written by Mrs. Farmer and read by W. G. Haskell of Marblehead.

Rev. John Adams' Ordination Sermon, taken from St. Paul's letter to the Galatians 3:28, "There is neither Jew nor Greek, there is neither bond nor free, there is neither male nor female; for ye are all one in Christ Jesus," emphasized the common fatherhood of mankind and the brotherhood of man. He declared the true Christian concept of the common humanity as one body in Christ sharing a common need of spiritual life and salvation. "Standing in opposition to this belief is any teaching which denies that all men are included in the covenant of God's saving grace." To preach the Gospel and to work on behalf of it he declared to be the work of the Christian ministry. Rev. Adams concluded by saying his presence at this ordination gave testimony to his belief in the role of women in the church, based on New Testament records, church history and present day achievements of women, particularly Universalist women. Of Rev. Hanaford, he remarked, "Her work and record with us thus far has been praiseworthy, and her call to the ministry and to the pastorate here has been made with an earnestness and unanimity which seems to warrant the propriety and justness of the rites we now perform."

Following the fervent Ordaining Prayer by Rev. Twiss of Lowell, Rev. Olympia Brown of Weymouth extended the Hand of Fellowship, welcoming the candidate to the joys, toils, sacrifices, trials, and blessings of the Christian ministry. With right hands joined, she told Phebe, "It will be yours, as a woman to sympathize with and aid suffering woman, who needs the sympathies of her sex." Olympia's prayer that Phebe Hanaford be a model for young women called to the ministry and seeking sympathy for their dreams gave resonance to Rev. Olympia Brown's role in Phebe's call to the ministry.

The charge given by Rev. H. R. Nye of Springfield expressed his esteem for the candidate. The morning service continued with a poem by Mrs. Munroe, read by Rev. G. W. Whitney, who had traveled from Beverly for the occasion. The edifying service expressed the genial spirit of the candidate, and unbarred windows and opened the doors of the soul. Rev. Phebe Hanaford rose and gave the Benediction. The social that followed the service rang out with gratitude for the gift bestowed on Rev. Hanaford.

The Installation Service began at two o'clock with an invocation by Rev. Eben Francis. Hymns and Scripture readings offered inspiration as did the prayer offered by Rev. Hewitt. Rev. Olympia Brown's sermon defined the role of pastor of a church. "In the installation of the pastor, the law of division of duties is recognized." Rev. Brown went on to list the duties of the pastor:

...as so responsible as to need the strength that can come only through that gospel which is the power of God unto salvation. These duties include the social and political evils of the times, injustice to the weak and powerless, wrongs which cry out for redress, wicked customs and bad laws which undermine the safety of the State.

In conclusion of a sermon that left no listener ignorant of the responsibilities laid on Rev. Phebe Hanaford that day, Rev. Olympia Brown turned to the newly ordained and said,

And so may you, my sister, find at last, satisfaction and joy in the thought that your work shall speak for you; and may you ever be sustained amid the difficult duties of the minister, by the consciousness that you are following in the footsteps of Jesus, that you are doing the Lord's will on earth. Amen.

Ordination did not change Phebe Ann Coffin Hanaford but affirmed who she was. A Quaker by birth and a Universalist by choice, her call to the ministry had begun years earlier as she sat in the silence of the Friends Meeting on Nantucket Island. Listening to Mary Farnum and reading letters from Sybil Jones, she remained filled with a desire to consecrate herself to the work of the gospel ministry. Phebe's grandmothers remained ever present reminders of women of wisdom who walked in God's light, as did her cousin, Lucretia Mott.

The editorial of *The Ladies' Repository* answered the letters received asking for an account of the services of the ordination of the first woman ordained in Massachusetts. The lengthy response concluded, "The tearful face of the candidate, with its expression of faith, purity, and consecration, together with the reverent mien of those who stood around, and the fitting and touching words of the prayer offered up—all were eloquent indeed."[89] Mrs. C. A. Winship's detailed article appearing in the *Universalist,* noted that "the hymns were all lined out for singing by men."

After her ordination Rev. Phebe Hanaford continued to serve as chaplain of the Right Worthy Lodge of Masons. One evening, to her dismay, she was asked to respond to the toast at the Masonic Supper, an honor never before in the Lodge's history offered a woman. Phebe's abhorrence of the use of alcohol had kept her active in the Temperance Movement. She had written articles on the evils of drink for the *Universalist.* Phebe noted in a letter to her "Co-workers and Pioneers," regarding one such article, "Benton altered it to its present appearance." Phebe acknowledged some tensions existed between herself and the editor of the *Universalist* regarding her involvement in the Temperance Movement. She frequently spent her own money for material for banners and paid her travel expenses to lectures. She spoke at the Temperance Convention in Concord to a large audience that included "Governor" Walter Harriman of New Hampshire, a strong advocate of abstinence from alcohol.

As a newly ordained minister, Rev. Hanaford received invitations to preach in several Universalist Churches. In the spring of 1868 Emily Ruggles' diary records she accompanied Rev. Hanaford to Cambridge, Brighton, Ipswich, North Reading, Fitchburg and Lunenburg. When asked to preach at Rockland House on Nantasket Beach, Rev. Hanaford chose a theme based on the words, "I shall be satisfied when I awake in Thy likeness." She illustrated her theme by referring to the struggles artists have in creating likenesses that will become masterpieces.

89   April, p. 308

Rev. Hanaford recalled Joanna Quiner's skillful hands, now idle in illness. Later that day she spoke with Harriett Hosmer, the famed sculptress, who sat in the congregation. Both women faced the discrimination dealt those who stepped outside the accepted role for women.

After repeated requests over a period of five months, Rev. Hanaford received her Certificate of Ordination dated July 13, 1868.[90] Of the men of the Committee on Fellowship, Ordination, and Discipline, whose five signatures appeared on her Certificate of Ordination, Phebe failed to understand why any of these men had justification for the delay. Learning that her friend had received her Certificate of Ordination, Emily Ruggles suggested they take a trip to Hoosac Tunnel.

After a comfortable ride, smooth and free of dust, the travelers arrived in Florida, New York. At the eastern end of the tunnel they were seated in a large stagecoach drawn by six gray horses. Their destination was North Adams. They would go through the White Mountain guided by Mr. William Fuller, a driver of considerable local fame. At North Adams, Phebe wrote that she stood enthralled with the beauty of the cascade and the sinuosity of the river channel and the effects it had had on the rocks over the centuries. The sun shone down upon the foliage that interlaced overhead, creating an arch, highlighting the trees and their roots that towered above them.

Riding into the western shaft, they saw the miners at work with pickaxes and shovels. Accounts of the excursion describe the wet atmosphere as they trundled along on the handcar for an eighth of a mile into the huge bore. At the western shaft the

90   Andover-Harvard Theological Library

group of tourists descended three hundred and eighteen feet into the heart of the mountain. At the Hoosac Tunnel House, Phebe and Emily described their experience in the tunnel to their hosts, Messrs. Rice and Henks, as like being in a dumbwaiter. Phebe noted the miners were wet even in their rubber coats and that they spoke with an accent. Awed at the feat of engineering but alarmed at such a dark, damp terrible place to work, Phebe wrote notes so that she could send an account of this adventure to the *Boston Journal.* The trip concluded with Rev. Hanaford's service at the Methodist Church in North Adams.

The two women then traveled to Marblehead, Massachusetts for the ordination of William Garrison Haskell and his Installation as Pastor of the First Universalist Church. On September 2, 1868 Rev. Hanaford and Rev. Olympia Brown stood with Rev. Haskell in the sanctuary as testimony to the fact that the Universalist Church promoted the cause of woman's rights by more than words. Later that month on the seventeenth and eighteenth, Mary Livermore's name appears in Emily Ruggles' diary when she "called on Mrs. H. in the evening." Olympia Brown's name appears in the diary in October "with PAH." The loss of Phebe's diaries denies us access to any conversations Phebe had with them, but as suffragists these three women were occupied with the reaction of Elizabeth Cady Stanton to the passage of the Fourteenth Amendment.

The ratification of the Fourteenth Amendment in July 1868 granting full citizenship to the Negro caused ongoing tensions within the Suffrage Movement. The issue of precedence of the Negro's over women's rights became intolerable to Elizabeth Cady Stanton, founder and president of the Equal Rights Association. She and the other women had worked hard for the rights of the freed slave, but she repeated, "It was never at the expense of woman's rights." Lucy Stone formed the New England Woman Suffrage Association with Julia Ward Howe as president. It is likely Phebe was invited to join the New England Woman Suffrage Association since "Mrs. Howe composed the Ordination Hymn" for Rev. Phebe Hanaford.[91] Phebe was soon listed among the "brilliant galaxy of speakers…on the woman's suffrage platform."[92] Of these women Phebe would later write, "They are good housekeepers, true mothers and faithful wives."[93]

As a mother Phebe had great influence over her son. She nurtured his interest in Universalism. When the time came to choose a school, Howard agreed to board at Dean Academy in Franklin, Massachusetts. He would be seventeen in December. Joseph considered him a man obligated to complete his studies each day as he had been taught. For Phebe, Howard wrote,

> Because I love my mother and appreciate her self sacrificing efforts on my behalf, I hereby promise that I shall strive to be an obedient and faithful pupil at Dean Academy and that in any debate in reference to the so-called woman question, I will never take any position opposed to woman's right to citizenship or to any sphere of labor for which she is fitted and to which God shall call her.
> H. A. Hanaford

Phebe wrote to her son for his birthday, December 10, 1868.

Dear Son, My precious boy, you have no idea how much I miss you. It was so pleasant to have someone at home who was ready

---

91 Miller, 1979, p. 556

92 Harper, p. 322

93 Hanaford, Phebe A., 1881, p. 348

to read every Universalist paper and was so ready to welcome the arrival of new books written by Universalists. My dear son can hardly realize what a comfort it was to have his sympathy in so many matters. I long to hear from you and know how you like your roommate, which is a very important matter.

I pray you will not forget to read your Bible daily and to offer your prayers faithfully. If you and young Eaton are to be ministers, you ought to begin now, and it will not be amiss for you to pray together every night. But do not omit <u>secret</u> prayer. God hears and answers prayer, and if you ask Him to give you Quickness to comprehend and memory to retain your lessons you will be helped by your heavenly Father and I shall hear that my darling boy is a good scholar. I am willing to work for you, my dear son, but I shall be greatly encouraged in my work by learning that you are faithful and successful.

Hoping to hear from you soon, my precious son, and commending you to the kind care of our Heavenly Father, I remain

Your ever loving
Mother[94]

An article by Lorenza Haynes, Waltham's first librarian, offers us a picture of Phebe at this time.

...let us glance at one who has dared to make such an innovation upon man's prerogative, the sacred desk. The face is spiritually beautiful, crowned by a dome of thought which would do honor to any man's shoulder. Glossy black hair lying smoothly on the temples and

gathered into a braid behind, black eyes of the soft and soulful expression. Her dress is black silk with collar and cuffs of linen; a little broach of some delicate stone fastens her watch-guard, and a little cross of the same pure stone as the broach is a pendant to it.
Her speaking described as a full, rich but feminine voice "carries the clear meaning to the heart of the hearer.... The sermon from John, XIV chapter and 8th verse, was ably treated and eloquently delivered...both morning and evening services were attended by many who stood patiently from beginning to end of the services. In manner she is easy and graceful, and her every word, tone and look carries conviction to the heart that she speaks as she feels, — that her heart and talents are consecrated to her great and good work.... One great charm in her preaching and in her whole appearance in the pulpit is her *womanliness*, which is borne with such modesty and reverential grace that all unjust criticism and prejudice is at once disarmed against women as a spiritual teacher.[95]

The concluding words identify a significant contribution Phebe made to the acceptance of women in the ministry. Miss Haynes admits that, "An article limited as this must be to treat other than briefly, discourses which for depth of thought, strength of argument and beauty of expression should be heard to be appreciated." On March 20, 1869, the Waltham Church committee met to discuss the appointment of Rev. Hanaford as preacher on an interim basis. Clyde Joslyn's unpublished "Universalism in Waltham, Mass.; 1836-1858" reports one dissenting voice. "One member of the Society resigned in disgust when Mrs. Hanaford

95   Haynes

was called to the pulpit, saying that if he had a hen that crowed, he would cut her head off." Waltham Church records reveal their impression that it was more than Rev. Hanaford's appearance but the "authority that radiates from this woman in spite of her small stature and ladylike manner." The Waltham Universalist Society offered Rev. Hanaford the position of regular minister at a salary of $1000 a year to preach twice a month alternating with her duties in Hingham. This salary would offset her lost income as editor of *The Ladies' Repository.*

On May sixth, Emily notes, it was Phebe's fortieth birthday, and "PAH came over in the evening and passed the night with me." Their shared lives, although lived in different styles, made for a remarkable friendship. Emily, standing over six feet tall, overcame life's obstacles with impressive physical strength. Phebe Hanaford, small in stature, worked within the restrictions placed on her. Emily, single and with a keen sense of the commercial market, earned her living by her wits. Phebe, the intellectual scholar, studied without remission and supported her family through her writing.

As Universalists, Emily Ruggles appears to have lived her faith privately, following her conscience; whereas Phebe's Inner Voice called her to lead others in their faith. Emily's visible support of Phebe could be measured in miles traveled and time spent in support during troubled times. Phebe's veiled dependence on Emily ran deep, overshadowed by her personal achievements. The assignment in Waltham would bring about a personal awakening in the forty-year-old Universalist minister, wife, mother and reformer, and a realization of who she was as a woman.

Phebe Hanaford
Author 1853

Ellen Miles
Waltham 1869

Rev. Phebe Hanaford
First Universalist Church of the Messiah
New Haven 1870

Rev. Phebe Hanaford
Jersey City 1877

Universalist Women who called Rev. Hanaford to
The Second Universalist, Church of the Holy Spirit
New Haven 1884

Phebe Hanaford, Basom 1918
89th birthday

CHAPTER FIVE

A WALTHAM MARRIAGE

Soul-sister! May the waiting years for thee
Pour out a largess of such joy
That earth shall seem the porch of heaven to be.[96]

Appointed as Pastor to Waltham Church in 1867, Rev. Hanaford took a keen interest in the Sabbath school, where she met Miss Ellen Miles. Ellen had begun teaching at the Sabbath school in Waltham before the Universalist Society had engaged Rev. Hanaford as their pastor. We learn from *Daughters of America*[97] that Ellen was born in Randolph, Massachusetts in 1835. Family circumstances brought Mrs. Anne Miles and her three daughters to Waltham when the girls were in their teens. In *Daughters of America,* Phebe Hanaford mentions Ellen Miles in six different chapters: "Literary Women," "Women Poets," "Women Preachers," "Women Educators," "Women As Readers-Actors-Singers" and "Women of Faith." Granting that Ellen Miles was a woman of faith and a splendid educator, the entries under the other categories are linked to her literary efforts as coauthor with Phebe. Ellen's personal talents and womanly characteristics are portrayed in the character "Helen" in Phebe's novel *Heart of Siasconset.* Ellen Miles' friendship with

---

96   Hanaford, Phebe A., 1871. *From Shore to Shore and Other Poems,*
        Dedicatory Sonnet,
97   Hanaford, Phebe A., 1881, p. 518

Phebe undeniably earns her a place in the life story of Phebe Hanaford.

Phebe's admiration for the Sabbath school teacher deepened during her ministry in Waltham. Emily Ruggles' diaries tell us that, in time, Phebe invited Ellen Miles to visit her at her home in Reading. This intrusion of Phebe's professional life into her family life demonstrates her view of the compatibility of career and marriage. In her writings Rev. Antoinette Brown Blackwell, "the first woman regularly ordained by public services in America, perhaps in the world,"[98] encouraged women to examine the compatibility of the two vocations, marriage and ministry. "Seven years into her preaching ministry and two years after her ordination, Antoinette Brown "became the wife of Samuel C. Blackwell, and since that time has retired from pastoral labors, and given her attention to training her five daughters."[99] Phebe chose a different path.

Phebe's choice of Universalism in the face of Joseph's continued refusal to recognize his wife's right to choose was an affront to society's hierarchical arrangement of marriage. Her ministry alienated her from Joseph as a Calvinist Baptist. Her financial independence, including her support of their children, had the effect of diminishing his role as head of the household. Their role reversal reduced their marriage to a legal contract. Phebe never annulled their marriage contract, legally or otherwise. Neither did society grant a woman the right to leave her husband to pursue a career.

The third Equal Rights Convention, the first convention held after the Civil War, took place on May 12, 1869. Phebe Hanaford, now recognized as a speaker for the New England Woman

---

98   Ibid, p. 422
99   Ibid, p. 423

Suffrage Association, was a delegate from Massachusetts. Traveling from further distances than previously recorded, delegates arrived in large numbers at Steinway Hall in New York City. Phebe Hanaford's name appears among the newcomers to the woman's suffrage platform. With Elizabeth Cady Stanton presiding, the meeting proved to be the most stormy and unsatisfactory Convention held to date.

Anti-slavery advocate, Stephen Foster from Massachusetts, suggested that Miss Anthony's and Mrs. Stanton's objections to the granting of citizenship to men regardless of race were contrary to the principles of the Equal Rights Association. He stated that the Massachusetts Society could no longer cooperate with them. He went so far as to ask Mrs. Stanton and Miss Anthony to withdraw. The attack was considered an insult to the two women who had brought the nation so far in its recognition of women's rights, and the motion was quickly overruled.[100] However, the issue of their approval of the proposed Fifteenth Federal Amendment remained in the forefront.

Frederick Douglass, backed by other members, wanted the Equal Rights Association to adopt a resolution indicating a grateful welcome of the pending Fifteenth Amendment prohibiting disenfranchisement on account of race and to earnestly solicit the State Legislature to pass it without delay. Elizabeth Cady Stanton continued to fight for the inclusion of the word "sex" in the proposed resolution. Susan B. Anthony pointed out that, with this amendment, 2,000,000 colored men would be given power over 2,000,000 colored women.

Newspapers reported Anthony and Stanton as anti-negro. This accusation cost them the support of powerful men including

---

100   Harper, p. 322

Horace Greeley of the *Tribune*, long their friend and an advocate of women's rights. Many women found Mrs. Stanton too radical in her approach. Susan B. Anthony stood with her friend. Ever the abolitionist, Lucy Stone gathered supporters for the proposed Fifteenth Amendment. Years earlier Phebe Hanaford forfeited her Quaker pacifism in favor of a war that would bring about the abolition of slavery. It proved impossible for her to abandon that principle. Phebe Hanaford, Julia Ward Howe and the Massachusetts delegates left the Hall favoring the rights of the Negro over immediate enfranchisement of women as full citizens as demanded by Elizabeth Cady Stanton and Susan B. Anthony.

Within weeks Elizabeth Cady Stanton and Susan B. Anthony quit the Equal Rights Association and formed the National Woman Suffrage Association. Women reacted to the news with concern for the future of the Suffrage Movement. Mary Livermore wrote to Phebe saying she would be in Reading on the twenty-first of May to discuss the next proposal to save the Woman's Suffrage Movement. Emily Ruggles records in her diary that Mrs. Livermore spoke at the Lyceum Hall on "Women and Her Wants" to a large audience, adding, "Mrs. Livermore and Mrs. Hanaford stayed at our house overnight." Emily recorded again meeting Mrs. Livermore on her arrival in Boston on May twenty-second.

The two women traveled to Hingham where Mrs. Livermore spoke at the morning and afternoon Universalist services. They then went to Weymouth where Mrs. Livermore spoke at the evening service. The following Sunday, Emily drove to Waltham to hear Rev. Hanaford preach. Emily traveled with Phebe to Mattapoisett on the twenty-fourth of June. Emily's diary indicates Emma Coffin visited Reading and Florence Hanaford traveled with her aunt to Nantucket the first week of July. Dr. Hanaford met Emily as she returned home from the station, reporting, "I am sorry but you missed them, Miss Ruggles, I just put them on the train for Boston. Mrs. Hanaford will return this evening."

In July, 1869 subtle changes appear in Emily's diary regarding her visits with Phebe. On July 1 she wrote, "Called on PAH in the evening, Nellie Miles returned from Westbrook with her." On the second she wrote, "Called on Mrs. Hanaford in the evening. She and Nellie Miles returned home with me and remained an hour or two." Emily joined in their evening's relaxations either at the Hanaford residence or at her home. Many summer evenings Emily hitched up "Kittie Lucas" and the three women took a ride around the pond to escape the heat. On the twenty-sixth, Emily wrote that "Nellie Miles returned from Waltham with Mrs. Hanaford." Interesting to note that in her diary, Emily always referred to her friend as Mrs. Hanaford but very soon referred to Ellen Miles as "Nellie."

Rev. Hanaford continued her trips to Hingham during the summer. On July 6 *The Hingham Journal* wrote of the Sabbath school anniversary celebration. "The church was beautifully decorated with flowers and afforded spectacles beyond description." The program, well rehearsed for weeks, included Rev. Hanaford's poem, "From Shore to Shore," sung by the adult and children's choirs. On July 30 Emily wrote, "Called on PAH in the afternoon, she and Nellie Miles returned the night before – they walked home from the store with me in the evening and we took Mrs. H.'s clothes to our house to pack with mine for our White Mountain trip." They traveled to White Mountain on August 2 and returned home on the fifth of the month.

Within a few days Phebe received Lucy Stone's August 5, 1869 circular letter written from the New England Woman

Suffrage Association initiating the formation of the American Woman Suffrage Association. It read,

Dear

Many friends of the cause of Woman Suffrage desire that its interests may be promoted by the assembling and action of a Convention, devised as a truly national and representative basis, for the organization of an American Woman Suffrage Association.

Without depreciating the value of Associations already existing, it is yet deemed that an organization at once more comprehensive and more widely representative than any or these is urgently called for.

In this view, the Executive Committee of the New England Woman Suffrage Association has appointed the undersigned a Committee of Correspondence to confer, by letter, with the friends of Woman Suffrage throughout the country, on the subject of the proposed Convention....[101]

Phebe Hanaford's friends, Caroline Severance and Julia Ward Howe, signed the letter along with Lucy Stone. "In response to the above circular, and by express authority of the signers," was issued the following.

WOMAN SUFFRAGE CALL

The undersigned, being convinced of the necessity of an American Woman Suffrage Association, which shall embody the deliberate action of the State organization,

---

101   Schlesinger Library

and shall carry with it their united weight, do hereby respectfully invite such organizations to be represented in a Delegate Convention to be held in Cleveland, Ohio, Nov. 24 and 25 A.D. 1869.[102]

Phebe Hanaford's name appears as a Delegate from Massachusetts to the first American Woman Suffrage Association Convention to be held in Cleveland, Ohio in November 1869. Other delegates from Massachusetts included William Lloyd Garrison, Lydia Maria Child, Julia Ward Howe and Caroline Severance. The formation of the American Woman Suffrage Association, while it offered a solution to the radical stand of Elizabeth Cady Stanton and her National Woman Suffrage Association, diminished the combined strength of the suffrage movement. Phebe's appointment as a delegate confirms her agreement with Lucy Stone's belief that Elizabeth Cady Stanton's organization did not represent the majority of women. As a delegate to the American Woman Suffrage Association Convention, Mrs. Hanaford went on the lecture circuit to explain the split in the woman's suffrage movement and promote Lucy Stone's plan for state amendments over a federal amendment for Woman Suffrage. On September 4, Emily Ruggles wrote, "PAH and Nellie Miles came from Connecticut the night before." Through September and October, Emily's diary shows entries regarding Nellie's frequent visits to Reading.

The November 15 entry in Emily's diary reads, "Went to Boston on the first train and went out on the Albany Road to ride from West Newton to Framingham with Mrs. Hanaford and Nellie Miles, who were on their way to Niagara and Antioch. I bought goods in Boston and left for home at 11. Wrote to PAH

---

102   Ibid

in the evening." On this trip Phebe and Ellen included a visit to Howard Hanaford at Antioch College. They reached Yellow Springs the night before Thanksgiving. In his invitation to Mrs. Hanaford, Antioch's President George Washington Hosmer encouraged Mrs. Hanaford to spend the whole day with Howard. In recognition of her recent ordination, he invited her to share in their chapel service and to preach. Phebe wrote an account of the event for *Pearson's Magazine* in 1903.

> *Antioch College which had Horace Mann and Thomas Hill among its presidents was open to both sexes, and that fact determined me to send my son thither from Massachusetts to Ohio, in the far-off sixties — while the good Rev. Hosmer was its president. I can never forget the joy of my soul as I preached the Thanksgiving Day sermon in 1869 in the college chapel, with the honored president at my side, and my son with his fellow-students — male and female — in my audience. What a dinner we had afterwards, with speeches and songs; and how admirably Ellen E. Miles, then a Massachusetts teacher on a vacation, read as an elocutionist to the delighted assembly! And how we sought for fossils the next day in the old quarry near the college! Behold is it not all in our memory books! This visit to the boys and girls of Antioch intensified our belief in coeducation so that when the Association for the Advancement of Women was formed in New York in 1873 we were ready to join the earnest advocates of that much needed reform in educational methods.*

Following this memorable visit, they continued on to Cleveland for the first American Woman Suffrage Association Convention. Of the men who attended the Convention, Henry Ward

Beecher accepted the office of president. This was in sharp contrast to the National Organization that barred men from membership. Mary Livermore of Illinois, Celia Burleigh of New York, Mrs. W. T. Hazard of Missouri, and Margaret Longley of Ohio were among the eight vice presidents. Lucy Stone became Chairman of the Executive Committee, and Rev. Olympia Brown served on the Committee. The Corresponding Secretary, Myra Bradwell, had served her country well during the war in the Northwestern Sanitary Commission and was currently Editor and business manager of the *Chicago Legal News*.

On November 4, 1869 the world mourned the death of business tycoon George Peabody. Thousands who had benefited from his generous spirit attended his memorial service in Salem to applaud their benefactor. Only a few months earlier dedicatory services had been held for the Peabody Academy of Science. "During the session of the American Association for the Advancement of Sciences, which was held in Salem, Mass., in the summer of 1869, the dedicatory services of the Peabody Academy of Science were held in the Tabernacle Church; the building owned by the academy being too small for the audience."[103] Mr. Peabody's early interest in the promotion of science and useful knowledge in the county of Essex, Massachusetts included his donation of $140,000 in 1867. His interest led to the formation of the Essex Institute of Salem. This early group of scholars became the Peabody Academy of Science. Joseph and Phebe Hanaford enjoyed the Essex Institute under the leadership of Dr. Henry Wheatland.

Members of the Essex Institute commissioned Phebe Hanaford to write a biography of this man who had been

---

103   Hanaford, Phebe A., 1870, p. 185

their benefactor. Phebe reached an agreement with D. Lothrop Company to write a compilation to include an enumeration of George Peabody's philanthropies. Phebe included his endowment of $15,000 for the expansion of the local library. At their request a portrait of Mr. Peabody, done in London, was on its way to Massachusetts.

Amidst the pressure of her writing, Phebe accepted an invitation to preach in New Haven at the Universalist Church of the Messiah. Emily Ruggles' diary records Phebe's departure for New Haven and New Jersey on December sixth. "Wrote to PAH at Bridgeport and New Haven." Rev. Hanaford was well received at the Church of the Messiah, and members of the Committee invited her to return in December. In light of the New Haven Universalist Society's search for a resident pastor, Phebe agreed on the date. Emily met Mrs. Hanaford at the depot on her return from New Haven. On the sixteenth Emily called on Phebe and "Nellie Miles was there." The next day Phebe left for Quincy on a lecture tour.

The close of Emily Ruggles' 1869 diary shows Phebe's continued travels for the American Woman Suffrage Association. Her December 30 note reads, "Called on PAH in the morning and walked with her and Nellie Miles to the depot. Mrs. H. went to Concord N.H. to attend a woman suffrage convention." The first annual New Hampshire Woman Suffrage Association convention held in Eagle Hall in Concord on December 31 included "Mrs. Phebe Hanaford as a speaker, Mrs. Julia Ward Howe, Mrs. Caroline Severance, Lucy Stone and H. B. Blackwell, A. J. and Mrs. Mary T. Davis of New Jersey and the successful worker of the woman's cause in the West, Mrs. Mary Livermore of Chicago, and many others in our State."[104]

....
104   New Haven Colony Historical Society

The success of the American Woman Suffrage Association had adverse effects on Elizabeth Cady Stanton's position as the leader of the suffrage movement. Her paper *The Revolution* gave the more radical views of the National Woman Suffrage Association. Lucy Stone's weekly newspaper, *The Woman's Journal*, devoted to women's rights, including political equality, promoted the ideals and goals of the American Woman Suffrage Association. Lucy Stone's husband, Henry Blackwell, managed the business details of *The Woman's Journal*, which was printed at the office of the American Woman Suffrage Association, located in the rear of Tremont House at Three Tremont Place in Boston. Mrs. Livermore, then the publisher of *The Agitator* in Chicago, agreed to edit *The Woman's Journal*. Initially all editorial letters and communications were sent to her through the office of Myra Bradwell's paper on Washington Street in Chicago. The first issue of *The Woman's Journal* on January 8, 1870 included a "Salutatory" by Julia Ward Howe inviting all to join in the common cause of woman's suffrage. The editorial begins,

> Rev. Phebe Hanaford now settled over the two parishes of Waltham and Hingham, Mass., has accepted an invitation to the pastorate of the Universalist church in New Haven, at a salary of $2,500 for the first year.... We make the above announcement with much pleasure and pride as it is a practical refutation of the oft-made statement that "women can't preach, you know," —the success of women ministers is very problematical–an experiment, whose result is yet uncertain.

The Woman's Journal[105] printed Rev. Hanaford's article, "Woman As Preacher." Phebe opened with the words "No genuine

---

105   1(1), p. 2

Christian will deny that every power of the mind and every faculty of the body ought to be consecrated unto the Lord."

Rachel Tedesco suggests that Phebe had several reasons for seeking the position in New Haven.

The first was that the weekly commute by horse and buggy back and forth between Reading and Waltham and Reading and Hingham must have been tiring. It must not have been the money because the salaries from the two part-time pastorates equaled the total she was to get from New Haven. The second reason was undoubtedly the opportunity to set up a separate household from Dr. Hanaford. The third reason may have been to be near the women's rights activists in New York, the center of the pro-suffrage action.[106]

The marriage agreement between Lucy Stone and Henry B. Blackwell, published in the *Liberator* years earlier, made it known that Lucy retained her independence as well as her name after their marriage. The husband and wife worked together to fulfill Lucy's goal to form the American Woman Suffrage Association. The goals for the Association were established and set forth as pledges.

We plead the equality of perfect justice.
Woman and man, black or white, wife and husband, sister and brother.
We plead recognition of the strongest moral power the nation holds—

---

106   Tedesco, 1998

The power that makes the home—the power that makes
the man—
that gives the essence of integrity and honor to public
and to private lives.
We seek purity in society and State,—purity in the in-
termingling of all social classes among a Democratic
people—in the contact of capital with female labor—in
the enactment of law, and in the administration of it.
We seek intelligence, virtue and wisdom through the
education of our educators—
through the enlightenment of a people's will.
The ballot is the greatest educator—
We are to organize victory out of a momentary defeat.
We are to rebuke by any irresistible demand the
  indifference of legislators to the necessities of reforms.
    WE WILL BE HEARD.

Emily Ruggles' diary offers the only information available
on Phebe's itinerary in early 1870. "Nellie" appears with Phebe
in most entries. On January 25, Emily writes, "Passed the night
with PAH. Dr. H. was on the Cape." Emily recorded that on
the twenty-sixth Mrs. H. took the train from Reading. On the
twenty-seventh she notes Phebe was with Nellie Miles. Emily
"met Mrs. H. at the last train and went and passed the night
with her." On the twenty-eighth, Phebe and Emily are at the
Horticultural Hall in Boston at a meeting "called to form a State
Woman Suffrage Association.... Nellie Miles, Mrs. Hanaford
and I came out together on the last train."

While deep into her suffrage work, Phebe's Letter of Call to
the First Universalist Church in New Haven dated January 19,

1870[107] indicated that earlier on the fourteenth the committee had approved her appointment by unanimous vote. The three-year contract granted a salary of $2000 a year and a bonus of $500 for the first year. These terms required a letter of acceptance from Rev. Hanaford. Phebe sent her letter of acceptance on these terms and confirmed she would preach at the Church of the Messiah at the end of the month.

On January 29, 1870 Phebe and Ellen Miles traveled from Reading to New Haven. After the morning service, Rev. Hanaford met with the Committee of the Church of the Messiah. They agreed Ellen Miles would be the Sabbath school teacher, as well as Rev. Hanaford's companion since Dr. Hanaford would not be able to leave his medical practice in Reading. Phebe and Ellen left New Haven the next day to go directly to the Suffrage Convention in Montpelier, Vermont. Emily Ruggles met Mrs. Livermore in Boston at the Tremont House for the trip to Montpelier.

The meeting lasted all that day with Lucy Stone and her husband explaining the plans for the American Woman Suffrage Association. Julia Ward Howe spoke of the need for increased membership to promote women's rights in the State of Vermont. Along with the other women from out of town, Emily, Phebe and Ellen boarded the night train. Ellen stayed with Phebe when they reached Reading. Emily's diary reports that Phebe finished the biography of George Peabody on February 18, 1870. The book was published that year and reached a sale of sixteen thousand and included a fifteen-page Introduction by Dr. J. H. Hanaford. This book would be the Hanafords' last cooperative literary effort.

Phebe officially completed her ministries in Hingham and Waltham on March 1. In affirmation of Rev. Hanaford, the members of the Waltham congregation issued a statement.

107   Nantucket Historical Association

RESOLVED that in her public ministrations she has exhibited those natural and acquired endowments which eminently fit her for the work in which she is so devotedly engaged, and has demonstrated to our judgment that, in providing for the needs of the Church, and for the great work of the Gospel ministry, God has not confined the bestowment of His gifts to the male sex.

RESOLVED that while we shall lose the inspiring influence of her fervid eloquence and direct, forcible and pleasing manner of presenting the great truths of the Gospel, we congratulate our brethren at New Haven upon their good fortune in obtaining a Pastor as well qualified to break to them the bread of life, knowing that what is our loss is their gain, and we sincerely invoke the blessing of Almighty God upon both Pastor and people.

The closure of Rev. Hanaford's ministry in Hingham and Waltham opened her career as a preacher and closed her life as a wife. According to Reading records the permanent separation from Joseph Hanaford, her husband of twenty years, never ended in divorce. Florence is not mentioned in Emily's diary for the nights of "March 23 and 24 when Mrs. H. passed the night with me," or on March 25 when Mrs. Hanaford "took a last look at the house. I walked her to the depot." That house may not have provided a happy environment for Florence due to the obvious tension between her parents, but nothing in the research of the Hanaford family life in Reading supports the idea that Florence wanted to leave her father. The only sign of Florence's interest in Universalism was her one-year enrollment in the Reading Liberal Ladies Benevolent Society. The Andover College Calendar for 1869-1870 lists Howard as an undergraduate.

Travelers leaving Boston on the Providence Railroad depart-ed from one of the most spacious and elegant stations in New England. The brick building housed five tracks in a track house that spanned over one hundred feet. To pass the waiting hours between trains, men relaxed in the billiard room or enjoyed the comforts of the barbershop. In the immense central apartment with its overhead balcony, people sought information on depar-tures and arrivals while shoppers bought theater tickets at the office and flowers from any of the several stands.

Emily Ruggles wrote in her diary on March 28, 1870, "Went to Boston in the morning and attended to business and then started for the Providence Depot to see Mrs. Hanaford and fam-ily as they left for New Haven—met Nellie Miles on the street... and walked with her to the depot." No longer a visitor, Ellen Miles would live together with Florence and her mother as a family. The relationship between Ellen and Phebe that began in Waltham moved to New Haven.

NEW HAVEN

New Haven surroundings had a large number of oyster plantations along the Quinnipiac River where the March winds blew off Long Island Sound. Oyster farming looked very differ-ent from the whaling industry of Nantucket. In contrast to the Atlantic Ocean as unlimited home ground for powerful whales, an oyster plantation is staked out by the farmer where he culti-vates oysters in great numbers.

Phebe Hanaford and her household took up residence at 19 Home Place. The name Home Place originated with the developer, the Home Insurance Company of New Haven. Rev. Hanaford's contract with the First Universalist Society dated

January 19, 1870 was written on stationery from "The Home Insurance Company of New Haven" and signed by Wm. Mc-Goodell, Clerk. His name also appears on the Company stationery as "Sec'y."[108] Home place became Court street in 1898. The house faced Worcester Square with its display of elm trees that gave New Haven the name "The City of Elms." Phebe enrolled Florence in "Miss Peny's Young Ladies Academy."[109]

Located in a quiet neighborhood, Home Place was a short walk to the Church of the Messiah on Chapel Street. From the New Haven Colony Historical Society, we read,

The first association of a few people in New Haven who rejected the doctrine of everlasting punishment for the unbelieving was considered a shocking affront to religion, and in orthodox churches prayers were offered in an indiscriminate way, for pagans, infidels and 'Universalists.' It required a great deal of courage for a pious person to be a Universalist. A few citizens who felt alike with regard to the teachings of the New England primer, met Sunday evenings in a quiet way, and while they formed but a small association, their meetings were occasionally held in the basement of the State House. An elderly citizen remembers seeing some Universalists sitting on benches placed along the wall, in the basement of the building, and looking to his imagination, very much as if they were conscious of doing something highly improper. At one time they met regularly in Saunders Hall on the northeast corner of Chapel and Orange streets, and the first church was not built until 1850. It was on

108   Ibid
109   1882 Coffin Genealogy

the southeast corner of State and Court streets. They afterwards worshipped in what had been the church of the First Baptist Society, now owned by Dr. P. C. Skiff. Moses Ballou, son of Hosea Ballou, known as the Father of Universalism in the United States, at one time ministered to that denomination in New Haven. Their pretty little church, with parsonage attached, on Orange above Elm street, is on land once a part of the large garden of Eli Whitney, the inventor. A second Universalist society worshipped in a chapel on Davenport avenue, they bought in 1883." Other stories tell of Universalism in New Haven that in 1866 folks met in the basement of the State House and in a room overlooking a glass factory or in homes for many years. Hosea Ballou preached to a large congregation but was in the end "unhappy with the response." It was not easy for a religious person to be a Universalist thirty years ago.

There is a story told that the president of Yale forbade his students to attend John Murray's services when he preached in New Haven on his way from Maryland to New Hampshire. In *Three Centuries of New Haven, 1638-1938,* Rollin G. Osterweiss records,

Universalism was first mentioned in New Haven in 1832 when the Society petitioned the committee of Properties of Common Undivided Lands for permission to erect a house for public worship on the West Corner of the West Green. This was denied in 1849. Universalists secured a permanent church home purchased for $6,200 on the southeast corner of State and Court Street. It opened in 1850.[110]

110   p. 215

"New England even before the middle of the nineteenth century became the center of gravity for American Universalism."[111]

The *Universalist* on 26 March 1870 published a series of debates on women in the ministry that indicate the continued resistance to women like Rev. Phebe Hanaford.

The inevitable debates took place over whether there was Scriptural precedent or authority for women ministers. The editors of *The Universalist* resisted the whole idea of a "woman ministry." Even though there was an acknowledged shortage of clergy in the denomination, they refused to concede an official place for women.... The majority would fail....a waste of money,...they would make the woman question an eternal one...One-half to two-thirds of those women would marry and would (and should) retire from the ministry.[112]

What women should do remained a political issue. On April 2, 1870 Mrs. Victoria Woodhull sent a letter to the *New York Herald* declaring her intention to run for President of the United States in 1872. In the letter she claimed the right to speak for the "unenfranchised" women of the country, and Mrs. Woodhull had the financial assets to do so. Her announcement came at a time when the suffrage movement remained dangerously weakened by its division and was in need of support from the press. *History of Woman Suffrage Vol. II* records Phebe Hanaford's visit in May 1870 to Horace Greeley, owner of *The New York Tribune*.

111   Miller, 1979, p. 641
112   Ibid, p. 558

Speaking with Horace Greeley a few weeks ago he replied to my query why he was not in favor of woman suffrage, by saying that he did not think women would gain the opportunity of suffrage or improve their opportunity if they had it until they should come to consider suffrage a duty, and he declared that he had never known anyone to advocate woman suffrage on the ground of duty.[113]

The following day Phebe heard Anna Dickinson speak to nearly three thousand people in the largest hall in New Haven, urging the women present "to consider their duty to this vast Republic in which we live, and whose starry banner is as dear to women as to men. A thousand times more dear than ever to women now since we gave our noblest and dearest for its defense."

On May 11, 1870 women from around the nation weathered the rain in New York City to gain admission to Steinway Hall to hear the speakers at the American Woman Suffrage Association Convention. Resolutions passed easily under the guidance of Lucy Stone. Men in support of woman's suffrage included Rev. Henry Ward Beecher and Senator George Julian. Celia Burleigh rose to introduce "now the pastor of one of the most popular churches of New Haven, and whose church I am glad to say is crowded every Sunday, the Rev. Phebe Hanaford." Phebe stood and thanked Mrs. Burleigh and, after a brief reference to her visit to Mr. Greeley, spoke of the recent talk of Anna Dickinson in New Haven. "The keynote of her bugle-call to the rescue was the idea of duty and that is the idea which inspires the women on this platform to-day." Phebe then delivered her talk, "DUTY," quoted here in part.

----

113   Stanton, Anthony, Gage, & Harper, p. 790

We women have been lectured in regard to our duty to the family ad libitum as far as the writers or speakers were concerned, ad nauseum to ourselves. We have been told our duty to the church till at this very hour the membership in all denominations of Protestants—to say the least—is composed more largely of women than of men. And now the leading reformers of the world are telling us in clarion notes, and in thunder tones, with the voice of warning or of appeal, that woman owes service to the state, and that it is her duty to strive earnestly that she may have that ballot in her own hand which shall be at once her educator and protector, her sceptre and her sword.

When the meetings ended, Phebe and Ellen took the train to Boston where they planned to meet Emily Ruggles and attend a meeting. Emily wrote that she "went to Boston to go to a Woman's meeting with Mrs. Hanaford who had come on to attend the anniversaries but found her sick so we came out on the next train and she spent the night with me." Phebe, rarely sick, recovered quickly and went to Melrose the next day to meet with Mary Livermore. That night she returned to Reading. The next day she and Emily rode in Emily's horse cart to Waltham where Nellie and Mrs. Miles joined them for a trip in the cart to Newton Upper Falls. Phebe and Nellie returned to New Haven on May thirty-first. While Emily's diaries provide pertinent news of Phebe's travels, the loss of Phebe's diaries unfortunately denies us details of the purpose of the visit to Mary Livermore and what she had to report of the meeting of the American Woman Suffrage Association. We are also denied a copy of Rev. Hanaford's appointment as chaplain of the Legislature of Connecticut.

In *Daughters of America* Phebe wrote of herself:

She was the first woman who ever, as a regularly appointed chaplain, officiated in the Legislature of Connecticut, which she did in 1870 and 1872 several times in Senate and in House of Representatives. She was the first woman in the world who ever officiated in such a capacity in a legislative body of men.[114]

On the morning of June 3, 1870, Rev. Hanaford offered the invocation in the State House. She prayed in part "that the time may come when the daughters of the State, not neglecting the duties of home, may take part in the State as in the church, to the good of the Commonwealth and the glory of Thy great name."[115]

The Commonwealth of Connecticut joined in the National observance of Decoration Day to honor those who fought at Antietam and Appomattox. There, as throughout the war, so many officers were killed, there was an expression that if a man were in the First Artillery, he would either be made an officer or be killed. The tattered flag in the State House bore witness to Connecticut's heroes. Rev. Hanaford, standing in the pulpit on June 5, expressed her deep feelings about the appropriateness of remembering the boys and men who had died in the recent Civil War and of honoring the women in town made poor by the deaths of their men. In her sermon "Honor to Whom Honor" she quoted from Romans 8:7. The next morning *The New Haven Daily Morning Journal and Courier* printed her sermon in full. This could only have been possible because, ever the journalist,

114   Hanaford, Phebe A., 1881, p. 428

115   *The Woman's Journal*, June 16, 1870, p. 188

Phebe sent the paper a copy of her sermon for those who would not attend the service.

> *The questions now arise, whom should we honor? Then comes the question When shall we pay the tribute and how shall it be paid?*
>
> *I do not ask if you all honor the soldier that died for his country. I take it for granted that you do, because I am sure that you ought; for whether persons agree in political views or not, on this one point all noble hearts can fully sympathize; and whether we all think the war a just one, or some of us suppose it was the effect of the mismanagement of politicians, and, alas, there is too much of that always — we can all surely render homage to the man who sacrifices his life for what he feels to be a principle.*
>
> *…Those who gave them to the cause of freedom deserve to be honored, and it is a solemn duty which this country owes to the dependent families of departed soldiers, that they should not be called to endure the additional hardships of poverty, when they are so patiently enduring the pangs of bereavement…. And if our nation would be just, giving tribute where tribute is due, the mothers of those strong souled men of middle life, those glorious young men, aye, those beardless patriot boys, whom they tenderly love, yet to whom they were willing to hand the shields…such noble mothers should have conferred upon them the privileges of citizenship; and since their dead sons may no longer go to the polls, their hands should hold the ballot and their votes be counted…. Even if no other woman in our land should vote, the mothers of our patriot dead should fill the citizen places which their boys vacated at the country's call.*

Rev. Hanaford continued her appeal to the New Haven Legislature.

> On June 6, 1870, at a second hearing before the Joint Committee on Woman's Suffrage, in the Capitol at New Haven, Rev. Phebe A. Hanaford of the Universalist church, Mrs. Benchley and Mrs. Russell were the speakers. During that session of the legislature, Mrs. Hanaford acted as chaplain both in the Senate and House of Representatives, and received for her services which she valued chiefly as recognition of woman's equality in clerical professions.[116]

At an earlier hearing of this committee, Mrs. Isabella Beecher Hooker was among the speakers. "Mrs. Hooker was ably sustained in her new position by her husband, a prominent lawyer of the State. While Mrs. Hooker held meetings in churches and school-houses through the State, her husband in his leisure hours sent the daily press articles on the subject. And thus their united efforts stirred the people...."[117]

Phebe never received Joseph Hanaford's support in her work as a suffragist, nor did he ever accept her role in the Universalist Church. We have no record of her seeing her husband on her occasional visits to Reading. An undated letter from Joseph written to Phebe after her move to New Haven explains the mental state of this man, once a practicing physician, father and husband. The first two pages of his letter are missing.

> ...I bear up against so much opposition. I just stay and endure. I am too sensitive but can not help that. I must suffer far more than you know & more than I would have

---

116   Stanton, Anthony, Gage, & Harper, 3(32), p. 327
117   Ibid

you suffer. (My head now aches from grief but my heart more still.) That you never understood me I am more & more convinced & often seem a mystery to myself. But I am not aware that my peculiarities have ever had malice for a basis. I am fully sensible of many, many blunders, but not of wishing to make you or my children unhappy (one of them knows the real me better than all of my relatives & yours with few exceptions). In reference to N.H. to understand my feelings just analyze yours when the realities of returning to this house to live are thought of, if ever it is. We are both sufficiently proud and high spirited & can not be humiliated without suffering. It makes me suffer as much in my own case, as you in the other. I do not ask you thus to humiliate yourself....When my self respect is gone there is not much of me left & I could not as I am made up live in N.H. & be other than a most miserable man, so often reminded of the fearful change since the days that I love to remember & cherish any more than you'd come to this house and be happy. To see that beautiful house etc etc in contrast with mine or rather to be reminded so forcibly of the real facts would be like once owning one such occupied by dear friends, wife & ch. & then look upon the ruins with all burned and lost. This may be my folly but true & real to me— nothing can make it unreal to me as I am made. And then those under whose influence you must be, those who hate me more than they love you! What could I expect but adverse influences? And then the fact that you are preaching a doctrine as diverse from mine—as your own men say as day & night light & darkness! And then the changed order of things—so different from Paul's doctrine! It is far less torturing to be a martyr here than there, a wreck, a nothing, irresolute, useless (things that I must be there). I resent that I must follow when though I had all of the comforts & kindness that you can bestow. The circumstances & not the individuals are in my way. It pains me to write in this strain but honesty demands it. It is not my intention to punish myself again...It gives my nerves a shock & takes away my appetite—am half sick from the influence of yours & H's on the thoughts suggested. I shall be far less miserable here alone <u>really</u> alone, than under different—outward circumstances. I prefer to be alone, alone morally, mentally, domestically, a hermit in spirit which I <u>must</u> be. You speak of an untidy house, cheerless etc. all true but it is the best that I can do or have the heart to do under the circumstances. Within a few days I have been tempted to leave all behind & go where I know not but somewhere where there will be less to remind me of my wretchedness, but the grave may be the only place. I may seek refuge in a few days for a time on the Cape where I have good friends—am not sure when I shall start—may be there on the 19th, so do not think it strange if I am not heard from as promptly as usual. –Be assured that I write all with kind feelings, with a heart sufficiently sad not to add full of sorrows by the indulgence of unkind feelings which I am trying to banish—in all cases as I have sufficient inward conflicts without any outward ones. I may have misunderstood F's note from a morbid state of mind but I will try to do right by her, as well as I have done by H.

Miserable[118]

---

118   Hanaford Family Archives

A very different letter arrived from Rev. Doctor Edwin Chapin of New York in which he agreed to preach the installation sermon.

Phebe completed the program for her Installation Ceremony. On the afternoon of the ninth of June the Church of the Messiah delighted the eye of all who entered. In the congregation were members of the legislature as well as friends. After the introductory hymn by the choir, Mrs. Julia Ward Howe's hymn was read by Rev. Mr. Dodge of Stamford and sung by the choir. Rev. Cyrus H. Fay of Middletown offered the introductory prayer. Rev. Chapin preached the installation sermon from Colossians 1:15. Who is the image of the invisible God?

His words reflected his belief that Sister Hanaford had accepted the call to this Church and had been installed, and that her work was important and that of the congregation none the less so. In his list of obligations he mentioned that the society must not expect their pastor to do all the work to build up a Church, but they must aid her in the discharge of her duties. He affirmed as an established fact that woman could sing in public, and "asked why should she not pray and speak in public?" He trusted that the congregation would take upon themselves the responsibility of calling Mrs. Hanaford to be their pastor, and recognize that she should receive her salary promptly. He exhorted them to be faithful to their pastor, and she would meet their expectations. He reminded them that when they had settled a pastor, their work was not done—they must help her as members of the Church. He told them their outside life must be beyond reproach; and that they should always be in their seats and listen to the words of their pastor, and believe what they professed—be united and charitable. Friend and mentor, Rev. Olympia Brown, expressed her regard for Rev. Hanaford, praying she would be "the Lord's anointed able to guide her congregation in the holy teachings of Christianity, and enable her to speak with earnestness."[119] Rev. Hanaford then listened to the charge given by Rev. William Garrison Haskell, that she:

> ...study human nature; understand the circumstances of your people that you may be faithful to your religion. Be constant in prayer; remember God helps those who help themselves.... You will need to preach Christ everywhere. Let none go away from your church without feeling the influence of your Christian belief.... Do not mix politics with religion, because the politics of the present time are too filthy; but put religion as much as you can into politics. Do what your conscience approves.

The service closed with the following hymn by Ellen Miles.

> Oh, Lord of Lords and King of Kings,
> Whose loving kindness knows no end,
> To whom the wide creation sings,
> We dare to call Thee Father, Friend.
>
> To Thee we come with reverent hearts,
> And ask thy blessing at this hour;
> Oh! Send Thy Spirit from above,
> Till all shall feel and own Thy power.
>
> Unite us in the bonds of love,
> Pastor and people guard and guide,

---

119   *The New Haven Daily Morning Journal and Courier,* June 10, 1870

Within our hearts may thy sweet dove,
With folded wings, for aye abide.

Bless Thou our Zion! in all hearts,
Oh, plant and seeds of Truth divine,
Till all our ransomed race shall come,
To worship at the heavenly shrine.

Charles Dickens' death on the day of Rev. Hanaford's Installation perhaps inspired her to write a biography of this writer whose sense of justice and sympathy for the downtrodden contributed to social reform in England and America. A biography of Dickens seemed as appropriate as her biography of George Peabody. Earlier Phebe sent Queen Victoria the special edition of the *Life of George Peabody* bound in smooth Moroccan leather. In return Phebe received a large engraved envelope from London. She sent a notice of the Queen's letter to *The Woman's Journal*, in which there appeared an article about the event.[120] "Rev. Mrs. Hanaford has an autographed letter from Queen Victoria, thanking her for a copy of her *Life of George Peabody*." The article noted the "Life" continues to sell well but "is not the best Mrs. Hanaford can do, it being mainly a compilation, which was all her publishers wished her to prepare."

In July the State Judiciary Committee considered a bill providing for the separate estate of a married woman to be under her personal control. George Pratt, Esq. declared it unconstitutional because it disturbed the vested rights of the husband and impolitic because it tended to disturb the harmonious relations of families. The debate on women's property rights drew

120   *The Woman's Journal,* July 30, 1870, p. 236

increasing attendance from numbers of citizens, and the discussions moved to the Court of Common Appeals.

The Joint Committee on Woman Suffrage submitted a report to the State House of Representatives on July twenty-first. It was the culmination of the previous discussions and seemed to be logically favorable to women. To Phebe Hanaford's disappointment and the dismay of those who thought they had won State suffrage rights for women, newspapers reported, "the conclusion of the Legislature did not comply with the prayers and petitions for suffrage or property rights." Years later Phebe reflected on this affront to women.

I have asked myself the question Why can I not have the ballot? Having power and authority ecclesiastical, which is acknowledged by the laws of the land, why can I not cast my ballot also, as a man does, and thus help make the law which governs pastor and people? As a voter, I could have said come where I have had to say go when moral questions have arisen which the pulpit of the land could not fail to notice.[121]

Following the failure of the proposed suffrage amendment to pass in the Connecticut Legislature, Olympia Brown called on Phebe in New Haven to discuss Mrs. Livermore's plan for a New Haven Suffrage Convention featuring William Lloyd Garrison as speaker. From a letter Olympia Brown wrote to Isabella Hooker after her visit, we learn the purpose of Olympia's visit was to "set Mrs. Hanaford straight." Olympia Brown told Phebe that the Connecticut Association considered itself independent of Lucy Stone's Boston group, and therefore the

---

121   Hanaford, Phebe A., 1890, "Twenty Years in the Pulpit"

American Woman Suffrage Association had no power to call a convention in New Haven. Olympia added that to call a convention without consulting Mrs. Hooker, Chairman of the Connecticut State Suffrage Association, violated their Constitution. She expressed to Phebe the importance of working through the Connecticut Suffrage Association. Assistance from outside Connecticut, especially from Mr. Garrison of Massachusetts, Olympia believed, was no help politically or religiously in Connecticut. Olympia wrote to Mrs. Beecher, "I think she saw these points and gave assent to them."

The idea that the Connecticut Association was not auxiliary to the American Woman Suffrage Association appeared to Phebe to be a new interpretation of the Connecticut Woman Suffrage Association Constitution. Olympia's concession to Phebe regarding Mrs. Livermore's request appears in her letter to Mrs. Hooker.

> I told her in that case I thought she should refer the subject to the officers of the Ct. State Suffrage Association who would take it into consideration whether or no the cause required a Convention this autumn & if so they would call one. She agreed to this and authorized me to say to the Executive Com. & Officers of the State Association that Mrs. Livermore & other friends in Boston deemed it advisable to have a convention held in New Haven soon after the opening of the college and she instructed me to ask the Com. & Officers to consider the subject & take action as they deem best.... She promised to prevent so far as she should be able Mrs. L. from organizing an association there, auxiliary to the American Woman Suffrage Association. I told her you live in Connecticut

now and should be an active member of the State Association which is entirely independent of either New
York or Boston. The members of the Connecticut Association are neutral or not aware of the factions. It is not
necessary to embroil them in it. Left to the residents of
Connecticut, the State Association is doing good work
and understands the issues better than advocates from
outside the State…. So much for Mrs. Hanaford.[122]

This, "much for Mrs. Hanaford," written in the letter reveals
the influence Phebe had among her peers and her position during
these days of division within the ranks of the woman's suffrage
movement. A letter from Isabella Hooker to Phebe postponed
the date for a meeting with Olympia Brown in Hartford until the
first week in September. The same letter invited Phebe to stay
at her home along with Miss Brown. In reply Phebe Hanaford
wrote from New Haven, Connecticut on August 29, 1870.

Dear Mrs. Hooker—

I have my bonnet on all prepared for Savin Rock, with visi-
tors, but I pause to answer your note which my son has just
brought to me.

I'm glad the meeting is postponed to Friday. I will stay
over, and so will Miss Brown, I think— i.e. if she is prepared for
Sunday.

But you do know I am always accompanied by a "sister
Pricilla," as a friend jocosely terms her—my friend and com-
panion and fellow student—Miss Ellen Miles, the teacher and
elocutionist, (of whom you may have heard) who is compiling
my poems now for the press, etc.—and if you have not room

for her also I shall be obliged to stop at the hotel. We always lodge together, so that only one room would be required for us. Otherwise I would gladly lodge with Miss Brown who is my very dear friend, and with whom I have lodged pleasantly many times.

Yours for Right
Phebe A. Hanaford

We cannot identify the jocose friend, but Pricilla we know from Acts 18:2. She is the wife of Aquila and companion of Paul in his travels to Ephesus.

Emily Ruggles wrote in her diary of her travel plans: "Went to Lynnfield in the morning to have the horse's shoes looked to and at 6 o'clock P.M. went to Waltham and passed the night with Mrs. Anne Miles to be ready to start on our journey to New Haven to spend a week with Mrs. Hanaford. Hope to be there in two days, possibly two and a half." The following day she reports that they covered 2 ½ miles to Auburndale by horse and buggy. The day's entry names the towns they passed and the miles they covered. They arrived at 5 o'clock in New Haven. The next day Rev. Hanaford "visited the sick in the buggy."

Florence's name appears in Emily's entries along with news of shared ice cream treats and sunset rides. Picnics included a ride in a horse car to Savin Rock. In her sermon Rev. Hanaford made reference to the beauty they experienced at Savin Rock the previous evening. Emily simply reports of Phebe's sermon, "Charles Dickens, Is he in heaven or hell?" On Saturday the twenty-third Emily wrote, "Mrs. Miles and I prepared for home and after we were ready to start we were photographed with the family standing on the steps."

On September 9, 1870 the Connecticut Woman Suffrage Association Conference convened in Allyn Hall in Hartford. As founder of the Connecticut Woman Suffrage Association, Mrs. Hooker stressed the need for suffrage societies in several cities with membership limited to residents of Connecticut. The reelected president, Rev. N. J. Burton, then presided over the meetings. Phebe Hanaford accepted a position on the Executive Committee chaired by Isabella Beecher Hooker. Writing away from home, Phebe contributed a detailed article, "CONNECTI-CUT WOMAN SUFFRAGE ASSOCIATION – THE ANNUAL MEETING," to the October 1st issue of *The Woman's Journal*. In her article she expressed some disappointment in the event.

> *As a result of limiting participants to Connecticut residence, the annual meeting was not heralded as the opportunity for the public to behold the brilliant stars of the Woman Suffrage galaxy, who shine beyond the little State whose officers were now to be chosen.*

She concluded with a personal touch.

> *This is all my sprained right hand will permit me to write for the Journal to-day, except a protest against hoops as a part of a woman's dress when getting out of a carriage, which is the voice of my aching thumb. No wonder men can do so much more easily in their part of the world's work than women, so long as they dress so much more sensibly.*
>

P.A.H. New Haven, Conn.
>

Rev. Hanaford's deep involvement in the suffrage movement never interfered with her service to the Universalist Society. In preparation for the Centennial Celebration of Universalism in America to be held in Gloucester, Massachusetts on September 20 and 21, 1870 Phebe wrote a brief history of the church, *Historical Sketch of the First Universalist Church and Society*. As pastor Rev. Hanaford published the pamphlet in 1873. At the conclusion of her paper, Phebe noted her new location at 13 Home Place.

> *Universalism in New Haven has been a plant of slow growth... In the year 1836, on the 27th of May a Universalist Society was organized in New Haven by eleven men... on Sunday, November 11th, 1838, I find the first mention of selecting a site for a Church... March 6th, 1850 three trustees were appointed to hold the deed in trust of a lot and church, on corner of Court and State Streets, was purchased for $26,000, and in this house the Society now worships.*[123]

An estimated 12,000 were expected to arrive in the tent city at Stage Fork Park located at the head of the Gloucester Harbor in the beautiful city of Gloucester. Phebe and Olympia Brown, as predicted by Olympia, were the only two women ministers with pastorates in Connecticut. Equally impressive was the fact that 13,000 women raised $35,000 through individual donations for the Murray Fund.

When the centennial of the denomination was celebrated in 1870, there were sixteen parishes in the state of Connecticut, of which six were either inactive or without regular pastors. Connecticut Universalists did have one unique distinction as of 1870. The first two women

---

123   New Haven Colony Historical Society

ordained in the denominational ministry both held pastorates in the state, Olympia Brown was serving in Bridgeport and Phebe A. Hanaford in New Haven.[124]

Phebe Hanaford received several responses for her proposed Lecture Series. She sent the agenda to the *New Haven Daily Morning Journal and Courier* (n.d.).

POPULAR LECTURES

Mrs. Julia Ward Howe	CULTURE	October 31
Rev. Olympia Brown	THE KANSAS CAMPAIGN	November 7
Mrs. Ada Bowles	MEDDLING WOMEN	November 14
Rev. Phebe Hanaford	WOMAN SOLDIERS	November 21
Mrs. Mary Livermore	QUEEN ELIZABETH	November 28
Miss Lucy Stone	WINNING HER WAY	December 12

In her reply to Rev. Hanaford, Julia Ward Howe wrote of her plans for a Woman's Peace Congress. Her goal, she wrote, "was to mobilize women to demand a peaceful settlement to the war that raged in Europe." Mrs. Howe invited her friend to address the group in Union Hall in New York on December twenty-third. In her speech, "Gospel Peace," Phebe reiterated women's right to speak out for the fruits of peace instead of the

---

124   Miller, 1979, p. 677

devastation of war because they had given birth to the men who would be killed.

Women go down to the very gates of death that those soldiers of France and Germany may commence life—have they not thus earned a right to say that the barbarism of war shall no longer shorten the lives of those whose existence at first they secured by the peril of their own? This surely is woman's work, just what we shall do, may not be easy at this time to say, but we must begin.[125]

As part of the order of business at the Woman's Peace Congress, members voted for officers. Julia Ward Howe remained as president. The sixteen vice presidents included Lucretia Mott, William Cullen Bryant, Rev. Henry Ward Beecher, Isabella Beecher Hooker and Rev. Phebe Hanaford. On her return to New Haven, Phebe preached on the futility of war on Christmas Day.

Early in the New Year, the first reproduction of the 1825 engraving of "Belshazzar's Impious Feast" was presented to the American public. Copies were sold for $4. In response, Phebe wrote her 1871 sermon on the Book of Daniel. Belshazzar is the name given to Daniel by the chief eunuch Ashpenaz in the court of Nebuchadnezzar, King of Babylon. Daniel's prophesy of the fall of the Babylonian Empire had come from the words written by the armless hand. Phebe saw it as more than the prophetic account of the destruction of a King who exalted himself and desecrated the treasures of the Temple. Phebe read the scriptural account as a possible clothing of history in the

125   Yale Divinity School Library

garb of prediction. On January 8, 1871, she delivered a lengthy sermon on Belshazzar's Feast from Daniel 5:27. She chose the word TEKEL, which translates, "you have been weighed on the scales and found wanting."[126]

Rev. Hanaford found much to be wanting during her rounds of the city. She believed the gambling houses in New Haven would close if women had the necessary vote. Phebe and Ellen Miles also visited the Home of the Friendless. They understood that few of the women housed there could find work that would keep them off the streets. As on a previous occasion in Nantucket, Phebe believed the women "more sinned against than sinners." Walking to the other end of town, Phebe identified what she believed to be a brothel. She turned her attention to those employing women in the brothels and saloons. Within a week she and Ellen entered a brothel to free the women. Two women left with them for the Home of the Friendless. In time their work for women came to the attention of *The Daily Lever.*

> ...At the present time, Rev. Hanaford is doing a very suc-
> cessful business in robbing the brothels of New Haven of
> their deprived inmates. She seems to enter upon this busi-
> ness with her whole soul, and is not afraid to go wherever
> duty calls her. She has visited many places where ladies
> would not, as a general thing, dare to go; but she enters,
> and has never yet been insulted by any one.[127]

Phebe Hanaford requested a correction in an article in which they wrote that she "was seen walking in the streets with these unfortunate creatures arm in arm." She pointed out that

---

126   Boston: B.B. Russell
127   *The Daily Lever,* 1871 (n.d.), Nantucket Historical Association

the statement was incorrect. "The management does not permit social familiarities and I do not wish to be represented as permitting any." She also wrote to *The Woman's Journal.*

LETTER FROM CONNECTICUT
NEW HAVEN, CONN.

Dear Journal: We are taught in the Good Book not to be "weary in well-doing," and some of the women of New Haven are trying to obey the injunction, albeit they render themselves liable to abuse and odium for their labors of benevolence. I have come in for my full share of misrepresentation because of my connection with the "Home for the Friendless" where, as manager and yet, when I think of the good which such institutions accomplish for the crushed and fallen ones of our sex, I am constrained to welcome reproach and "persecution for righteousness' sake" and resolved to continue in the work of saving the lost. Let me give you the copy of a letter from a poor girl who was rescued from suicide by drowning last summer, and carried to the station-house in this city. Miss Miles and I went to her, and were soon joined by the missionary of the Home, Miss Sarah M. Hadsell, (a noble woman who is performing a noble work), and then the trio of managers carried the fallen one to the Home. After about a fortnight the missionary accompanied her to the home of her parents in Massachusetts. She thus wrote lately to the missionary:

Jan. 15, 1871

You don't know how very happy your letter made me: I received yours and one from Sister Mary at the same time. I have read and read and read it over and over again, and I cannot help but feel grateful for the true, earnest friends I think I have, but when I think of the terrible way in which I left them, I cannot help but shudder, it seems like some terrible dream as I look back upon it now. Oh how I wish I could blot it all out! If I could only live my life over again, what a different life I would lead!

I have not received the box darling_____ sent. Mary wrote me about it, but as I was going home this week, I think I would not have her send it. When I read about it I could not help the tears from starting, when I thought how unworthy I was to be remembered with so much kindness by her. I would love to see you at your Christmas gathering; you must have had a delightful time. Are the girls all there that was there when I was, and how is poor Johanna? I think of her very often. And Maggie—does she think sister Lizzie will come back? Please remember me to them all. Tell them I have not forgotten them or their kindness to me while I was there. In fancy I often hear little Mary's crutches, thumping along, and poor Emily's fingers wandering round to know by feeling what she can't by seeing—comical Jane and chatty Maggie, and then Joe's hacking cough breaks in—the pleasant little French lady and her cooing baby, and poor old grandma, and last, not least, placid gentle Miss N_____; how good she is, ain't she? How can they help being happy with such good people as Mr. & Mrs. Paddock? Please remember me to all the ladies; tell them I am soon well, I remain your friend.

Phebe described the inmates of this home as, "mostly invalids and all of pure lives; they are among the despised." We can see the influence of the young Mrs. Hanaford visiting the Seaman's

Home in Nantucket, praying with those isolated from society. The difference from the young wife and mother was that Phebe now had her personal and professional life integrated. Now she lived in a committed relationship with Ellen Miles who shared her interests and supported her in her work. Together they prepared a book of poems for publication. Phebe dedicated their shared project of *From Shore to Shore and Other Poems*[128] to Ellen.

TO ELLEN E. MILES

Friend of my later years, whose tender love
Has filled my home with blossoms, sweet though late,
Whose noble heart my spirit must approve,
As duty's path thou tread'st with willing feet:
Thy welcome service, at Love's bidding mine,
As these my rhythmic waifs are gathered now,
Calls for a grateful tribute, and I twine
This simple wreath, dear NELLIE, for thy brow,
Soul-sister! may the waiting years for thee
Pour out a largess of such holy joy
The earth shall seem the porch of heaven to be,
And songs of praise thy tuneful lips employ!
Then while eternal years shall onward roll,
Still may share Love's summer of the soul![129]

In the Preface Phebe wrote,

These poems are offered only to those, who, through love, will not view them with a critic's eye. They have not been wrought

---

128   Hanaford, Phebe A., 1871
129   Ibid, Dedicatory Sonnet

with patient labor, neither have they been quarried from mines of thought, but have sprung spontaneously from seeds which sympathy has planted. The manifold cares of a city parish forbid much pruning or trimming; and hence they are given to the public in much the same form as when they first appeared in the various newspapers and magazines whose "poet's corner" they helped to fill. If they may only, in their present dress, gratify the many friends who have asked for them, and in some way bless humanity, and thus glorify God, the writer will be satisfied.

  P.A.H.

  19 Home Place, New Haven[130]

With the infrequent mention of Florence or Howard, it is difficult to assess Phebe's family life. In 1871 Howard's homecoming from college brought news that he wanted to study for the Universalist ministry. He agreed to transfer from Antioch to Tufts School of Divinity in Medford, Massachusetts, a fulfillment of all that Phebe wanted for her son. In addition, Phebe took pride in the fact that the first woman who voted in Wyoming, Louisa Swain, was born on Nantucket Island. Phebe sent an article of this event to the Nantucket *Inquirer and Mirror*. The *Woman's Journal*, October 15th issue, included Phebe's article, "Yesterday for the first time in the world, Wyoming put into practice the theory of female suffrage.... Ninety-three ladies voted at the polls in this city...The first being Louisa Swain." In conclusion, Phebe wrote enthusiastically about Connecticut women and Mr. Hickox's excellent tract on the "Legal Disabilities of Married Women in Connecticut." She ended her article saying she was "off to Bristol, Connecticut to present the woman's

---

130 Ibid

suffrage cause before the inhabitants under the auspices of the Young Men's Christian Association."

Phebe's interest in women's rights spanned the gamut from educated professionals in the suffrage movement to the prostitutes in the brothels and the residents in the Home for the Friendless. She dedicated her biography of Charles Dickens "To the Women of America." B. B. Russell published both *Shore to Shore and Other Poems* and *Life and Writings of Charles Dickens* in 1871. With Phebe's encouragement, Ellen sent botanical articles to the *Guiding Star*. She also sent prose and verse to *The Liberal Christian, The Woman's Journal* and *Voice and Peace*.[131] Ellen Miles devoted her talents to the children's religious training in the Sabbath school that followed Rev. Hanaford's morning service.

"Devoted" describes Ellen Miles. Beyond the Sabbath school, Ellen visited those in need. Six years her junior, Ellen stood inches taller than Phebe. She carried herself erect without appearing to tower over her friend. Her handsome face and high forehead, crowned with a full head of brown hair, carried a look of one with concern as to how she appeared to others. Her strong voice, trained in elocution, belied any weakness. Ellen absorbed confidence from Phebe's inward strength while Phebe depended on her friend's talents and generous spirit.

The homemaking that Ellen managed with considerable ease and artistic touches provided the comfort they both enjoyed. Above all else her efforts in their home allowed Phebe her many commitments. They had been together less than a year and already their relationship had matured to a partnership of spiritual equality. With their separate works, there existed a balance as between Pricilla and Aquila. Phebe and Ellen "taught

---

131   Hanaford, Phebe A., 1881, p. 220

the way of the Lord" (Acts 18:2). As in everything, they shouldered criticism and rejoiced in success. They were two halves of a circle that admitted few intruders. There are no records indicating that Dr. Joseph Hanaford intruded on this relationship. The Hanaford Family Archives provides two 1871 letters from Joseph to his wife.

Reading Feb. 4 1871

Mrs. H. I have just closed a letter to H. I am about leaving for the Cape & will spend a few moments in replying to yours last, occupying your old study which I have appreciated. I have no lecture written that I would give in N.H.—am writing one which I intend to give in Boston at Bro. Cook's as soon as I can get to it & intend to write another on Human Progress—the increase of the length of life in modern times. I cannot now say about N.H.—must think of it. My friends do not advise it. There would be many embarrassing circumstances, not to say humiliating. Many things make me unhappy & I feel that I cannot easily bear many more. I am unhappy & cannot but remain so under the present circumstances. Personally I do not allow myself to indulge in otherwise unkind feelings toward any human being. Yet my circumstances are peculiar & I must remain as a waif or a helmless vessel on a turbulent sea.

I am glad to hear so good a report of Fl. I often think of her & then the tears will come. This is an unnatural life for me & happiness is out of the question for me as things now are. There is a noisy family now about me, one with whom I have but little sympathy & can have but little though I have never exchanged an unpleasant word. I should much prefer a small family, one child & a Baptist family instead of Infidels. I think that I may have such in the Spring. This family I had supposed came in for a short time but still remain, & do not like to move as it seems, thought or talked of buying but have nothing to buy with. —offered to board me 5 years for it, but I should not wish to board so long. J.H.H.

Joseph Hanaford's second letter begins in a friendly manner to "Mrs. H." but also demonstrates a disciplinary tone regarding Howard, now studying at Tufts Divinity School.

Reading Dec. 8, '71

Mrs. H. I write in haste this time to send you some quills which I have since obtained –If you take a penknife & make a slight incision you can thrust the point in & let it remain 20 minutes—that will do. I enclose H's letter. Have not had time to see him as I am still kept here awaiting a case here & one on C. Wrote him strongly recommending economy—has some more to learn in that direction. J.H.H.

Throughout the first month of 1871, Washington DC turned its eyes briefly from the war in Europe to Victoria Woodhull. Senator John S. Harrison of Louisiana had earlier presented the "Victoria Woodhull Memorial" to the Senate, as did Congressman George W. Julian in the House of Representatives during the Christmas holidays of 1870. Few believed Mrs. Woodhull herself wrote the interpretation of the Fifteenth Amendment protecting the voting rights of citizens thereby eliminating the need for a Sixteenth Amendment guaranteeing women the right to vote. As a proponent of the Woodhull Memorial, Mrs. Woodhull spoke before the Judiciary Committee in Washington on January 11th, becoming one of the first women to do so.

Susan B. Anthony and Elizabeth Cady Stanton planned for Isabella Beecher Hooker to run the National Woman Suffrage Convention in Washington. Suffragists cancelled their session to attend the hearing. In the audience to hear Victoria Woodhull's message to the committee sat Isabella Beecher Hooker, Elizabeth Cady Stanton, Susan B. Anthony, Lillie Devereaux Blake, Olympia Brown, and Pauline Wright Davis. In spite of the defeat of the Woodhull Memorial in the House Judiciary Committee headed by John A. Bingham of Ohio, Victoria Woodhull remained a person of great interest to the suffragists attending the National Woman Suffrage Association Convention in Washington. With the Woodhull name in every newspaper, the National Woman Suffrage Association Convention barely received any publicity. Mrs. Woodhull gathered allies from among the leading suffragists for a variety of reasons, not the least of which was her money.

While the National Woman Suffrage Association identified their cause with that of Victoria Woodhull, the American Woman Suffrage Association, known as the Boston Group and headed by Lucy Stone, made every effort to distance itself from Victoria Woodhull's propaganda. In *The Woman's Journal,* the American Woman Suffrage Association consistently rejected Mrs. Woodhull as a voice for the suffrage movement because she was also the spokesperson for "free love." *The Woodhull & Claflin's Weekly,* which had been circulating for the past few months, presented "free love" as part of the platform of the

Woman's Rights Movement with no resistance from the leaders of the National Woman Suffrage Association.

Phebe contributed to the growing tension between the two suffrage organizations by objecting to the appearance of Victoria Woodhull on the suffrage scene. She did not understand how, in spite of Woodhull's position on "free love," Susan B. Anthony and Elizabeth Cady Stanton could have supported Woodhull's announcement of her candidacy for the presidency. Amid the talk of Victoria Woodhull's ambitions, there arose the question of her true motive for her work for woman suffrage. Supported by Isabella Beecher Hooker, Elizabeth Cady Stanton and Susan B. Anthony, Victoria Woodhull became the spokesperson on constitutional equality. A deeper division and the weakening of the suffrage movement seemed inevitable.

In her work for the American Woman Suffrage Association, Phebe went on tour in New York State to encourage members of local Suffrage Associations to attend the upcoming Convention in New York City scheduled for May 10, 1871, the twenty-third anniversary of Seneca Falls, and the birth of the Woman's Rights Movement. On May sixth Phebe wrote to Olympia Brown from Rochester telling Olympia of her plans to be at the Belvedere Hotel on the corner of Fifteenth and Irving in New York City prior to the American Woman Suffrage Association Convention.

...I shall be there on Wednesday—now can't you come over Wednesday P.M. or better still—morning—and we can go over the Ex. Com. Report and resolutions with me—so as to see that every good thing is remembered. We must have a business meeting at 2 P.M. Wednesday to cut & dry to plan things safe and sure—so as to have no balks Thursday. If we can get through the first day—the momentum gained will help us through a

second — So let us fix It — you meet me by 2 P.M. Wednesday — or earlier if you can — for the brunt of this Convention must come on you and me very largely — I mean for the strong utterances.

Your plan for the Ct. work all right — only I half fear nobody will pay the quarter in this season of [illegible] — but we can try & see — I hope to get to New York by Monday — but will not be in my hotel until Wednesday —

So plan to meet me at the Belvedere. I hope you can stay through to the end and make the valediction.

With Love

P.A.H.[132]

Lucy Stone opened the American Woman Suffrage Association Convention in Steinway Hall on May 10, 1871. The tone of respectability at the meeting guaranteed that the enfranchisement of women would ensure equality within the home, thus preserving constancy and the permanence of marriage. Isabella Beecher Hooker, now aligned with Stanton and Anthony, opened the two-week National Woman Suffrage Association Convention at the same time in Apollo Hall. The topic of Constitutional equality, according to Victoria Woodhull, included equality in the matter of "free love."

Victoria Woodhull, who viewed herself as a unifying factor, unwittingly became a major source of division. Woodhull detractors brought out loyal supporters for the American Woman Suffrage Association, and among them was Horace Greeley. During the meetings of both suffrage associations, his *New York Tribune* headlined "Woman Suffrage and Free Love," linking Victoria Woodhull with the National Woman Suffrage Associa-

---

132   Schlesinger Library, Olympia Brown file

tion. While the article inadvertently drew attention away from the American Woman Suffrage Association Convention, women across the nation withdrew from the National Woman Suffrage Association as Woodhull's policy of "free love" became linked with women's rights.

The American Woman Suffrage Association remained distinct from the National Woman Suffrage Association as the press hurled scathing accusations of "free love" against Stanton's policies. Phebe learned in a letter from Olympia Brown, who now headed the Connecticut Woman Suffrage Association, that they had severed their ties with the National Woman Suffrage Association. The Connecticut Woman Suffrage Association would work exclusively for woman's suffrage. Phebe and her New Haven friends of suffrage traveled to Bridgeport to visit Olympia. There, Olympia verbally assaulted Phebe for her rigid stand against Mrs. Woodhull as the voice for women's rights and asked Phebe to leave her house. Phebe's zeal to disassociate the Woman Suffrage Movement from Victoria Woodhull came from her abhorrence of "free love" and her belief that the existing connection would serve to destroy all they had worked for.

Scandals involving Victoria Woodhull and her family were reported by the press through the summer months. Of interest to Phebe was the fact that through it all, Isabella Beecher Hooker remained a loyal friend of Mrs. Woodhull. In July, Isabella Beecher Hooker wrote letters to Phebe to which Phebe, after explaining the delay in her reply, wrote,

New Haven, Conn.
Aug. 9, 1871

Dear Mrs. Hooker,

...I have now read them all and the accompanying documents, and must confess that I am not convinced by them of anything save that you are fascinated by Mrs. Woodhull personally, that you overlook the unlawful and disgraceful life she is leading, if, as I understand from these very documents, she is living as a wife with a husband from whom she is divorced. That she was divorced in order to live with him in defiance of the law, or, as you say, as a protest against a law which she does not consider proper and binding, does not make the matter any better. As well might a thief living in open defiance of the law against stealing, and he would not be so great a sinner. Instead of upholding the course of such a woman, or permitting the world to place such a construction upon your action when you might avoid it, as I think every drop of Beecher blood in your veins ought to cry out against her life of shameless disregard of propriety, and her utterance of loose demoralizing sentiments in her paper. You and I do not believe in legal prostitution—why do you countenance illegal prostitution thinly veiled with the threesome marriage! If I have been rightly informed in regard to the past life of this woman she enticed Col. Blood from his first wife. Let any woman dare do that with Mr. Hooker, or even attempt it, and you would at once see the error of giving loose rein to free-love ideas. They may so in a world where grace reigns, but in this world they only result in license and anarchy. I bear Mrs. W. no malice, but I would have her publish a purer paper (which does not sanction the licensing of prostitution) and live a better life. I cannot sanction her course, and I do not wish to be understood as favoring her as a leader in the suffrage movement.

I have resigned today as one of the Exec. Comm. (Connecticut Woman Suffrage Association) — therefore I shall not be likely to report any thing again that should be kept secret. I hope a more judicious person will be chosen in my stead. I am glad the money is forthcoming for the tracts. If I were able you would have many hundreds from me, for I consider all the tracts thus far published invaluable, especially that on "Legal Disabilities," which was so much needed to open the eyes of women.

I saw Mrs. Chandler in the parlor of the Woman's Club Room last Friday, after the Boston meeting, she spoke to the ladies present, I think the result will be the formation of a Woman's Hygiene society — which is perhaps the thing needed. I read your good letter to her with great interest. I never saw Mrs. Chandler before but she comes to me well recommended by a dear friend — Miss Amanda Lane of Gloucester. Olympia knows the latter lady I think. Anything that I can do in the movement I shall be pleased to attempt.

It seems to me that, in our State especially, you need a leader of natural right — a born Queen in the moral realm — at least a woman born to call others around the standard of reform, and I cannot help regretting that your influence should in any degree be lessened by your acceptance of Mrs. W. as an associate leader, or as your superior in rank. She does not rank you in morals, in intellect, in social position, or in anything, and yet she is leading you, and heaven alone knows where this will end.

As for my relations to Olympia, they are changed only as her own spirit has changed. I have no quarrel with her. I do war with her opinions, and I do not care to be told to leave her house, when I make her a friendly call, just because I differ with her in regard to upholding women-suffragists whether they are free-lovers or not. "He who permits oppression shares the crime," and those who uphold as leaders and public co-workers in the suffrage reform, free-lovers, share the stigma which these free-lovers deserve.

If Miss Brown did not wish any one to know how insultingly she talked, she should have curbed her temper before so many — two New Haven Ladies were present with me at the time. I fear she will lose her parish in Bridgeport if she does not let free-lovers alone. I do not think I deserved her censure. I know I did not. She may call me a hypocritical Pharisee, a thousand times more, if she chooses, and I shall not change my views of free-love. If she desired to keep her conduct to me private, then why did she tell a Hartford lady who asked for me that I was "too virtuous to be there?" That was a sneer which called for explanation to the lady which of course I gave. I hope Olympia will see the propriety of changing her course toward one who has always been a friend to her. She talks of Christian charity enabling her to take up Mrs. Woodhull, but I do not see that her Christian charity hinders her from dropping Miss Miles and my self, because we do not choose to be counted in with free-lovers. She is an able woman, and I had always far rather she would speak before Legislatures than myself, for she likes it and I never did. Your letter seemed to ignore the existence of a National Society. Then why such an array of names of officers to the National Wom. Suf— & Educa. Soc? Surely the word "Educational" does not alter the fact that there is designed to be a National W.S. Soc.—I think we had better join our forces under the "American" flag. If Mrs. Woodhull was a real lady it seems to me of her own accord she would refuse to hold office, where her acceptance causes so much trouble. A repentant Magdalen I can accept as a co-laborer, even in office and before the world—but a woman who "glories in her shame"—never!

That paper is hurting the cause more than all her money will help it. And as for the dreamy, mystical, impractical non-sensical stuff that Andrews publishes—bah! The "Revolution" as steadily advances till it is now almost, if not quite, free from any objectionable features, and I hope the "Weekly" will do the same. Then it will do good.

I have written thus plain because I ought to be frank with you, but I so wish I could be with you on these points. I am willing to be convinced, if I am wrong, and toward yourself, I have none but the kindest feelings, and I am,

Truly your friend (and not less because I tell you what I believe to be the truth.)

Phebe A. Hanaford

I think you ought to have sent Mrs. Stevens' letter to the "Tribune." It did not belong in the "Weekly" where the same readers would not see it that would have welcomed it in the Tribune.[133]

On August sixteenth Phebe Hanaford traveled to Oxford, Connecticut and then journeyed three miles to Nottingham Station to speak at the Grand Temperance Mass Meeting in Clynick Grove the next day. The event sponsored by the Minnehaha Lodge included talks by Honorable Neal Dow and Rev. Thomas Poulson and others. The exhausting day included dinner and supper.

Within a few days Phebe received a request from Mrs. Isabella Hooker to speak at the Church of the Messiah. After consultation with the Prudential Committee of the Church, in Phebe's response she refers to Mrs. Woodhull as "darling queen," the term affectionately used by Isabella Hooker.[134]

---

133   Stowe-Day Library
134   Goldsmith, p. 293

New Haven, Conn.
September 23, 1871

Dear Mrs. Hooker,

In reply to the message from yourself, brought to me by Gen. Roberts, yesterday, I shall be obliged to say that as neither the Trustees of my Church nor myself owe any sort of allegiance to your "darling queen," the notorious mistress of Col. Blood's affections at the present date, it will not be agreeable to us to invite you to speak in our church.

For you, personally, we have great admiration and respect, mingled with the deepest regret that you should place yourself before the world as the loving subject of such a Cleopatra. New Haven reverences the Beecher blood in you, and until now, no woman in the State would have received a warmer welcome than yourself, but I fear your influence with a woman whose claims to inspiration and to purity are alike denied by the larger portion of those who watch painfully your course, and long for your eyes to be opened. Your allegiance to that "darling queen" hurts both yourself and the cause you desire to serve. Am I less your friend because I tell you the truth?

If you wish my pulpit to repudiate the claims of that "darling queen" to your allegiance, and to state that you place yourself firmly on the Christian platform of the Am. Wom. Suf. Association, then, it may be obtained, but not while you appear to sanction free love or free-lovers.

Sadly, but frankly, your friend,
Phebe A. Hanaford[135]

Olympia Brown heard of this and wrote Mrs. Hooker. This correspondence gives evidence of the divisiveness Victoria Woodhull brought to the suffrage movement and the damage to friendships.

---

135   Stowe-Day Library

Bridgeport, CT
Sept. 26-1871

Dear Mrs. Hooker,

Yours just rec. I am so sorry your letter requesting to preach at Mrs. H's church went to Gen. Roberts. It was just the chance she wanted to show her own purity.

As you women will do meaner things than men not because they are worse but because they have been so cramped in their education & view of life—what can we expect of Mrs. H. for years a believing member of a close communion Baptist church all unaccustomed to liberal ideas—for years having a man like Dr. Hanaford so mean & narrow that he grudged his wife & children the food they ate. From childhood having no higher aim before her than that of being more flattered & admired than other Nantucket school girls. Both her religion & her social life and her education have contributed to make a mean narrow selfish trifling character. Six years of broader faith than she has known, three years of the new gospel of liberty for women are not sufficient to undo the influences of the past and make her a noble woman it is nothing against the sex but against a mean church which inculcates self righteousness & against a shallow education and a false ideal—Her professions of love to you were only to keep your favor & should the tide turn she will flow around you & tell you how she has loved you all the time—I shall come on the morning of the 4th shall go at once to the Music Hall.

Yours,
Olympia Brown

P.S. Be careful of yourself don't fail us at the meeting. I shall never promise any friends however near not to sit on the platform with Mrs. W. I will sit on the platform with the vilest sinner on earth if necessary to advance the cause of truth or to save a single soul—still more when there is a possibility that the condemned person may be innocent & more noble than all her accusers—I do not sit in judgment on Mrs. Woodhull. I do not know her character nor understand her circumstances—she is in the hands of one that knows her altogether. I should not invite her into this state. Last spring when she was to come here she had been invited by Mrs. Middlebrook. I assented to her appearing in our meeting which however was not a meeting under the auspices of the state association—but a private enterprise of Mrs. Middlebrook's & mine. I would not favor inviting her into our state because it is not necessary but if I am thrown in her company I shall treat her as I would any other worker in the cause—If she comes here of her own accord & I am invited to sit on the platform I shall no doubt do so. Mrs. Middlebrook is twice as odious here as Mrs. Woodhull but in defiance of my society & all the prejudice, I have worked with her and shall no doubt to the end. Mrs. Hanaford would be loudest in the praise of Mrs. W. if it were popular but the pious dodge is one long familiar with Mrs. M. and one very sure to find favor with the people.

Olympia Brown[136]

Without evidence, Woodhull gave names of women she believed lived out her theories of "free love" while they hypo-

---

136   Ibid

critically persecuted her for practicing "free love" openly and honestly. She added names of members of the American Woman Suffrage Association to her list including Phebe Hanaford, who had "moved to New Haven without her husband." In September during a "spiritual transformation" that occurred while on a speaker's platform, Woodhull publicly accused many women of "free love." Interesting to note, Phebe's shared life with Ellen Miles did not come under attack.

Unpopular or otherwise, Phebe Hanaford conducted a campaign to separate herself and the American Woman Suffrage Association from the supporters of "free love." Lucy Stone endeavored through lectures, correspondence and articles appearing in *The Woman's Journal* to gather "clean souls" to the cause of suffrage. Unafraid of Mrs. Woodhull's accusation, Rev. Phebe Hanaford went on with her work in New Haven with women caught up in prostitution. Phebe and Ellen entered brothels in the morning to offer shelter to the women willing to accept the forgiveness of a kind and loving God. In her sermons Rev. Hanaford preached about what she saw on the streets of the city, including evidence of gambling, ignoring unsigned letters of criticism regarding her work. She would not be the first pastor terminated for identifying those involved in the city's gambling.

Rev. Hanaford accepted the letter of invitation to the Ordination and Installation of Celia Burleigh on October 5, 1871. The ceremony was to be held at the First Ecclesiastical Society (Unitarian) in Brooklyn, Connecticut, one of the oldest churches in the country. Rev. Burleigh would be the first woman ordained and installed as a Unitarian minister. At this service, people sensed the presence of Rev. Samuel J. May, one of the earliest voices inviting women to ordination. If there were any doubters in the community, the ceremony converted them to the wisdom of women in ministry. The day recalled the obstacles that Rev. Antoinette Brown had faced as the first woman to be ordained in America. The next week Rev. Antoinette Brown Blackwell's name appeared in the local paper as a guest speaker. Phebe wrote to her.

New Haven, Conn.

Nov. 3 – 1871

Sister Brown,

I see by the paper this morning that you are to be in town Monday next, and write to invite you to my home to dinner and tea that day, and to sleep Monday night.

I want to talk with you about Mary's Ordination. I have written her a hymn, at her request.

And I want to speak of Mrs. Sarah M. C. Perkins, as a lecturer and perhaps preacher, and see if you want her to lecture for you, when she comes to lecture for me.

I am expecting Mrs. Mary C. Webster here on Sunday next to speak in the afternoon, as I wish to hear her before I get her to supply for me. If she is as good as I hear she is – (Mrs. Conner heard her in your pulpit and liked her) I shall be glad to employ her instead of a man to preach for me when away. She may not come but I expect her.

I am very glad that Bro. Willis has recovered. We wished very often that we had been near enough to be of some service in his sickness. Please extend the invitation to him to come here on Monday, with you.

I suppose you rec'd the Celia Burleigh report which I sent you. I have one of your circulars about the Course of Sermons. I have planned a Sunday evening course. I would like to talk to you about.

In great haste,
P.A.H.

P.S. I only invite you and Mr. W. not Mrs. Middlebrook, as I am but slightly acquainted with her. If Mrs. Seymour should come she will be welcome here.[137]

Isabella Hooker's support of Mrs. Woodhull remained firm throughout 1872 in spite of her immoral life detailed in Horace Greeley's *New York Tribune*. On November twenty-first the newspapers reported Mrs. Woodhull's appearance at Steinway Hall where on the previous evening she spoke to some three thousand people on "The Principles of Social Freedom Involving the Question of Free Love, Marriage, Divorce, and Prostitution." The paper reported that Theodore Tilton escorted Mrs. Woodhull to the stage. Tilton's endorsement of Victoria Woodhull sharpened the differences between the American and the National Suffrage Associations. Susan B. Anthony, Elizabeth Cady Stanton and Isabella Hooker saw Victoria Woodhull as the person to lead the fight for suffrage. Others saw Mrs. Woodhull as the cause of division within the National Woman Suffrage Association. Phebe continued in her lectures to advance the woman's cause and to separate that cause from "free love." Olympia Brown wrote in her autobiography, *Acquaintances, Old and New, Among Reformers* that Victoria Woodhull's "free love doctrine was most injurious to the progress of the Woman Suffrage cause."[138]

Neither here nor in her chapter "Some Later Reformers" does Olympia mention Phebe Hanaford; however she writes kindly of Mary Livermore. *The Annual Journal of the Universalist*

---

137 Schlesinger Library, Blackwell Family Collection
138 p. 91

Historical Society 1963 Vol. IV is devoted entirely to the biography of Olympia Brown, as recorded by her daughter, Gwendolen B. Willis. She quotes Olympia in the chapter, "The Ministry," as follows. "I have already mentioned Phoebe (sic) Hanaford, whom I had persuaded to enter the ministry, and it was at this time that I was instrumental in establishing her as pastor in New Haven where she preached successfully for several years."[139]

During her years at the Church of the Messiah, Rev. Hanaford gave a series of "Biographical Lectures" designed to illustrate moral and religious truths. She advertised these lectures on cards printed by Hoggson & Robinson. People could hire seats, and ushers reserved them until the ringing of the bell. A collection was taken up to defray expenses. Rev. Hanaford also conducted the Bible classes in the Sabbath school, where she instructed the children in God's universal love. She greatly approved of the annual Children's Sunday recommended by the General Committee and included children's baptisms in the service. She recorded these baptisms and adult baptisms in the parish register which she instituted. During her ministry the church established a constitution and bylaws that were printed along with a register of past and present members. To this she added the Universalist confession of faith. Ellen Miles and Phebe prepared a Sabbath school library catalogue. Phebe preferred literary activity to sewing circles, believing the sewing circles to be a potential source of parish gossip.

Throughout 1873 Rev. Hanaford presided at the Friday evening prayer meetings at the Church of the Messiah. *The New Haven Daily Morning Journal and Courier* published the program

---

139   Willis, p. 39

with names of speakers and their topics for the entire season. This information gave the members time for reflection on the topics and an opportunity to ask questions. As pastor, Rev. Hanaford did not believe in pulpit exchanges and limited them to gifted preachers. She exchanged pulpits with preachers in local churches, reflecting her acceptance beyond her parish. The Free Masons showed their regard for Rev. Hanaford by asking her to officiate at the funerals of their most respected members. She preached at the funeral of Daniel Bostwick, honored as the oldest Free Mason in America. She was the first woman invited to attend a Masonic festival.

On the political front, Elizabeth Cady Stanton invited Victoria Woodhull to conduct one of her Spiritualist sessions in the opening weeks of 1872. Coverage in the New York and Washington newspapers included Mrs. Stanton's reference to the Woodhull Memorial and Victoria Woodhull's appearance earlier before the Senate Judiciary Committee. Stanton's uncompromising position in the dispute over Mrs. Woodhull did not weaken over the winter months. Olympia Brown wrote to Isabella Beecher Hooker.

Bridgeport Ct.
Jan. 26, 1872

Dear Mrs. Hooker,

Yours rec, have sent it direct to Mr. Gallagher. Have done little lately, been waiting for you to come back. I went to a conference at Norwich in the hope of finding friends to get to our meeting and sure enough I found friends who offered the Universalist Church and wished us to come—but in the afternoon Phebe Ann came and preached and took them by storm and told them privately what bad folks we were. Said we had "gone to the Devil."

Congratulated Mr. Steere on not being willing to pray for us when we were at Meriden and sent word to Mrs. Lewis how sorry she was that she should have got mixed up with such company, told 'em all we were free lovers etc. etc. I don't know when we shall ever reach the bottom of that woman's iniquity. I have not heard from the friends at Norwich but I shall write them. Have held a debate at the Stanford on Suffrage.

Mrs. Woodhull has lectured here since you left, I had an engagement on that evening but left it to attend the lecture, had to leave and go to my engagement before the lecture was quite finished whereupon—Mrs. Middle-brook was very indignant called me a coward and everything bad. So you see I catch it on all sides. I sent my article on our Association to The Woman's Journal. Lucy declines to publish it on account of her desire for peace, I hope you will come back soon, I can do little without you. I don't know what to do about the programme you propose, am not a politician and think it a first rate programme. I do not know what to do to carry it out.

Olympia Brown

Don't see how I can go to Washington but would go to the hearing if really needed.[140]

Due to the divided positions in the leadership, membership waned in the suffrage movement as women's clubs mushroomed across the country. While Phebe remained embroiled in her struggle to distance the suffrage organizations from "free love,"

---

140   Stowe-Day Library

Celia Burleigh, third vice-president and a founding member of Sorosis, a professional woman's organization, presented Phebe Hanaford and Ellen Miles for Sorosis membership. At the April meeting under Charlotte Wilbour, President, and the membership committee agreed the achievements of Mrs. Hanaford and Miss Miles qualified them for membership. Ellen and Phebe were accepted as members at the business meeting held two weeks later. At the June meeting Phebe and Ellen took the Sorosis pledge and received their gold membership pins. Their trips to Manhattan from New Haven twice a month for meetings became part of their ministry to women.

The American Woman Suffrage Association Convention booked the Apollo Hall in Manhattan for May 9, 1872, a date that coincided with the National Woman Suffrage Association Convention to be held in Steinway Hall. There Victoria Woodhull hoped to gain women's support for her run for the presidency. Failing to gain their support, Victoria Woodhull disappeared from the woman suffrage movement. With Victoria Woodhull out of the way, the two suffrage organizations could now focus on the means they would use to gain the vote. Lucy Stone and her Boston group agreed to continue to work solely for state suffrage in all the states. Mrs. Stanton demanded a Federal Amendment to the Constitution and remained firm in her fight for a woman's right to divorce. Efforts to unite the two suffrage associations met with failure, with Lucy Stone refusing Susan B. Anthony's peace offering and invitation to unite the groups. Phebe remained a member of the American Woman Suffrage Association.

After a brief holiday on Nantucket, Ellen Miles went to visit her family in Waltham and Phebe went to Reading. On July twenty-second Emily Ruggles took Phebe Hanaford to the depot for her second trip to Bangor, Maine to preach. Upon her return Phebe had a brief visit with Emily in Reading and went on to Boston where she met Ellen on the thirty-first. They traveled together to New Haven, arriving in time to resume their duties on August first.

Phebe received a letter from Mr. Augustus Morse, her former school principal on Nantucket. Mr. Morse was coming to New Haven for the meeting of the Association of Teachers to be held at the College Street Congregational Church in August. He and his wife visited Phebe at her home for an evening of reminiscence. They discussed Nantucket Island's revival in recent years as a tourist attraction. The industrialization following the Civil War had brought a new middle class to Nantucket where they could get away from the effects of the very industrialization that enabled them to buy summer homes on the Island. Large homes, converted into hotels, opened their doors to tourists who came to enjoy the summer breeze. All through the years Phebe and Ellen vacationed on Nantucket Island.

In 1872 Rev. Hanaford was elected to the Universalist Church's Committee on Fellowship, Ordination and Discipline.[141] During the Universalist Convention she recommended that ministers prepare a history of their parishes for publication in the *Gospel Banner*. Because several ministers resisted, for a variety of reasons, the proposal was shelved for one year. The Women's Missionary Association of the Universalist Church agreed to raise funds for the foreign missions. The proposal for the first Convention of Women Preachers to be held within the year gave evidence of the future of women in the church. Rev. Hanaford's invitation to offer the dedicatory prayer at the church

---

141   Universalist Archives, Andover – Harvard Theological Library

in Waterbury was the first time this honor had been extended to a woman. The year proved fruitful for her ministry, and during the Christmas season the parishioners presented their pastor with a generous gift of one hundred dollars.

In her third year as pastor of the Church of the Messiah, Phebe sensed a growing dissension within the parish. For years the congregation had remained divided economically as well as theologically. Her work in the temperance and suffrage movements had raised questions about the appropriateness of this work for a minister. The overt influence of a few men with financial power made the woman pastor an easy target for latent patriarchal attitudes. Rev. Hanaford's words spoken fearlessly on women's rights were deemed unfitting for her sermons. Never one to compromise her commitments, Rev. Hanaford refused to accommodate her critics. Opposition to the renewal of her contract spread within the parish.

From the First Unitarian Universalist Society: Bound volume: Records of the Prudential Committee, First Universalist Society 1870-1895,[142] we read,

January 17th 1873 meeting called to take into consideration the retaining of our pastor Rev. Mrs. P. A. Hanaford.
January 19th 1873 entry,
The committee appointed to confer with Sister Hanaford reported they had met with her to explain the doings of the Society meeting on Jan. 17th and they reported she requested a written statement from the Prudential Committee or the clerk. A written communication was received from our pastor which was read by the clerk,

142   Yale Divinity School Library

a reply to his letter to the pastor informing her of the Society's call and acceptance of the same for the year commencing.

While Rev. Hanaford received limited support from her congregation, Rev. Henry Ward Beecher's *The Life of Jesus the Christ* enjoyed great literary success in the early months of 1873. Yale School of Divinity invited this theologically liberal Congregational clergyman to deliver a series of lectures. Rev. Hanaford wrote for a ticket. The response to her request acknowledges her status in the community.

New Haven
March 17th, 1873

Dear Madam,

I thank you for recalling to me my life in Massachusetts with which some of my happiest memories are associated and I am truly pleased at your kind mention of my books.

In regard to Mr. Beecher's lectures, the tickets for them will not be ready until Thursday morning, when it will give me pleasure to send you a ticket for the course. We have been obliged on account of the smallness of the room to limit our invitations to ministers, the faculty of the college and members of the senior class who are intending to become ministers; therefore though I regret being obliged to do so I shall not be able to send tickets for your ladies as you request. Even the ladies of our own families are denied the privilege of attending since we expect the house to be entirely filled by ministers and students who are really the audience that Mr. Beecher desires to address, who will be most benefited by his lectures.

Very respectfully,
Samuel Harris[143]

Yale College, including the Divinity School, a bulwark of male strength, remained closed to women students. The corner of Chapel and College Streets echoed the restrictions on women's higher education and their role in the Church. Phebe understood personally that without adequate education, women remained dependent on their husbands for their well-being. Education had qualified her to assume the position of pastor of the Church of the Messiah. Further, interference from church authority regarding their private lives troubled women in the ministry more than it did their male counterparts.

The need for women in the ministry to unite was met with the first Women's Ministerial Conference. The first Convention of Women Preachers in modern times was held in Boston at the Church of the Disciples on May 20, 1873.[144] The invitation, given without sectarian limitation, called together quite a number of women from various parts of the country, all engaged in the work of the Christian ministry. From page 1 of their archives, we learn,

On May 29, 1873 Julia Ward Howe, now in her nineties, invited women from many denominations, or as she put it without sectarian limitation, to the first meeting for women ministers. At the Church of the Disciples in Boston, women preachers arrived from around the

143   Ibid
144   Universalist Archives, Andover – Harvard Theological Library

country. Of these only three women were ordained ministers, other women were engaged in Christian ministry, called to this service by a deep interest in the religious well-being of the Community, and a belief that this would be greatly promoted by the direct initiative of women in the Christian church. The interest of this meeting was such as to lead to the plan for a second convention for June 1875.[145]

In the face of the conflicts between the woman's suffrage movements, Lucy Stone did not call for an American Woman Suffrage Association Convention in 1873. Jane Croly, founder of Sorosis, making use of the void generated by the absence of the annual American Woman Suffrage Association Convention,

> ...determined in consideration of the present demand for unity of method among women interested in like subjects, to take preliminary steps for bringing the representative women of the country together in a Woman's Congress, that we may take into careful consideration the more important questions that affect our woman's life.[146]

A call was prepared for distribution

> ...to all women who by voice or pen or practical work, have conquered an honorable place in any of the professions or leading reforms of the day, and they were invited to signify their approbation and sympathy with this effort, by sending their names to affix to the formal call

---

145   Ibid
146   Sophia Smith Collection

for a Woman's Congress to be held in New York City in Oct. 1873.[147]

Sorosis disclaimed any intention to take the lead in the Congress, declaring "after it shall be assembled; it will select its officers and govern itself." Meantime it constituted itself a local committee for the preliminary business. The message was signed by Mrs. Charlotte B. Wilbour, Mrs. Romelia L. Clapp, chairman exec. committee, Mrs. Alice Fletcher, recording secretary, and the other officers of the club. One hundred and fifty women responded to this message.

Rev. Hanaford sent a message to the Prudential Committee that the Church of the Messiah would be closed during July. Phebe and Ellen Miles took the train to New Bedford, and then boarded the *River Queen* for Nantucket for their summer holiday. Once in Nantucket Sound, Phebe always left the pleasures of sea travel to Ellen and coped with her seasickness. The view of the Island with its ancient houses and modern cottages appeared when the dense fog lifted and the winds dropped to a sea breeze. Capt. George traditionally waited to take them to Siasconset in the family carriage. The ride provided time for hearing news of the family before the start of the season of visits to friends as described in *Heart of Siasconset*. The visits always passed quickly and Phebe was back at her desk at the end of the month.

Victoria Woodhull broke onto the scene again in September, 1873, with the exposure of Rev. Henry Ward Beecher's affair with Mrs. Elizabeth Tilton. The news became a national scandal, which led to Beecher's resignation as President of the American

---

147   Ibid

Woman Suffrage Association. Phebe's respect for Rev. Beecher made it difficult for her to do anything but blame Victoria Wood-hull. She believed Woodhull's ongoing propaganda about "free love" had discredited Rev. Beecher and given rise to the incessant negative press coverage that had destroyed the woman's suffrage movement.

The Call for the Woman's Congress was issued for October 1873. At a business meeting, preliminary to the public sessions, a Constitution was adopted.

> The Association shall be known as the Association for the Advancement of Women. Its object shall be to receive and present practical methods for securing to women higher intellectual, moral and physical conditions, and thereby to improve all domestic and social relations.[148]

Mrs. Wilbour's plans for a Woman's Congress materialized on October 15th and 16th, 1873 at the Union League Clubhouse in New York. Among the hundreds of women interested in the advancement of women, there were included ministers, Rev. Phebe Hanaford, Rev. Antoinette Brown Blackwell, Rev. Olympia Brown, Rev. Augusta Chapin and Rev. Celia Burleigh. Among the educators were Maria Mitchell of Vassar College for Women and Dr. Mary Putnam, founder of the Association for the Advancement of Medical Education of Women. Mrs. Caroline Soule of the Universalist Society, chaired the opening meeting. She announced that at the preliminary meeting the previous evening, the Association for the Advancement of Women had been effected and that Mrs. Mary Livermore of Massachusetts had been chosen to be the president. Fifteen

148   Sophia Smith Collection

vice presidents representing fifteen states were named. The list of secretaries included Ellen Miles and Phebe Hanaford. Twenty-one women were named to the Executive Committee. These women represented the women's rights movements from across the nation.

The next morning Mrs. Livermore delivered an acceptance speech and Rev. Hanaford opened the business meeting with a prayer. At this point Julia Ward Howe asked to be heard. She objected to the actions already taken at the preliminary meeting since, along with others present, she believed the future of the organization would be determined by the Congress, which had not yet begun. Sympathies for the complaints as well as explanations and justifications were offered for the decisions taken at the preliminary meeting. Mrs. Howe stated she was prepared to read her paper if they wished but not under the current terms as a member of the Association. Since there was no solution, Elizabeth Cady Stanton advised them to accept the officers and the constitution and get on with the business at hand believing the important question was whether women had brains enough to retain a constitution and act as an association. Mrs. Stanton's frankness brought the dispute to an end and Mrs. Howe read her paper, "The Association of Women for the Amelioration of Society."

The needs of children were addressed in the afternoon session and included the statistic that half the children born in the world did not reach maturity. This directed the goals of the Association beyond the nation's borders. Mrs. Fairchild stressed the importance of educated mothers as well as fathers capable of the self-control within marriage required for the spiritual well-being of the mother and physical well-being of the children. Dr. Tracy Cutler of Ohio continued in the same vein, stressing knowledge as the foundation of mothering. Additional comments came from Mrs. Slocum who said that the bonds of social servitude had to be lifted before women could be good mothers. Good mothers must demand equality in the home. Mrs. Stanton carried the issue beyond equality in the home to the right to the same freedom as men. She believed that only when they understood and experienced freedom could women be fit to be the mothers of statesmen.

Following the paper, "The Co-Education of the Sexes" given by Mrs. Allen of Alfred University, the Association adopted a resolution approving co-education. The topic "The Necessity of Higher Education of Women" by Sarah Perkins of Cooperstown, New York concluded the afternoon session. The Legal Status of Women covered in the evening session was open to the public. Mrs. C. B. Hooker described women's present legal status as that of a political slave, the peer of the alien, the criminal and the lunatic. The quality of the papers and the participation of the women made it obvious these women had strong opinions about women's advancement and were well able to speak their minds.

On the second morning it was estimated there were about fifty men in the audience as Mrs. Soule addressed the issue of professorships for women in co-ed colleges. She defined higher education as that which develops the whole woman. Daughters deserved the same education as sons and women deserved to see women in professorships as well as men. She added this should not be seen as a threat to family life in this generation.

Elizabeth Cady Stanton's practical mind approached the issue of co-education from an economic view. "Why should taxpayers have to duplicate institutions to teach the same subjects?" she asked, stating that equality of education was the

real issue. She went on to say "woman's biggest enemy is organized religion." She illustrated this by saying, "In the past week
at the meeting of the Evangelical Alliance, women, who by the
way worked very hard for the church, were not permitted a
voice at the meeting." She urged members of the Association to
begin right there in New York by demanding the admission of
women to Columbia College.

Other papers included "Enlightened Womanhood" by Mrs.
Cooper Bristol and "Prison Reform" by Mrs. Elizabeth Chase.
Rev. Celia Burleigh in her address said contemporary dress
made quadrupeds of women since they used all four limbs to
climb stairs and get in and out of carriages, making it almost
impossible to be useful when dressed as styles demanded.
Rev. Hanaford addressed the group on "Women in Church
and Pulpit." In conclusion the Association agreed to an annual
Congress, the next to be held in Chicago in 1874.[149]

Rev. Hanaford accepted Rev. Isaac Atwood's invitation to
speak at the First Universalist Church in Jersey City, New Jersey.
The lack of a resident pastor had led to a decline in membership
and the closing of the church. In December Phebe preached at
the morning and evening services. Those who came to the Universalist Church on Ivy Place saw "a woman in her mid forties
with a round face and a broad intelligent brow. She took care to
maintain a feminine look and always wore a simple black dress
with a lace collar as her clerical outfit."[150] By a unanimous vote
of the Prudential Committee, Rev. Hanaford was invited to return in a month for further discussion. "In 1870, in this densely
populated state (New Jersey), there were only six Universalist
parishes and only three ministers in residence. Only three of

149   *The New York Times*, October 16, p. 2; October 17, p. 5
150   *The American Standard* (n.d.)

the parishes (Newark, Hightstown and Irvington), had regular preaching; Irvington did not even own a meeting house."[151]

At home in New Haven, in the Church of the Messiah, the power of a few continued to override those who supported Rev. Hanaford as their pastor. Believing it better to part in harmony if reconciliation was not possible, Phebe prepared to complete her services. Her letter and the response of the Presidential Committee are recorded in the First Unitarian Universalist Society: Bound volume: Records of the Prudential Committee, First Universalist Society 1870–1895.

> *Gentlemen*
>
> *Believing it to be my duty to accept the unanimous call of the church in Jersey City, N.J.—I hereby repeat the notice given before you all at the Social meeting—that I shall close my labors here on the 1st of April next and I desire through you to thank this Society in New Haven for the large majority vote in my favor at that meeting and for the emphasis given to that vote by the prompt subscription to the salary. Had the vote been unanimous I would have remained with this Society not withstanding the advance of salary offered by the Jersey City Society. But feeling that I need the rest and change I am more reconciled to the thought of leaving those who have been so kind to me and mine, and I invoke the choicest of Heaven's blessings to rest upon them all, and trust that a greater spirit of unity will prevail on this Society in coming days, that the pastor may thus be able to perform the needed work and that still greater prosperity may attend the Society—than it has ever known. Happy in the thought that I shall leave you in a state every way*

---

151   Miller, 1985, p. 720

more prosperous than when I came to you, and wishing only
good to every member of the Parish.

I am respectfully your Pastor
Jan. 6, 1874[152]

The recorded response reads,
"Moved that the Clerk call a meeting of the Society on January
13th 1874 for the purpose of supplying the pulpit and settling a
pastor to continue the lease.

On motion adj.
Attest. L. P. Sherry Clerk"

An undated letter from the Prudential Committee reads,

Whereas, the relation of pastor and people has for
nearly four years existed between this Society and the
Rev. Mrs. P. A. Hanaford is about to be dissolved and
she to remove to another people in another State; and
whereas she will, wherever she may go, take with her,
from us, largely of that love and sympathy which are ever
the spontaneous outpouring of human hearts towards
those who have been instruments of good to them, as she
should a token of our esteem; therefore

Resolved: That the years our sister has been with us,
mingling freely in the family circles, and sitting at the
family board; and, as our pastor going in and out before
us; breaking unto us the Bread of Everlasting Life, and
preaching the doctrine of the ultimate and complete

152   Yale Divinity School Library

growth in holiness of every human soul, have served to inspire us with the fullest confidence in her moral and religious integrity, her purely Christian character, and her ability and her unqualified fitness for an efficient ministry of the religion of Him who went about doing good: as they give evidence of her social and loving nature, her sincerity of purpose, and unassuming love and good will to all.

Resolved: That as our pastor she has been untiringly devoted to the duties of her calling; joy and gladness have attended her labors everywhere—in the social gathering, in the Sabbath School, the Pulpit, and at the Communion table. And if in now parting the brightness of that joy be dimmed, and, the remembrance of those meetings be touched with sadness, the thought that she still lives and labors in the service of the same Good Master: still strives for the upbuilding of the same precious faith, shall brighten again our hopes and strengthen our purpose. With one united heart and voice we bid her God speed, and pray for Heaven's richest blessing to go and be with her in her new field of labor. May she still find willing hearts and ready hands, and may peace and prosperity be the portion of the people of her charge, nor will we forget that though miles of territory may separate us, yet are of one common family owning "one Lord, one faith, one baptism." So to us, there comes no farewell, but an earnest looking for a future reunion, which we are assured, may, in the providence of God, be in the life that now is, but shall be in that which is to come.

Dominick Marble
Joseph A. Newhall
Edmund Hersey
George Hersey Sr.
Franklin Hersey[153]

Rev. Hanaford again visited the Universalist Church of the Good Shepherd in Jersey City during the second week of January 1874. By mutual agreement, Rev. Hanford signed a contract for three years at a salary of $2,500 a year. It no doubt gave her some satisfaction to know that her salary equaled that of the highest paid pastor in the Universalist Society. The committee members agreed to hire Miss Miles as a Sabbath school teacher. Rev. Mr. Isaac Atwood served the Church of the Good Shepherd in Jersey City through the month of March. Rev. Hanaford delivered her farewell sermon, "The Finished Work," at the Church of the Messiah on Palm Sunday, March 29, 1874. The text "I have finished the work Thou gavest me to do" from the Gospel of John introduces her accomplishments as their pastor. "Including the sermons of this day I can speak of four hundred and five sermons preached since I became pastor of this church."[154]

In a letter to Olympia Brown, Phebe opens a small window into her feelings at this time. She writes, "I have left my pastorate in New Haven. The men in the congregation oppose me and asked for my resignation.... I do not think that I will continue my work in the church because of the treatment accorded women ministers."[155]

---

153   Ibid
154   *Daily Evening Union,* March 30, 1873 p.2, col. 3-6
155   Schlesinger Library, Olympia Brown file

Rev. Hanaford's work as pastor in New Haven came to an end. With the loving support of Ellen Miles, Phebe continued the work God gave her to do. Their relationship, begun in Waltham, grew with their years of mutual dependence and shared commitment to their work. They honored each other with a love that would remain throughout their lives. Phebe always wore the symbol of their reciprocal love, the treasured gold ring inscribed "E.M. to P.H."[156]

CHAPTER SIX

THE JERSEY CITY YEARS

...if I were to tell what was said and done by men who thought themselves doing God service by blocking a woman's way, I should put before the public a book which would cause both laughter and tears.[157]

It becomes our task to "put before the public" an honest account of Rev. Hanaford's ten years in Jersey City. These years represent almost half of her twenty-two years of service as a regularly ordained Universalist minister.

The brief history of Universalism in New Jersey reads,

One of the paradoxes of Universalist history at the state Level was the failure, comparatively speaking, of the denomination to flourish in the very area where John Murray had landed in 1770. In 1856, when the cornerstone of a new church of the First Universalist Society in Newark was laid, there were only two other denominational meeting houses in the state, one in Hightstown and one in Sussex County... there was not a free State in this whole Union where there are so few Universalist organizations....[158] The editor of the Universalist Register commented in 1841, "the cause advances but slowly if at all in New Jersey."

---

157   Hanaford, Phebe A., 1890, "Twenty Years in the Pulpit"
158   Miller, 1979, pp. 719

Jersey City Universalist Society records were lost in a fire. Universalism in Jersey City appears in the history of Essex and Sussex Counties.

> The Church of the Good Shepherd (First Universalist) corner of Grand Street and Summit Avenue, Jersey City, was organized on December 10, 1871. The ecclesiastical organization was effected June 2, 1872. The society met at Library Hall from December 10, 1871, until October 20, 1872 when it occupied the present edifice, corner of Summit Avenue and Grand Street....Rev. A. A. Thayer, April 1, 1872 to April 1, 1873; supply from April, 1873, to April 1, 1874 with no regular pastor; Rev. Phoebe (sic) A. Hanaford, April 1, 1874; Rev. J. Hazzard Hartzel, from November 18, 1877 to April 1, 1878....The first officers of the church of the Good Shepherd were as follows: D. L. Holden, Albert Munson, Amos T. Farrar. Of these officers, only D. L. Holden remained in office in 1884.[159]

When Rev. Hanaford assumed her position as pastor of the Church of the Good Shepherd in 1874, the church had been without a regular pastor for one year. During that time the Officers had the responsibility of attracting visiting clergy for weekend services. Among those clergymen, none came to an agreement regarding a three-year contract. Churches without regular pastors usually do not experience growth in membership. It can be asked, did they offer a three-year contract to a woman because Rev. Hanaford appeared the only hope open to the Officers of getting a resident pastor? Phebe, with her daughter, Florence,

---

159   Shaw, p. 1185

and her companion, Ellen Miles, moved into their accommodations at one of "The Seven Houses" on Summit Avenue, which the ladies of the congregation had newly carpeted.

The Jersey City newspaper, *The American Standard,* dated April 6, 1874, printed,

Mrs. Hanaford in Jersey City

The congregation of the First Universalist Church some time ago invited Rev. Phoebe (sic) A. Hanaford to take charge of the church. She deliberated on the offer for some time. It was a difficult matter for her to reconcile herself to the idea of dissolving her connections with her three thousand parishioners, but she finally decided to accept the offer, agreeing to commence April 1st. She has since preached once in the church to the intense satisfaction of the congregation. Tomorrow she assumes pastoral charge. It is anticipated that half of Jersey City will flock to the First Universalist Church near Library Hall to hear her tomorrow.

It is difficult to imagine how the journalist arrived at the figure three thousand as the number of Rev. Hanaford's parishioners. We cannot confirm that half of Jersey City attended her first service as pastor on Sunday. No doubt, wearing her black dress and lace collar, Rev. Hanaford faced the trustees in their seats, including Deacon Holden. A gentleman from *The American Standard* attended the service. His article appeared under the heading, "**Mrs. Hanaford Yesterday.**"[160] The journal-

---

160   April 13, Vol. xxvi, No. 87

ist's attention to her style speaks to the importance of preaching in the church and the attention the press gave to local church matters during this period.

> Mrs. Hanaford is one of the most captivating pulpit orators in the country....Her style of delivery is animated, yet of exceeding grace....The attendance has so much increased since Mrs. Hanaford's installation that campstools will hereafter be provided in the aisles between the pews. Mrs. Hanaford should be heard to be appreciated. And those who hear her once will not care to hear any one else.

The Jersey City and Bergen Railroad companies had several lines of horsecars throughout the city, making travel within the city convenient. Rev. Hanaford had her business cards printed to include directions to the church from the ferry.

In her sermon for Decoration Day, May 24, 1874, Rev. Hanaford noted that the church in which she stood, built in 1852, served as a symbol of hope for unity within a nation torn by civil war.

> *However it is our loved dead that are in God's hands, it matters not how or where, for God is love. The Universalist faith is that all souls enter into a new light and see with clearer vision these things which before were hidden or misty. This strewing of flowers is not a consecration of the war, but a consecration of the soldier's self-sacrifice. We have need of soldiers — the need is greater now in the spiritual field than ever before, and it is the highest warfare to put down intemperance and fraud, and shield and uphold the oppressed.*

In June Rev. Hanaford traveled to Wellfleet on Cape Cod for her son Howard's ordination. Wellfleet remained an isolated town and may have been the only invitation Howard received. We have no words from Phebe regarding her feelings on her visit to Cape Cod after so many years or any personal record of her participation in the ceremony. Rev. Phebe Hanaford delivered the Ordination Prayer, making her the first woman to participate in her son's ordination.[161] Howard soon married Mary Weston Landerkin of Wellfleet in the Methodist church with Professor Charles H. Leonard of Tufts College and Rev. E. S. Macreading, Pastor presiding.[162]

The American Standard carried an article, "Rev. Phebe A. Hanaford", detailing events already shared in the telling of her story. In conclusion, the journalist wrote,

In personal appearance she is of medium size, dark complexion with black hair and eyes and judging from a phrenological point one would say self-esteem and veneration were prominent traits of character. She is an earnest and enthusiastic speaker, a thorough believer in woman's suffrage, Vice President of Sorosis Club of New York and an active worker in all the reforms of the day.[163]

To attend the monthly Sorosis meetings Phebe and Ellen Miles took the Grand Avenue trolleys to the ferries going to Manhattan. Members of Sorosis wore their gold S-shaped pins available at Tiffany's for $4.50. Women wore their pins with pride and objected to Tiffany Jewelers selling them to nonmembers.

161   Miller, 1979, p556
162   1882 Coffin Genealogy
163   June 22, 1874 Vol. xxvi, No. 146

On Phebe's recommendation her daughter Florence was accepted as a member of Sorosis at the traditional May festival. This celebration provided an opportunity to explain how Sorosis served the needs and interests of the women ever since its founding by Jane Croly in 1868 and how the name expressed the goals of the club.

"Sorosis is a botanical term found in Henstow's Dictionary and defined as a compound fleshy fruit, formed by the close aggregation of many flowers whose floral whorls become succulent. It is derived from the Greek Soreusis meaning aggregation. Cooke's *Manual of Botanical Terms* identifies it as a fleshy fruit, resulting from many flowers as the pineapple. The pineapple therefore was chosen as the emblem on their banner." Those who still maintained that the word Sorosis was not understandable for a club such as theirs were told that a group of women gathered together to sew or raise money was understandable but not a club like theirs where women asked: "Is it possible?"[164]

In the spring of 1874 Mrs. Wilbour went abroad leaving 1st Vice President, Rev. Phebe Hanaford, to fill the presidential chair, which she did with marked ability, contributing many valuable papers to the literary work of the club, and impressing the strength of her conscience and convictions upon the general tone and spirit of the membership.[165]

This entry in the *History of Sorosis* remains the only reference to Phebe's contributions to the Sorosis meetings. Women

164   Sophia Smith Collection
165   Croly, p. 29

accepted the presidency and then left the 1st vice president in charge. Believing Mrs. Croly, the founder of Sorosis, would be traveling abroad in the coming months, Phebe Hanaford ran against her for president in 1875. Phebe lost on the fourth ballot with twenty-one votes to Mrs. Croly's twenty-four. Phebe Hanaford remained 1st vice president for eleven years, 1875 to 1886, under Jane Croly. Organizations pay tribute to presidents, not vice presidents. It took considerable research of the club archives to find the contributions Phebe Hanaford made to Sorosis over the years.

The church calendars published in local newspapers included several announcements as to where ministers would be taking their summer vacation. Of Rev. Hanaford the notice read, "The Rev. Mrs. Hanaford, of the Universalist in Bergen, goes to the Catskills. Her sermon yesterday, on the text "Come ye apart into the desert place and rest awhile," had special references to vacations and their uses."

Their choice of the Catskills was unique since every year Phebe and Ellen vacationed on Nantucket Island. A letter on Sorosis stationery from Glasco-Ulster Co. N.Y. Aug. 28, 1874 to a dear friend details how this busy woman spent her vacation. "...I have obeyed the injunction—As ye go, preach." I have preached once in the hotel and six times in the two Methodist pulpits since my vacation began." She concluded, "I go to Europe next summer if nothing prevents. This time I think I shall accomplish that great desire of my heart."[166] There is no evidence that Phebe ever traveled to Europe.

The Universalist Convention held in New York City September 15-17, 1874 preceded Rev. Hanaford's installation

166   Schlesinger Library

as pastor of the Church of the Good Shepherd. She sent notice of her Installation Ceremony to *The American Standard* church calendar for September 18. Her Letter of Transfer from the Connecticut Universalist Convention dated August 31, 1874 officially removed Rev. Hanaford to Jersey City.[167] As planned, Rev. Hanaford's Installation as pastor took place in a simple evening ceremony attended by Convention members who traveled from New York to the Church of the Good Shepherd.

Rev. Hanaford invited Mrs. Caroline Soule, National President of the Murray Grove Association, to Jersey City to discuss the Potter Memorial Fund for the erection of a church in Murray Grove. Since it seemed the owners of the property were never going to sell their land to the church, Mrs. Soule proposed purchasing the lot next to Mr. Potter's grave. "The idea was proposed by Caroline A. Soule in 1874 at a conference in the Jersey City Universalist Church. Phebe Hanaford, the pastor, made the first contribution ($1.00) to a Potter Memorial Fund established to raise money to build the church."[168] It marked the beginning of the Potter Memorial Fund and soon reported a total of $30.30.

The Argus replaced *The American Standard* in 1875 and in the summer published an article titled "MRS. HANAFORD'S SERMON." The entire article appeared in *The Woman's Journal,* no doubt sent by Phebe. A portion of the article reads,

When Mrs. Phoebe (sic) A. Hanaford ascended the pulpit of the Church of the Good Shepherd, on Summit Avenue, opposite Library Hall, old Bergen, yesterday morning, the pews of the church were comfortably full. When she first came to this city, by invitation of the officers of the

167   Nantucket Historical Association
168   Miller, 1985, p. 220

church, the congregation was a rather slim one. Her ministrations have largely increased it. Besides these, a large number of persons who are not members of the church, gather regularly within the walls of the little edifice to listen to her sermons.

Mrs. Hanaford is certainly the most captivating pulpit speaker in the State....In text her sermons are models of rhetoric and in the chasteness and elegance of her language and the wealth and beauty of her illustrations few preachers in the country can equal her....Bergen (N.J.)

In the age of Revivalist "hell and damnation" preaching, Universalists relied on Sunday schools to teach God's universal love. "Sunday Schools were to be considered simply one of the instrumentalities of the Parish and were not to comprise a distinct power; they were like Bible classes or conference meetings, merely auxiliary organizations."[169] The Sunday school played an important role in Rev. Hanaford's ministry. With Miss Miles' talents as a teacher, the school was an effective tool to attract members. Applied with her forceful manner, Ellen's skills frequently met with rebuke. Considering the nebulous role of the Sunday school in the Universalist Society, Miss Miles required the trustees' approval. Though her defense of Rev. Hanaford against those who criticized the pastor's beliefs expressed in her sermons, brought disfavor on Miss Miles, her loyalty to Phebe remained boundless.

Within the parish criticism of Phebe went beyond her sermons. Most outspoken were those who criticized her membership in Sorosis, deeming it inappropriate for a minister. Phebe Hanaford considered this an invasion of her private

---

169   Ibid, p. 280

life and chose to ignore it. She chaired both Sorosis business and social meetings now held at Delmonico's Restaurant's new location, Twenty-Second Street and Fifth Avenue. Presiding at the business meeting on December 7, 1879, Phebe informed the members that due to failing health, Rev. Celia Burleigh had resigned as pastor in Brooklyn, Connecticut. The members took up a collection to show their gratitude to Celia for her friendship during the early years of the club.[170]

The census for 1880 shows Phebe Hanaford as head of the household, with Florence Hanaford, daughter, Ellen Miles, teacher, and Mrs. Kenny, servant at 770 Grand Street across from Arlington Park. Presumably they moved from Summit Avenue's church property to distance themselves from the invasion into their private activities. At the January Sorosis business meeting, Mrs. Hanaford suggested Peter Cooper, considered the leading philanthropist in the city of New York, as the first man to be invited to address the club. A highly successful businessman, Mr. Cooper founded the Cooper Union to provide education to those who could not afford tuition. Advocates of education among the members proved stronger than those who preferred women speakers. In appreciation for his work, the club resolved to support Peter Cooper's intention to run for a political position.

On the death of Rev. Celia Burleigh on July 25, 1875, Phebe offered a resolution that the members of Sorosis gather for a memorial service to honor the first woman ordained to the Unitarian ministry and founding member of Sorosis. Phebe suggested the service be held at the Church of the Good Shepherd in July while the church services were suspended. The resolution

170   Sophia Smith Collection

passed and within the week the members of Sorosis arrived by ferry in Jersey City. Rev. Hanaford based her sermon on Rev. Burleigh's handwritten account of her ordination, where Rev. Hanaford had offered a prayer and reading from Scripture.

In October, 1875 Rev. Howard Hanaford was installed as pastor of St. Paul's Universalist Church in Little Falls, New York where he remained until 1877.[171] Howard and Mary's son Charles Leonard, born on August 10, 1875 in Little Falls, was Phebe's first grandchild.[172] Letters from Phebe to her grandson, known as "Lennie," are among the correspondence saved in the Hanaford Family Private Collection.

The program for the 1875 Association for the Advancement of Women held in Syracuse during October included Rev. Hanaford's talk, Statistics of the Woman Ministry. Referring to her topic, she said,

It has been reserved for the new world—yes, for America—for the United States in her first century, to show that "all are one in Christ Jesus" by consenting to the fact that ecclesiastical functions are the heritage of the daughters as well as the sons of the Lord Almighty, when the Divine Voice says to any soul— pointing to the pulpit and pastorate—"Go work today in my vineyard."[173]

Phebe's passionate regard for the role of women's work in our nation's history led her to write *Women of the Century* in 1876. She did not want the celebrations of the nation's centennial to ignore women's contributions to the growth of the nation. Her

---

171   Universalist Archives, Andover – Harvard Theological Library
172   1882 Coffin Genealogy
173   Sophia Smith Collection

first biographical dictionary was "a record of the *women of the first century whose lives were full of usefulness and therefore worthy of renown and imitation*" in twenty-six chapters:

Women of the Revolution, The Wives of the Presidents, Women Leaders in Society, Philanthropic Women, Women during the Civil War, Literary Women, Women Poets, Women-Scientists, Women Artists, Women Lecturers, Women Reformers, Women Preachers, Women Missionaries, Women Educators, Women Physicians, Women as Readers, Actors, and Singers, Women in Business, Women of Faith, Women Inventors, Women Lawyers, Women Journalists, Women Printers, Women Librarians, Women Agriculturists, Women Historians, and Women Travelers

Phebe acknowledged her sources including *Noble Deeds of American Women, Pioneer Mothers of the West* and *The Queens of American Society.* In her Preface she wrote,

The centennial of American existence cannot properly be observed without a reference to its women, as well as to its men. Other pens may write eloquently of its patriots, its inventors, its warriors, its professional and literary and other men in public life, who have left their mark upon the century, and won the world's honors and favors of the good and wise; but the writer of this unpretentious record will be abundantly satisfied if she may but so present the truth about American women as to prove "before all Israel and the sun," that the nation is indebted for its growth and prosperity as a people, and for its proud position among the nations of the earth, to its women as well as to its men, to the mothers and daughters of the Revolutionary struggle, and to those brave sons of worthy ancestors whom we tenderly "called our boys in blue." The foremothers should be remembered with the forefathers, –the women who bore heavy burdens and did noble work in the time of the Rebellion, as well as those dear to their hearts, who fought and suffered and died for the 'dear old flag.'

...Each true life, whether public or private, which any woman of the century has lived, goes to make up the character and glory of the land and the age; and every high soul rejoices in the welfare of her native land, whether her name be found on the scroll of its famous women or not....But, imperfect as it necessarily must be, may this record help to impress upon the men and women of the future a sense of the obligation which the nation is under, and the respect and honor which the world owes to the women of the first American century!

P. A. H.
Jersey City Heights, N.J.

The terms of publication limited her to four to five hundred pages to be published in 1877 and sold by subscription for $2.50, or $3 for Morocco binding. With her eleventh book accepted for publication, the fifth by B. B. Russell of Boston who advertised the work as a "GRAND ENCYCLOPEDIA OF AMERICAN WOMEN," her pen had served her well over the years. Never having the luxury of an office outside her home, Phebe's literary career challenges Jane Croly's words from her address "Women in Journalism," "if women write from home they will be cheated out of their pay."[174]

---

174   Ibid

Women in need of pay during the Civil War had taken their home skills to the open market. Since the Civil War the number of patents issued to women had increased at a greater rate than those issued to men. During the preparations for the Centennial Exhibition to be held in Fairmont Park in Philadelphia in May 1876, women demanded a Woman's Pavilion to adequately demonstrate their inventions. Pressed for the completion of her book, *Women of the Century*, Phebe Hanaford did not take an active role in the work of the Woman's Pavilion. She did take issue with the disdainful words journalists used in describing the women's exhibits as "useless objects." In articles she argued that "genius inhabits both sexes equally but that women diverted their initiative and genius into practical channels, notably the home." Tempers flared at any defense of the exhibition of "household and other conveniences," believing it did damage to the cause of women's rights. Phebe understood from personal experience that women who stepped out of the home to express their genius often endured strong criticism.

In accord with the centenary celebrations, the Association for the Advancement of Women held their meeting in Philadelphia. Their honored guest, Lucretia Mott, abolitionist and supporter of the Woman's Rights Movement since 1848 in Seneca Falls, appeared in her Quaker garb and gentle manner. In a more dramatic style, Susan B. Anthony and Matilda Gage, having been denied participation in the July fourth official ceremonies, read the Declaration of Women's Independence at Independence Square. Women continued to demonstrate in public for recognition of their rights.

As always Phebe used her pen as her weapon of choice. In her chapter on Women Inventors she acknowledged the variety of inventions of women that went far beyond the home.

The question is sneeringly asked sometimes, Can a woman invent? The great Centennial Exposition answered the question satisfactorily to the believer in woman's capabilities and those who saw and heard the dish-washer and the women who were displaying their own inventions there will not soon forget them....Some woman with sufficient leisure would do royal service to her sex and the cause of woman, if she would prepare a volume in which, with all detail, it might be shown the help of women in the onward progress of society in regard to household and other conveniences. It would then be perceived, that, if woman had not done as much as her brothers in the way of inventions, it was not because the inventive genius did not belong to both sexes, but because women's energies and genius had been directed to other channels.[175]

In a private ceremony Florence Hanaford married Thomas Warner on "September 18, 1876 at 770 Grand."[176] With her mother performing the service, Rev. Hanaford became "the first woman to officiate at the marriage of her own daughter."[177] Phebe Hanaford entrusted her daughter to Mr. Warner who proved to be a protective husband.

Within days of the wedding ceremony, the Church of the Good Shepherd hosted the 1876 New Jersey State Universalist Convention. As secretary of the State Convention and ex officio member of the General Convention, Rev. Hanaford officiated at the religious services preceding the sessions. The *Jersey City Journal* reported that at the opening session on September twenty-second, D. L. Holden, President of the Universalist

---

175   Hanaford, Phebe A., 1877, p. 546
176   1882 Coffin Genealogy
177   Miller, 1985, p. 556

Society in Jersey City and chairman of the missionary committee, reported that, due to financial depression, the committee
was "unable to support a permanent missionary in the State.
Rev. Phebe A. Hanaford, pastor of the Church of the Good Shepherd, has preached twice in Bayonne and once in Elizabeth."
The article went on to say,

> Rev. Hanaford made a warm, earnest appeal for the
> Irvington congregation. She said the Newark society
> should extend a more fostering care over the unfortunate
> congregation and not allow the church at that place to die
> so long as there was one Universalist family in the town.
> A resolution was offered by Mrs. Hanaford "that this
> convention heartily endorse every Christian effort for the
> suppression of intemperance in our land, and pledge to
> the good work our earnest sympathy, toil and prayers."[178]

A report of the Business meeting of the New Jersey branch
of the Women's Centenary Association appeared in *The Argus*
on September 22, 1876.[179]

> During the year there had been raised the sum of $170,
> which had been divided between the Potter Memo-
> rial Church and a poor but worthy student in the women's
> Theological Seminary....Rev. Hanaford later presided at the
> meeting where Mary Parker of Scotland, President of the
> International Christian Woman's Temperance Society, again
> introduced the issue of Temperance. The closing remarks

178   *Jersey City Journal*, September 22, 1876
179   p. 1, col. 2

were made by D. Holden Esq., president of the convention. The convention adjourned to meet in Newark next year.

Early in the New Year *The Argus* reported "rumors wild and startling" in Bergen about "a terrible church war." Almost every church fell victim to the rumor with everyone guessing and no one knowing which church was involved. On the evening of January 31st the question shifted from which church to what is happening at the First Universalist near Library Hall? Men and women "dove nervously into the basement and disappeared into the dimly lit room." A journalist from *The Argus* joined the group "numbering about two hundred of the best known citizens of the Hill, with many from old Jersey City." The noise became oppressive as people shouted, "Read the motion."

On February 1, 1877 people read a lengthy article beginning on the front page of *The Argus* quoted here in part.

ANOTHER CHURCH WAR:[180]

Trouble in the First Universalist Church— Mrs. Hanaford Deposed from the Pastorate—A New Church to be Organized for Her—Excitement on the Hill.
Deacon D. Holden, a cashier at the Bergen Savings Bank, sat in the chair, unable to bring the meeting to order.... The motion was read. "Resolved, That the trustees of this church be empowered to employ a male pastor." With tears in his eyes Deacon Holden pleaded for moderation and a spirit of unity and forgiveness. He offered the advice that "the church far from being a business was a community of friends banded together to educate each other, to cultivate and ennoble the human character." He recalled their

---

180   P.1 six columns

early days with few members. "In the last few years we have risen to among the largest in numbers and wealth in the city but we lack the unity we once shared."

In Halden's soon to be forgotten words remain the evidence of Rev. Hanaford's success as their pastor. The article went on to quote Halden's prediction that all this would lead to the establishment of a new church. With the removal of the word "male" from the resolution, the "main question remained to be put to a vote. Should we dispose of our pastor, the Rev. Mrs. Hanaford?" The local reporter asked people, "What is wrong with Mrs. Hanaford?" From several people he learned that "the old maids of the congregation want a young man to preach to them." Others thought Mrs. Hanaford was not strong enough and a third group said, "The women are jealous of the female assistant of Mrs. Hanaford." One gentleman simply shrugged it off saying the storm had been brewing for a long time. Only when someone turned off the gas did the meeting end with no agreement on the cause of the difficulty.

The Argus had more to report the next day on February second. The journalist found the situation humorous enough to report and that this author finds this event too tragic to omit.

THE CHURCH WAR,
Secret of the difficulty...Conflict of Societies

The secret of the dissension in the flock at the Church of the 'Good Sheriff' has been discovered, and it is funny. Miss Miles is the companion of Mrs. Hanaford, the pastor. They have lived together ever since the separation of Mrs. Hanaford from her husband. She is a lady of great activity and has taken a prominent part in the society matters of the Church of the Good Shepherd. For a time she was Superintendent of the Sabbath School, and was in a fair way to become an assistant or real pastor over the congregation when it was discovered that there were other women in the church besides Miss Miles. They too were unmarried, and candidates with the fair Miss Miles for the favors of the flock. They were jealous of Miss Miles and began to criticize her conduct in the sewing circle. The gossip was so loud at the meetings of the Mite Society whether present or not, Miss Miles heard all that was said. One evening at a meeting of the Dorcas Club Miss Miles proposed to raise funds to buy a sewing machine for a destitute member of the Social Union. This was stoutly opposed to by a member of the Organ Fund Association. The Home Mission at its next meeting passed a resolution that all the sewing machines intended for a destitute member of the parish should pass through its hands. Now the war was opened in earnest. A committee from the Mite Society met at the house of the President of the Dorcas Club. Contrary to rules, they sent a petition to the Organ Fund Association demanding that Miss Miles appear at the next meeting of the Home Mission and give all the particulars about the destitute family who were in want of a sewing machine. The whole matter for the time being culminated in a joint meeting of all the societies of the parish....The anti-sewing machine party at once demanded of Rev. Mrs. Hanaford that she dismiss Miss Miles from her household. Mrs. Hanaford neglected to comply with the terms of the demand and hence the opposition to

Mrs. Hanaford developed at the meeting night before last and was reported in *The Argus* yesterday.

The request by a joint meeting of all the societies of the parish to dismiss Miss Miles represented the will of a large portion of the active members. This venom directed at Ellen Miles appeared in newspaper accounts pointing to Ellen Miles as the source of the problem. The *Daily Tribune* described her as obnoxious. Believing herself to be the cause of the trouble, Ellen Miles offered to resign. Phebe never considered Ellen's offer and did not see Ellen as the cause of the problem or her dismissal as the solution. Phebe's membership in Sorosis, her political activities as a member of suffrage organizations, and her lifestyle as a married woman living apart from her husband and her relationship with Ellen Miles did not interfere with her pastoral duties. Phebe believed that if she agreed to interference in her private affairs, as distinct from her pastoral duties, such accommodation could affect the future of woman's role in the church.

In search of another approach the board of trustees informed Rev. Hanaford that owing to the depression of funds it would be necessary to reduce her salary. Coming at a time when the church was in a prosperous condition with increased attendance, the real issue remained woman's role in the church. Since the interests of the church remained her interests, she left the question of the salary in their hands. It was not the position they expected her to take. The *Evening Journal* on February second wrote, "The motives which actuated the movement are the outgrowth of personal feelings of a nature not at all creditable to a church organization. The close of Mrs. Hanaford's engagement will be April 1st."

Phebe denied reports that she had placed herself in a position antagonistic to the congregation and, to the contrary, she repeatedly received from the officers of the church the assurance that she had performed her duties well and to the entire satisfaction of the members. From later correspondence we learn Rev. Hanaford believed a second vote allowing all of the members to vote would reinstate her for the remaining months of her contract. If she were not reinstated by the second vote, there would be no question of renewing her contract and she would leave at the end of her term with the parish united. When a second vote was considered by the trustees to be a violation of the by-laws, Rev. Hanaford agreed to the formation of a second church. She regretted the division that would weaken the church and perhaps cause death to the Universalist cause in Jersey City. In the meantime she would remain as pastor of the Church of the Good Shepherd until her contract expired at the end of March. The press wrote, "The whole trouble is caused by the bickerings of a few female members and are unworthy of notice."[181]

News of Phebe's troubles reached Nantucket during the spring of 1877. A Letter to the Editor of *The Inquirer and Mirror* (n.d.) confirms the request that Phebe dismiss Ellen Miles. In excerpts of this letter we also read evidence of Ellen's character.

Messrs. Editors—...What true woman would respect Mrs. Hanaford had she for the sake of re-election as Pastor of the Church over which she had been settled, dismissed, as some of her Parish desired, this faithful co-worker...In this case, a valued member of Mrs. Hanaford's

---

181   *Evening Journal*, February 2, 1877

family is disliked by some of the church, and so is made the target of attack. That the people are well satisfied with Mrs. Hanaford, is apparent from the fact that one of the opposition declared their minister had performed all and more than they had a right to expect of her, and if she would discharge the objectionable "minister's wife," she would have a unanimous invitation to remain longer in the pastorate. The offending person is Miss Ellen E. Miles, a lady of great executive ability, added to which, she is an intelligent and zealous worker in the Lord's service.

Miss Miles has, by her unselfish devotion, built up the Sunday School. She has gone down to the canal boats lying near by for the children; stood by the bedsides of the sick and dying, and with no fear of contagion, has always been ready to answer any call for services, such as only the gentle hand of woman can render, until she has endeared herself to the common people to such an extent, that even the children cling to her with the unfailing instinct of childhood's confidence in a true friend.

...Miss Miles, to whom I allude, is a staunch, talented woman, full of energy and executive ability; and I am sorry to say, it would seem that some of the sisters in the church have been jealous of these qualities which she possesses. It was not of Mrs. Hanaford that any of the congregation were jealous.

One of Many[182]

We gather information on the legalities of the procedures from a letter from New York dated February 21, 1877.

---

182   Nantucket Historical Association

...I venture to add just a word or two to what you have already published concerning the trouble in the First Universalist Church of Jersey City....By the constitution of the organization, the parish and church are separate bodies. The parish is composed of such persons as have signed of the roll, the existence of which they were in ignorance of, and in some cases, the parties were members of the church in good and regular standing. By the arbitrary enforcement of the rule referred to, quite a number of Mrs. Hanaford's staunchest supporters were not allowed to vote. Or else the result would have been quite different. Leaving out of the question therefore the matter of woman in the pulpit, which really has but little to do with it, I am sure your readers will sympathize with Mrs. Hanaford in the unjust treatment she has received..., and will be glad to know that in nothing can a syllable be uttered to her discredit; and that Nantucket may still take pride in her success. Her friends in the church, really the majority, are urging her to go with them, and form a new organization, promising her a new chapel at once; but she has not decided what to do, except that she will vacate the pulpit of the First Church when her term of service expires in March.

Very truly,

W. F. B.

The members willing to form a new church society met for the first time in the home of Mr. J. J. Gear of Summit Avenue on February nineteenth where the finance committee agreed to raise funds. A second committee organized to procure a suitable hall for holding church services. *The New York Times* published the following: "The friends and supporters of Rev. Phoebe (sic) A. Hanaford, to the number of about 60, have held a meeting and decided to organize a new church, to be known as the Second Universalist Church of Jersey City...." The article referred to Mrs. Hanaford as "the well-known pastor of the Universalist Church in Jersey City, unremitting in her efforts to increase the membership and her labors has been crowned with success." [183]

Rev. Hanaford attended the meeting on February twenty-ninth when the committee reported that the New Church Hall in town would be too small for their purpose. Because "Library Hall served as the Universalist Church in 1871 and 1872 before the purchase of the church on the top of Ivy Place," and despite the fact that Library Hall was directly across from the Church of the Good Shepherd, the committee chose the City Common Chamber in Library Hall for Sunday services. The finance committee reported donations of $2,500 for the new church, to be ready by the first Sunday in April.

During the months of February and March opponents of Rev. Hanaford stayed away from her services at the Church of the Good Shepherd. *The Argus* on February twenty-sixth reported that the proposed pastor for the Church of the Good Shepherd, Rev. Smith of Hightstown, was not acceptable to some members because of his young wife. The article recalled to the readers that the original complaint against Mrs. Hanaford included the preference of some of her opponents to "set under the preachings of an unmarried male divine."

An article in *The Evening Journal* reported the following under the heading "Universalist Church No. 2,"

---

183   *The New York Times*, City and Suburban News section, February 24, 1877

One of the leading members said to a *Journal* reporter this morning that the reason for the vote not to renew her contract was because they did not require her services. We hired her for three years and her contract expired the first of April. She had been notified six months ago that the church deemed it better that another pastor be engaged because they did not consider her possessed of the necessary mental qualifications for the pulpit.[184]

The "leading member's" closing remark about her lack of "the necessary mental qualifications" opened up a new and unfounded cause for the decision not to renew her contract. Rev. Hanaford's supporters decided the accusation against her mental qualifications deserved a public recant by an eminent phrenologist. Phrenology, a study of the shape and protuberances of the skull to analyze one's character and mental faculties, originated with members of the medical profession to demonstrate that women have smaller brains than men. This pseudoscience had considerable credibility in its day, and women were willing to subject themselves to it as a way of proving their intellectual equality. There is no evidence that Phebe objected to it.

The Argus in a March twentieth article, "Rev. Mrs. Hanaford's Head," detailed the phrenological performance on the front page. Twirling the tape line around his finger, Prof. Graham, noted phrenologist, estimated Rev. Hanaford to have good powers to reason on any subject that she might take an interest in. He reckoned she, as a preacher, "has all the mental, moral and spiritual powers to make her a first rate occupant of the pulpit." In conclusion the journalist quoted one woman's words

184   March 13, 1877, p. 7

echoing the feelings of many in the crowd. She believed that "if they got Prof. Graham before that awful meetin' which rejected her proposition to stay...all the trouble we've had to start a new church would have been avoided."

The New York Times under the heading, "Rev. Mrs. Hanaford's Head," described the experiment with sarcasm and disdain for the pseudoscience of phrenology. "According to the eminent phrenologist, Mrs. Hanaford's bump of veneration was simply enormous. It was diffused all over the top of her head, and by careful triangulation, its extreme height was proved greater than that of any living male."[185]

Out-of-state papers carried the story of her dismissal. *The Leader* added their comment, "From the account in *The New York Sun*, it seems that no one objected to her because of her lack of ability, or because they did not like her as a preacher, but the request was made because a majority desired a man for their minister...."

From *The Providence Journal* (n.d.),

Woman vs. Woman...The woman question is destined to a vigorous agitation; there are equities connected with it which cannot be ignored; there are also certain considerations which are ignorantly or willfully kept out of sight....The action against Mrs. Hanaford violates a principle upon which "woman's rights women" ought certainly to be agreed...that everybody is entitled to so effect that which by nature and education they are well qualified to do. The only objection to Mrs. Hanaford is

---

185   March 22, 1877, p. 4

that she is a woman, and the objection is only made by women.[186]

Rev. Hanaford prepared yet another farewell sermon.

On the last Sunday of March, in fulfillment of her contract, Rev. Hanaford faced the congregation of the Church of the Good Shepherd. She began as she always did,

And the peace of the God, which surpasseth all understanding, keep your hearts and minds through Christ Jesus. The circumstances under which we meet tonight may not justify us in accepting these words as exactly descriptive of the situation, but that does not prevent one who loves the souls of men and women among whom she has labored, who has rejoiced in their joys, and grieved in their sorrows to speak to saint and sinner, to friend or foe, to those who are of one faith and those who have not yet come into its nameless light, concerning the peace which is the dear heritage of every child of God.

After referring to differences in the early church, Rev. Hanaford continued.

From that day to this there have been differences of opinions in the various churches in each branch of Zion, and these have always been the subject of strife. A peaceful separation has always been better than a continual quarrel. And no peace is in store for any of us except through victory over evil, which is not to be obtained by any sacrifice of principle....Time is a great healer, and nothing more than disagreements of opinion.

186   Nantucket Historical Association

With all my heart I shall hope for a day to come in the sunnier future, when we all who have worshiped here together, shall see eye to eye, and sympathize heart with heart. Though accused of preaching Christ too much, I trust strength will be given me to preach Christ as long as I live, and when I die, wherever I may be, I would give that precious name last upon my lips, the name which speaks of the compassion of our Father and the boundless love of God.

How could I be true to my duty as a minister of Christ's gospel and not preach of his mission and works?

The Evening Journal carried this Letter to the Editor on March 27.

Preaching Christ

Hoping to correct an erroneous impression which may have been made in the minds of those who listened to a remark made in a sermon recently preached by Rev. Phebe A. Hanaford, at the Church of the Good Shepherd, which remark was repeated substantially to the very large audience assembled last evening to hear her closing sermon at the church, to the effect that complaints had been made "that she preached Christ too much," thereby conveying the thought that that was one of the causes of the recent division, I feel called upon, as an officer of the Universalist General Convention and as moderator of the First Jersey City parish, to say that no minister can obtain or hold the fellowship of denomination, who fails to preach Christ as the "Son of God and the Saviour of the World," and no person can be eligible as a candidate for the pastorate, who does not have, and continue to hold the fellowship of the general convention, and the very brief but comprehensive "Confession of faith" spread in full view of every worshipper there, must serve as a constant reminder that they will hear, again and again that "There is none other name under heaven, given among men, whereby we must be saved," but the name of Jesus. When New Jersey State Convention will claim and take possession of the church property as its own; there is no immediate fear of a change in the title. The pulpit will continue to be supplied each Sabbath by able Christian Universalist preachers of the great truth through the mediatorial reign of Christ, and in due time a pastor will be chosen. In the faith, and under the sign of the cross, we humbly hope to conquer.

David L. Holden, 19 Clifton place
March 26, 1877

Rev. Hanaford's letter to the "Editor of *The Evening Journal*" appeared Thursday, March, 27.

Permit me to say, in response to the article under the head of "Preaching Christ" published last evening, that the complaint in regard to preaching Christ too much, which I have mentioned publicly, was made to me through a trustee, not as his own complaint, but as the complaint of one who is a member of the first parish, and it has also been made to me, personally, by others connected with the parish. No member of the church has made such complaint, and we true Universalists will do so, for, as Mr. Holden truly says, "no minister can obtain or hold the fellowship of our denomination who fails to preach Christ as the Son of God and the Savior of the world."

Phebe went on to name the preachers who preached the Universalist belief in Christ from this pulpit. Also as an officer of the New Jersey State Convention and a member ex officio of the Universalist General Convention, like Bro. Holden, she wished to correct any such impression that Universalists do not believe in Christ. She concluded,

> *The Second Universalist Church, as well as the First, cherishes the faith of the cross, and its motto is also Thanks be to God which giveth us the victory through our Lord Jesus Christ!*

> *Phebe A. Hanaford 770 Grand St.*
> *March 26, 1877*

SECOND UNIVERSALIST CHURCH

On Friday evening parishioners gathered at the Church of the Good Shepherd where the members of the Second Universalist Church appeared in a group as required by the rules of the Universalist Convention. Sixty parishioners asked for and received Letters of Dismissal from the Universalist Society of the Church of the Good Shepherd. Rev. Hanaford thus met the requirements for the legal separation from the Church of the Good Shepherd. In the home of Mr. Egar on Saturday evening, the Messrs. Munson, Hendrickson, Crary and Shaffer assumed their office as deacons. Miss Miles accepted the appointment of Superintendent of the Sabbath school. *The Argus* church calendar for April listed the Second Universalist Church for the first time.

SECOND UNIVERSALIST CHURCH,
Library Hall, Jersey City Heights,
Rev. Phebe A. Hanaford, PASTOR.
Services Sunday at 10:30 a.m. and 7:30 p.m.
Morning sermon, The Glad Disciple, John XX.
Confirmation of children and communion after sermon.
Sunday school at noon.
Easter Sunday school concert in the evening.
All are invited. Seats free.

The Argus reported the first service of the Second Universalist Church on Easter Sunday morning in the Council Chambers now beautifully decorated with flowers. Rev. Hanaford read from a paper, "They as a body did not separate from the Church of the Good Shepherd from any resentment, but to maintain principle." Asking those with Letters of Dismissal from the Church of the Good Shepherd to stand, Rev. Hanaford pronounced "the Second Universalist Church of Jersey City organized according to the rules of the Universalist State Convention and the General Convention."

The legalities completed, the choir sang with Professor Wagner at the organ. Rev. Hanaford delivered her Easter message. Five candidates then received confirmation and a communion service concluded the first ceremony. Sixty-four children remained for Sabbath school. Rev. Hanaford postponed requests for admission to the new church, pointing out that this day was for the children. In the evening church members and local residents packed the hall for a concert. A collection taken up for the Sabbath school yielded $28.32. *The Evening Journal* described the events under the heading "The Enterprise

Launched." Rev. Hanaford distributed her hand written cards identifying herself as the Pastor of the Second Universalist Church, Jersey City, New Jersey.

A scrapbook in the Hanaford Collection[187] contains an article entitled "The Rival Universalists." From it the reader gains a view outside Library Hall where "handsomely dressed ushers were stationed at the doors of each to beckon passersby. The one from the new church took his position on the sidewalk and announced this is the church where the lady preaches." Phebe, not wanting to create an atmosphere of competition, may not have felt responsible for this conduct. However the positioning of her new church did just that. Unflinching in her appearance, privately she struggled to find the best course to take for the survival of Universalism in a state where it was not well rooted.

Believing Universalism represented the working class, Rev. Hanaford addressed the social evils of the day and the resulting poverty of many working people. In her sermon, "The Common People," Rev. Hanaford asked, "Who were the common people of that day and land?" She answered, "The people who heard Him with delight." Phebe described them as the strength and glory of that land who remain undistinguished by worldly standards. She believed the greater portion of those who listened gladly to Jesus were the ones He spent His time with; and, in turn, He gave them recognition they had never known. From the remainder of this published sermon we learn of the value Phebe placed on work; her intellectual work and the work of others.[188]

---

187   Ibid
188   Hanaford Family Archives

From her childhood she understood the value of physical labor and, while not placing a higher value on one over the other, this did not deny her preference for the intellectual and artistic. Phebe identified with people interested in poetry and culture. In Beverly she fed her mind with the interests of the Essex Society and she found like-minded women among the Reading Readers. In New Haven she attended classes at Yale and began a Social Readers meeting in the parish. Phebe welcomed intellectual stimulation wherever she found it. In Jersey City she found it in Mrs. Erminnie Smith's Aesthetic Society.

Mrs. Erminnie Smith's home at 203 Pacific Avenue contained an impressive collection of precious stones. Mrs. Smith had a long interest in geology and had studied crystallography in Freiberg when her sons were studying in Germany. A graduate from the Emma Willard Academy for Girls in Troy, New York, she grew up in Marcellus, New York, where she had Iroquois Indians as her neighbors and was conversant in their language. Phebe and Erminnie's meeting marked the beginning of a wonderful friendship bound by shared interests. She invited Erminnie Smith to join Sorosis. Ellen and Phebe joined the Daughters of Aesthetics monthly meetings where members presented papers on a variety of subjects. Phebe soon learned that Mr. Smith was the president of the Daughters of Aesthetics.

In the summer months Rev. Hanaford anticipated the confirmation of the Second Universalist Church as a church in good standing at the New Jersey State Universalist Convention scheduled for September, 1877. She had followed all the regular proceedings for the formation of the Second Universalist Church. Early into the Convention the issue of the Second Universalist Church in Jersey City came up for a vote. Headed by Deacon Holden, the secret ballot declared Mrs. Hanaford's church schismatic. This vote voided Rev. Hanaford's credentials for the various committees in the Universalist Society. Phebe believed someone had tampered with the ballots cast for her membership in the State Convention but did not believe anyone could prove it.

The *Christian Register* of Boston, an organ of the Universalist Church, quoted the *Orange Journal* in their September 29, 1877 issue.

We learn from the Orange Journal that Rev. Phebe A. Hanaford, though by previous appointment Secretary and preacher of the New Jersey State Convention of Universalists held this week in Newark, did not succeed in getting her new church admitted to fellowship. The church is objected to on the ground that it was organized in a schismatic spirit on territory previously occupied.

Rev. Phebe Hanaford as pastor of the Second Universalist Church wrote to the *Orange Journal* from Jersey City on September. 29, 1877 regretting the misinformation regarding her church, and asking to be permitted to deny that her church was organized, as the *Orange Journal* said, "in a schismatic spirit on territory previously occupied." Both articles appeared in the *Argus* on October 10, 1877 under the heading "Mrs. Hanaford's Church Not Schismatic." In part Phebe wrote,

A minority of the First Church preferred a man minister. The majority desired me to continue my work. D. L. Holden, moderator of the parish meeting where the question was decided advised those who still desired Mrs. Hanaford to preach for them to "withdraw quietly, form another parish and God speed." Those were his words...

As regards the location, Phebe understood the proximity of Library Hall to the Church of the Good Shepherd added to the appearance of a schism.

We remain on ground we have a right to occupy as it has always been ours from the first. She spoke of the ninety-seven families, one hundred and thirty-five Sunday school members, and fifty-five Church members. *Since Easter day, when we commenced, our Sunday school alone has raised nearly $500. We can afford to wait till our claim to live is acknowledged by all; for we have the sympathy of this community with us, and we are on the side of right.*
> *Respectfully,*
> *Phebe A. Hanaford*
> *Jersey City, N.J. September 29, 1877*

The decision regarding the admission of her church to the New Jersey State Convention was postponed for a year by the votes of the nine delegates, three of whom came from the First Universalist Church, "to plague us, as one of those against us said." Oliver Johnson, editor of the *Orange Journal*, made the following correction: "The *Orange Journal* did not say that Mrs. Hanaford's church, in Jersey City was formed in schismatic spirit. It said only that this was alleged to be the fact by her opponents of whom we are not one."

On learning their church had been declared schismatic and denied admission to the Convention, some returned to the Church of the Good Shepherd. Of the surviving correspondence of this period, we have only one.

Montrose, New York.

October 1, 1877

My dear sister; my much abused and persecuted friend, I have just this moment finished the reading of Br. Gunneson's report of the New Jersey State Convention. And I must say that I am filled with indignation, that a man professing sincere love for the cause and occupying such a prominent position as he does should so far allow his prejudices to control him as to wrong any one. I feel that you are grossly insulted and your band of faithful workers. Since neither would be permitted in council to make a report and thus present it to the world in the Minutes of the Convention, I want you without delay to give in *The Leader* the exact figures in reference to the families, church members, Sabbath School, the addition that has been made to your numbers, and thus show the glaring falsehood of the "net loss" in Jersey City. You owe it as a duty to yourself and to your church. Br. Lee will give you space, for I have just written to him a sharp rebuke for his manifest unfairness to you and the church of your charge, and forewarning him that if he persists longer in his course and does not do full and impartial justice, all who are now the patrons of *The Leader* in your parish will withdraw, and patronize *The Star* or *The Banner*.

Tomorrow I hope to be able to send to *The Leader* an article entitled "the door of mercy shut" in which I make reference to the action of the late Convention, I hope it will do some good...

Arrin Roberts

If Phebe received letters from friends such as Mary Livermore and Julia Ward Howe, they have not survived. From a letter dated January 15, 1881 to Rev. Olympia Brown, her mentor, we see that she did not step forward in Phebe's defense when her church was labeled schismatic. Phebe's letter, written years after the event, gives insight into the sense of isolation she felt during the trials of Jersey City.

Dear Olympia,

I never knew why we were separated; I have no bitterness for you.... I have grieved more than you know. It is a solemn fact...that there was a majority of the church, the parish and the Sunday school came with me (or rather I went with them, for they formed the Second church when I was out of town, and called me.) That majority had in it men who had sup-ported the cause here ever since it was started by Pullman and Holden, and yet did not vote for me because their names were not in the parish roll, and they were not allowed to place it there after it was known they would vote for me. Members of the church did not have a vote in the parish. And strange as it may seem — I am told by men and women there were 87 votes cast that night several times for various matters, and although four went out at the last vote 87 votes were still cast. Mr. Bostwick, one of my friends, was one of the tellers, and he called the attention of the chairman Holden to the fact that three votes were rolled together, though each voter advanced and put one vote in the box — or pretended to do so. Yet the chairman said "count them." These were all "no" i.e. against me, and were probably put in by some ballot-box stuffer who thought they would not be noticed. Over in Holden's bank the Pullman brothers were heard talking about the fact that my time was nearly up, and R. H. could take it. A woman had brought it up to a point where it was worthwhile for man to take it! The whole proceedings were disgraceful. Nine of Holden's imme- diate relatives were voters against me; one being a member of Dr. Booth's Presbyterian Church in New York City—yet her name was signed by her uncle to our parish roll, so that she could vote. A kind of rascally perjury!

They made a false issue saying—as Holden said to me—that if Miss Miles would go away I should have a unanimous vote, but I told him I should take no parish which I must get by dealing unjustly with anybody. Then she wrote them a note and said she would go, and they did not accept her word, showing that the is- sue was false. It was the <u>woman</u> question all the way through.

I warned Holden and told him if he would only secure a vote by which the majority could be satisfied, I would go away of my own accord, at the end of the year, and leave them a united parish—but that if he persisted in not calling another meeting there would surely be a division and hence a weakening of the 1st Church, and perhaps death to the Universalist cause in the place. I stayed to save the majority of our denomination. And I did it.

Regarding the State Convention of 1877, Phebe continued.

I believe Edwards, the man who wrote the statistics to be unprincipled, and he altered the figures. If the truth was known and the facts presented it would be seen to be great on our side in every way.

Some of our families have moved away. Some have died. Some had to make changes. But still we have our church pretty well attended. We live Universalism here and so I stay. I don't leave because I love my people.

PAH[189]

Guest preachers at the Church of the Good Shepherd included J. C. Vail and Henry A. Westall. Rev. J. Hartzell served from November 18, 1877 to April 1, 1878. In The *History of Essex and Hudson Counties,* it is reported, "There is no permanent pastor until Rev. O. L. Ashenfetter serves from September 1, 1879 to May 1, 1882 at which time the Rev. I. P. Coddington was installed and remains to the present day."[190]

The continued parting of the Universalist churchgoers into the Church of the Good Shepherd and Library Hall represented the larger division within the Universalist Society regarding the role of women in the ministry. The future of her church remained in the hands of others. With a regular salary of $1500 and the success of *Women of the Century* and other publications, Phebe and Ellen enjoyed a degree of financial security and the privacy of their home at 770 Grand Street.

In her private life Phebe sensed her son's loss of faith in the teachings of universal salvation. Rev. Howard Hanaford wrote from the Boston Grocery and Tea House in Cambridgeport, Massachusetts on November 12, 1877.

Dear Mother,

I came to Boston last Friday. I was obliged in the prosecution of my plans to visit Rev. Mr. Wilcox of Reading. When I promised not to go to Reading, I meant to

---

189   Schlesinger Library
190   Shaw

his house <u>to see him</u>. I did <u>not</u> see him or _____on Saturday but went quickly to Mr. W.'s near the station and remained with him from first to last. I was requested by him to join his Church after he was informed that I wished to unite with some evangelical church. As no better way appeared I gladly consented. I was examined by the Committee of the Bethesda Church and <u>approved</u> as a <u>member</u> yesterday morning. I preached in the <u>Bethesda Church</u> to a very large and deeply attentive auditory.

The injunction on him not to visit his father reveals a different Phebe Hanaford than heretofore portrayed; the cause remains a mystery. His compliance to his mother's demand indicates the influence Phebe maintained over her grown son. Howard wrote that he preached in the Bethesda Church to a large audience where "Father was there alone. We both observed your wishes as far as possible." From this letter we learn something of Howard's search for truth.

Mrs. W. Barrows and many others spoke with me and I never was so inexpressibly happy as yesterday. If my joy is your pain, please remember that for many months my heart has <u>ached</u> in view of the sorrow which might visit kind hearts because of my necessitated action. I have longed to join the people of God with whom I am now in fellowship for several years. I wrote Prof. L. two years ago that were it not for one doctrine (endless punishment), I should join the Cong. surely. M, you must with many others have noted my tendencies. Ray Polinus poems! What Unitarian would want that book! I have been always at heart a Bushnell Trinitarian since I was at Antioch. I am satisfied that universalism is not taught anywhere on the sacred page. I therefore cannot conscientiously teach it. I can say no minister, layman or <u>relative</u> has had the smallest part in influencing this change in me. When last April I became fully convinced that I could no longer work in connection with the Univ. ch. I wrote Rev. Mr. C. of Wellfleet. In August last I wrote Dr. Hanaford on the same subject and still later Mr. Northrok of Schenectady. They kept my secret so closely that few if any in L. Falls knew when I left that town what my plans were. For Mary's sake and to avoid unnecessary collision with those of opposite convictions I kept still until such time as I could pay all my debts and leave honorably. I believe I pursued a kind and prudent course.

Ellen Miles would understand, as no one else could, the pain Howard's decision caused her friend. Ellen never showed any great affection for Howard. She appreciated him only for the happiness he brought to Phebe. Sensitive to each other's joys and sorrows, Ellen understood his words, "I have always been a Bushnell Trinitarian" to be a personal betrayal of Phebe. Howard's reference to his wife, Mary, shows her surrender to her husband's choice in religious matters.

Mary knew nothing of the matter when you visited us. A feeling that she did not sympathise with me <u>could not</u> and would not alter my choice. Together with that my unhappy and most painful position caused me to be unusually irritable and sensitive. I thank God we are <u>one</u> now. She never was a Universalist, she says, and saw many things to distress her among them, though with me she dearly loved the people for their goodness to her. As for that debt to the Convention it will be provided for specially. And now, may God help you to be charitable and to believe that under the circumstances I am your loving son.[191]

Phebe honored Howard's request for charity when he separated from his Universalist Society. She understood that Howard's position as pastor of a Universalist Church added to his difficulties in following his conscience. She gave her charity as a mother and as one once trapped in a conflict of faith. Since her years on Nantucket as a Baptist, Phebe lived by the philosophy of Judge Storz, "Consistency of character and consistency of opinion are not necessarily identical. Never to change an opinion would be remarkable, nay unworthy in a wise man, as never to be stable in any opinion." Phebe recognized the charity he requested sprung from the spirit of Universal salvation that he no longer preached. Howard's decision had further ramifications.

Little Falls November 11

Dear Mrs. Hanaford,

In my trouble I must cry out to someone who can appreciate my feelings as well as you. I am so disappointed in my estimate of one so dear to you & to us all. We have just received a letter from our former Pastor telling us indefeasibly of something which he thinks we have already heard of, which we have not since his departure. There were stories afloat that he was about to, or had already changed his faith, but we could not for one moment entertain the thought that we had another Hibbard amongst us. God forbid that it should be so for we as a society have had trouble enough, do write to tell us what he means, we feel we ought not to add one pang to your dear Mother heart & if we have <u>forgive us</u>, remember next to a son we loved him & his.

He says in his letter he must follow his Savior now that is <u>best</u> if you will forgive the word, for who pray do we follow as best we <u>can</u> but our Savior. I fear he has followed Howe & Aekler of Little Falls too much. We can see many things now which we in our charity & love <u>would</u> not see before that convinces us his heart has been wandering for some time if not even since he came amongst us, but by & by he reconciled, we sincerely hope he may find as good friends in his new field of labor as he has left behind. If you could see the bitter tears I have shed over his letter you would certainly think he was dead & indeed he is dead to us. Now if you can write us a word of comfort do & if you can say this is all imagination do.

We heard Mr. Pernber of Mass. last Sabbath & engaged him, he commences his labors with us the first Sunday in Dec. remember me to our dear Miss Miles & except (sic) the love of your friend.

S.C. Benedict[192]

During the winter months of 1878 Phebe received sympathetic letters from Universalist friends who had learned of Howard's decision to seek an evangelical ministry. News of Rev. Olympia Brown came only from friends and that

---

192   Ibid

included news regarding her move to Wisconsin. Rev. Brown assumed the pastorate of the Universalist Church in Racine, and Dr. Anna Shaw became pastor of the Universalist Society in Hingham.

Phebe received a letter from Mary Hanaford written on March 28, 1878 from North Square Mariner's House in Boston where she lived with the children "until H. gets a settlement." From her letter we see a wife following her husband's guidance and, in doing so, trying to be happy.

> We are trying to be happy and contented. We have good friends trying to help Howard but the prospects of a settlement look rather dark just now for there is a perfect stagnation in the Minister market just now. I am sorry that you and Nellie are suffering so much lately. Wish you both were as healthy as I am but I fear you never will be in Jersey City. I am superstitious about its atmosphere. I am glad that Nellie is better both for her own dear sake and yours for I can imagine how heavily the care presses on you when she is ill.[193]

Nothing in Mary's letter assured Phebe that Howard had found the recognition and friendship he had known amongst his Universalist parishioners in Little Falls. A closer look at Howard's activities comes from *The Reading Chronicle,* Sunday April 13, 1878.

> Rev. Howard A. Hanaford supplied the pulpit of the Bethesda church last Sunday. In the evening, he gave some account of his experience in the Universalist ministry, and his reasons for leaving that denomina-

193   Hanaford Family Archives

tion. Inasmuch as Mr. Hanaford spent his boyhood days in this town, considerable interest was taken in his sermon, and the church was filled. Previous to entering the Universalist ministry, he studied the writings of all the leading liberal preachers and visitors. He thoroughly believed in the doctrine of universal salvation. At the commencement of his first pastorate, one of the first troubles he experienced was the lack of spiritual life evident in his church. His experience showed that as long as you let men indulge in the hope of final salvation, it is almost impossible to move them, even if your discourses are very pointed and earnest. If he preached that in addition to the punishment they received in this life as they went along, the wicked would be punished for a longer or shorter period in the life hereafter, they did not like it. From his experience in the Universalist denomination he thought they expected of their preachers, either the holding up the Orthodox religion to scorn and ridicule, or a discourse on the beauties and ultimate triumph of Universalism. A preacher might also indulge in a discourse on the beauties of nature, or the wonderful love of God. He found preaching a limited duration of punishment hereafter distasteful, even to his congregation in Central New York, where Restorationist views are more generally held, than in the rural districts of Massachusetts. He became very much discouraged. Owing to the lack of religious life in the church, and the lack of power in his preaching to affect the people's characters and lives, he was finally led into a thorough examination of the teachings of the Bible and Orthodox religion. The result of his examination was that last November he left the Universalist denomination. He now believes in the leading doctrine of Evangelical religion, including everlasting punishment. In closing, he urged his hearers to give Liberalism a wide berth. He could speak from experience that it was dangerous having anything to do with it. "Avoid it, pass not by it, turn from it and pass away." His discourse although one hour long, was listened to, with great interest to the close. Every denomination in Town was represented in the audience.

To advise an audience of every denomination in the town where his mother had first walked into the light "to give Liberalism a wide berth" condemned the faith that had made her a renowned preacher. When asked for, she had honored her son's request for charity. Added to this affront was Joseph Hanaford's consolation when he learned of his son's restored faith.

Outside her family concerns, Phebe learned from friends of the trouble Pastor Rev. Ames had encountered because of his views against gambling and tobacco in New Haven. The rich and influential members of the Universalist Church of the Messiah including Mayor Shelton and Paschal Converse resented Rev. Ames' continued reference to the workingmen whom he believed they exploited. The current disharmony came from the same people who had objected to her as pastor and had led to her resignation five years earlier. The dissension eventually led to the formation of a Second Universalist Church on the corner of Davenport and Ward, echoing Phebe's earlier recommendation to them "to separate in peace rather than remain together in disharmony."

Harmony within Sorosis was expressed in May when Phebe received only one vote in her second run for president in 1878. The members reelected Jane Croly as president and Phebe Hanaford as 1st vice-president. Returning from the Sorosis meeting on her forty-ninth birthday, Phebe found her house decorated with flowers and adorned with friends. Mrs. Soule presented the gift from the parishioners, a statue by Randolph Rogers, part of his group of statues entitled "The Fugitive Story." The gift reflected how well her friends understood her love of art, her memory of the Civil War and why the war was fought. Phebe introduced Mrs. Caroline Soule to her friends as the Editor of the Universalist paper the *Guiding Star*. Mrs. Soule spoke of her plans to go to Scotland as an evangelist to preach the doctrine of Universal salvation. Speaking with her, Phebe shared her respect for those who traveled abroad as disciples of the truth and invited her to preach the morning service on Sunday.

During the summer months Rev. Hanaford prepared for the 1878 Universalist Church State Convention in Hightstown to be held in September. She intended to defend the right of a woman to preach and of a church to employ her. She would maintain her position as pastor of the regularly organized Second Universalist Church in Jersey City. With Ellen Miles at her side, she left for Hightstown.

With no surviving archives of the Convention, we rely on the press for information. *The Argus,* long a fair reporter of Rev. Hanaford, reported the following on September 20, 1878.

Rev. Mrs. Hanaford Admitted to Fellowship
... she is opposed to the Use of Tobacco

The New Jersey State Convention of Universalists met in Hightstown Tuesday and continued in session until yesterday…. The question of the admission of the Second Universalist Church of Jersey City, of which the Rev. Mrs. Hanaford is pastor, was introduced by Dr. J. E. Forrester, who, after stating that he had opposed its admission last year, said he now believed that according to the usage of the denomination, the Society should be recognized. A motion to that effect was adopted without discussion by the convention with only two negative votes. Mr. Bostwick, Miss Ellen Miles and Mrs. Miles were admitted as delegates Wednesday morning. Mrs. Hanaford introduced a resolution opposing the ordination of young men who used tobacco. After a discussion during which it was suggested that a proper preliminary step would be the expulsion of the leading clergymen who need the weed, the resolution was adopted in a modified form. The new Church in Trenton and Revs. J. Hartzell, Wm. Taylor, F. Hitchcock and J. Billings were admitted to fellowship.[194]

The Evening Journal on the same day informed its readers that the two dissenting votes came from the First Universalist Church on the Heights.

Phebe Hanaford's major contribution to the Woman's Rights Movement was her remarkable ingenuity in integrating her ministry as an essential part of her work for women. The time had come to cast "the mantle of oblivion" on the men who had tried and failed to deny Rev. Hanaford her rightful place in the ministry. Her success in confronting "the woman issue" in the church established a precedent for future women ministers.

....

194   Second edition

In June 1879 Mrs. Hull, a member of Sorosis, was murdered. *The New York Times* had this to say on July first regarding Rev. Phebe Hanaford's Sunday sermon.

...Her discourse was a delicious specimen of feminine logic. She informed her hearers that she had often felt that the press of this country should be placed under official supervision, as in France. This theory she had discarded on learning that it was a newspaper reporter who had discovered the murderer of her friend and she now favors the utmost freedom of the press. Then it appeared that she had always been opposed on the principle to capital punishment, but the Rev. lady is now convinced of her error, and is sure that the best thing to do with burglars and murderers is to hang them. It is time, said Mrs. Hanaford, for sickly sentimentality and maudlin sympathy for criminals to cease. Her change of opinion seems to be thorough, for in her judgment the brokers of Wall-street would do better to reward the Boston reporter than to subscribe for the benefit of the criminals in the Smith-Bennett case. All of which most charmingly illustrates the truth of the old saying, that it makes all the difference whose ox is gored. Many people have had their friends murdered before Mrs. Hull was killed: but Mrs. Hanaford failed to see in this a reason why murderers should be hanged; and the public press has done some service to society before the Boston reporter recognized the Negro Cox, but she could remain convinced that it ought to be subjected to official supervision. It is a fearful thing to reflect that if the unfortunate Mrs. Hull had been a stranger to the Rev. Mrs. Phoebe (sic) Hanaford, that lady would be still firm in her convictions as to what society ought to do with murderers and the press.

The argument presented here shows *The New York Times* covered Phebe Hanaford. As a Quaker, Phebe had always opposed capital punishment. In 1871 when a convicted murderer was hanged, Rev. Hanaford delivered a sermon in which "she flayed the state and called the execution judicial murder." The *Universalist* criticized the use of her language regarding capital punishment in their November issue, but according to Miller, "...she replied by refusing to modify her position in any way."[195]

In family matters as well, Phebe on occasion refused to change her position. The following letter written by Howard's wife, Mary, illustrates one such instance. In 1879 Howard received a new position as pastor of the Methodist Church on Nantucket. Omitting her effusive language regarding the children, we read Mary's letter written from Nantucket.

March 25, 1879

Dear Mother H.,

I did not see or know of the letter which H. wrote you to which you replied last week, but I am very sorry if he wrote anything which grieved you. I certainly feel only the kindliest friendship for Nellie and gratitude for her many acts of kindness to me & mine and she will always I hope be a welcome guest in our home. I shall always think that it was unfortunate that anyone but yourself should have written to H. in that critical and unhappy time, knowing his unreasonableness in writing and since

---

195   1985, p. 567

it was properly a matter only of interest between you and himself.

Mary is correct in stating that Howard had a right to expect his mother to consider his predicament a private matter between them. She seems to imply that Howard was upset that Ellen Miles had written to him during the time of his conversion, and that this prompted him to write a letter to his mother about Ellen. Ellen's history of interfering with Phebe's relations with both Florence and Howard, and her lack of feelings for Howard, were indeed a source of friction for the family. This combined with the offensive manner Ellen Miles had come to employ in her defense of Phebe had become an intrusion into the family relationships.

Ellen's interference in family matters had begun when she first arrived in their home in Reading over a decade earlier. Mary's affection for Ellen may have blinded her to Ellen's coldness toward Howard, and she "accepted or let fall all that came from Nellie knowing that her motives were those of kindness both to yourself and H." Deep feelings surfaced in Mary's discussion of Phebe and Ellen's possible visit to their home, as she continues in her letter.

He only fears that something might be said to hurt his feelings and cause him to retort, but I know you are both wise and we'd respect his feelings…. I still hope you will both come and should feel much disappointed if I did not hope to see you. I thought that perhaps Mrs. Starbuck and the S'conset people might demand more of your time than I should be happy in giving but if Nellie would come and stop chiefly with me, I could be very happy. Can't she arrange to visit her family before or after your visit here so as to be here all the time that you are?" Now Mother can't you see as I do why H. opposes my desires concerning Nellie and tries to make himself believe that he dislikes her. I don't sympathize with him and he not with me. I don't know what to do to make everything pleasant, so I have confided in you, and ask you to advise me impartially.

Writing in defense of her husband's treatment of Ellen Miles, Mary also justifies her regard for Dr. Hanaford.

There is a reason why H. has seemed so ungracious both to you & me in this matter of Nellie visiting. You are aware also of many reasons why we should both be grateful to his father for I have rec'd only the kindest & most respectful treatment from him when I have occasionally seen him, but feeling a strong love & deep sympathy for yourself and wishing first of all to respect your feelings since I knew that H. often needlessly sounded them, I have always met & received H.'s father's kindness with so little politeness & friendship that I know he must look upon me as being very ungrateful & uncivil. While H. was in N. on trial & Lennie was so sick in Cambridge, I was almost wild with anxiety and knew not what to do, for the lady of the house told me of the exorbitant prices of good physicians and convinced me that just when I could not afford to employ one unless his case was critical, and so almost in despair I wrote to H's father asking him to come in and advise me. It was humiliating to me to have to do it after my mean treatment of him, but he came immediately and was very kind and greatly relieved my mind.

...I love you devotedly and will not if I can help it do anything to grieve you if you cannot feel happy in H's & myself sending an invitation to his F. to come <u>alone</u> and make us a quiet visit it <u>shall not be</u>, but if you could feel reconciled to it it would be a source of great happiness to H. and cause him to give Nellie a most cordial welcome thus helping me out of a most trying situation. I have not talked this over with H. but write you <u>privately</u> and hope you will not mention it to him, it would only cause me unhappiness but please write to me <u>privately</u>. H. will not open it if you write to me and tell me just how you feel about it.[196]

Howard has decided that as long as Phebe's injunction against his father visiting his family remained, he would maintain his injunction against Phebe's companion visiting his home. Once again Ellen Miles became the center of the storm that broke out in Phebe's life. There was one moderating force this time, however. Mary liked Ellen. Mary also liked Dr. Hanaford. This situation placed her in the role of arbitrator.

Mary's letter explains why Howard had never replied to his mother's letter in which she denies them the right to invite Dr. Hanaford to visit. As a parent Joseph kept in touch with his family and in time earned Mary's affection. Mary, nevertheless, out of respect for Phebe, kept Dr. Hanaford from visiting. Phebe and Ellen, however, accepted Mary's invitation to visit. Once on the Island, Phebe's rounds of visiting and requests to speak filled her days while Ellen "stopped mainly with

196   Hanaford Family Archives

Mary." Howard made arrangements for his mother to replace him in the pulpit, enabling him to excuse himself gracefully. The tension between mother and son remained throughout the year.

The first meeting of the Aesthetic Society held on January 3, 1880 in the Lafayette Reformed Church included the recitation of Phebe's poem "New Year Greeting." The verses refer to the aims of the Aesthetic Society, namely to "learn of Nature's works and ways." Meetings of the Aesthetic Society were recorded in their publication, *Echoes of the Aesthetic Society*. Years later one W. H. Richardson purchased a copy of their publication for 7 cents. He so admired Mrs. Hanaford's poem "New Year Greeting" that he wrote to *The Jersey Journal*. His article appeared on August 24, 1917 and can be found in the Jersey City Library.

REV. PHEBE A. HANAFORD'S POEM

The position occupied in the *Echoes* by a remarkable poem by Rev. Phebe A. Hanaford gives no clue whatever to its chronological order in Aesthetic annals, but it does give us one fine thought about our Aesthetic heroine. Mrs. Hanaford was very well known to a large circle of Jersey City folk, and her attachment for Mrs. Smith, even if not confirmed by the testimony of surviving friends to-day, was amply set forth in this poem and in other current newspaper and documentary evidence.

Mrs. Hanaford's poem, printed on pages 82-85 of the *Echoes* is entitled simply "New Year Greeting" and it was intended to convey a message to the members at the dawn of 1880. It abounds in references to the aims of the society; this talented lady seemed to catch and crystallize, as her realization of its purpose, at any rate, the thought that these attempts to "learn of Natures' words and ways were,

A chalice each, with draughts from Wisdom's
fountain;
We quaff with eagerness; for they impart
The life-elixir that the spirit needeth,
The panacea for many an earthly woe,
The knowledge that, once gained, the spirit speedeth,
Still more and more of God's great work to know.

Of these few lines of her poem, Richardson wrote,

And plain, ordinary everyday life, wherever it is lived today, does not get enough of the impulse to know "still more and more of God's great work" that Mrs. Hanaford tried to tell the Aesthetic Society it needed at that memorable meeting of January 3, 1880.

I count myself very fortunate in having had access to the program for that meeting as well as to the mind of a man who was present and who set down what he thought of the people who flitted across the platform of the Lafayette Reformed Church that afternoon.

The census of 1880 calculated the population of Jersey City to be 120,728. It listed Phebe Hanaford as the head of the household at 770 Grand Street. Her occupation "minister" appeared with an asterisk. Ellen Miles was listed as a teacher and Mary Kenny as the housekeeper. For this family, the most important addition to the nation's population in 1880 was Maria Mitchell Hanaford born on Nantucket Island on July tenth. The birth announcement of Phebe's first granddaughter came in a postcard from Howard. He writes, "4:45 A.M. Saturday July 10 fine

<u>daughter and all well.</u> Mrs. Worth will write you. Am busy. Had no rest till after breakfast this morning. H"

The Massachusetts' census listed Joseph Hanaford's "wife" as Harriet, living with him in the Hanaford family home in Reading. With this information we understand the reason for Phebe's injunction against Howard inviting his father, Dr. Hanaford, to visit his family. In any case, Howard and Mary ignored Harriet, and she remained the unnamed party. On the subject of Harriet, Mary wrote,

> She could <u>never</u> enter <u>my door</u> though I know H.'s father would not think of such a thing as exhibiting her to us."
> In the same letter, Mary shows a spark of her inner feeling about Phebe's family – in this instance, Capt. George Coffin. "H's Grandfather was in town yesterday but did not come to see us. H. is quite indignant. I really don't think he has the over measuring desire to see his grandson which you imagine he has."[197]

Vacationing on Nantucket Island continued to present complications for Phebe and Ellen. Phebe found justification for her continued demand that Dr. Hanaford not be entertained in Howard's home, while Howard maintained his father's right to visit them, so long as he did not bring his companion. Howard believed his mother's demand gave him justification for his continued refusal to receive Ellen Miles in his home. His dislike of Ellen Miles predated the business of the woman now living in the family home. Phebe planned to stay with her son and see her new granddaughter, Maria, and her grandson, Lennie. To avoid ten-

---

197   Ibid

sion with Howard, Ellen went to Waltham to care for her sister, Jennie.

Correspondence during this time provides a look into the depth of their emotions. Without a date to identify how soon after she had left for Waltham, a letter comes to Phebe from Ellen in Waltham,

> My darling, I just finished you a pair of scarlet bed shoes…. It seemed to me that, I left all the world behind me when I left you in that horrid depot, and could not keep the sobs down all the way out. If it is foolish, I must be foolish. I had very little sleep last night and spent the night in trying to plan. I am feeling well. I wish you were here this minute….Tell me of your plans and send me a postal often. All my heart full of love to her I love so truly, so fondly. I am going to make some calls this week. If you feel like coming, come any day. My arms, my heart are ever open to receive you, if I do sometimes seem to close them. Your own[198]

A photo of the proud grandmother with Maria survives to show that Phebe visited Howard and Mary on Nantucket. During her time there both Howard and Phebe were invited to attend a "Meeting of the Executive Committee of the Coffin Family Reunion to observe the 200th anniversary of the death of Tristram Coffin" scheduled for the following year. On August 21, 1880 *The Inquirer and Mirror* published a report stating that the business at hand did not get underway until the second day. The secretary, Allen Coffin Esq., called the assembly to order on

---

198   Nantucket Historical Association

Tuesday morning and Judge Coffin of Peekskill was invited to preside.

The time for the Reunion was fixed for Tuesday, Wednesday and Thursday, August 15, 16 and 17, 1881; the place was to be Nantucket Island. The motion, after free discussion, was carried unanimously. The chief argument being that August, being vacation month, more of the Coffin descendants could be on the island than in October, the month in which "on the second day, two hundred years ago Tristram Coffin departed this life." The consideration of a motion to perpetuate the memory of Tristram Coffin with a bronze statue on a granite or marble pedestal was next in order. Recommendations for the memorial to be a school or a home for aged mothers of the island did not pass. The article went on,

> Rev. Phebe Hanaford, of Jersey City, favored a monument though, she had formerly agreed with Allen Coffin's expressed thought, that an educational institution of a higher grade than the Coffin School would be a good memorial; but she felt it a duty to suggest that the Coffin descendants owe as much honor to the wife of Tristram as to the worthy patriarch himself. Why should not Dionis Coffin be held in honorable memory as well as her companion? Franklin owed far more to his mother than his father, and who knew, but that the Coffin traits of energy and integrity came from Dionis rather than Tristram! At any rate, we know that together they founded the Coffin line in America. Therefore, believing that we should honor our foremothers as well as our forefathers, she moved an amendment to the motion, so as to secure a bronze statue for husband and wife, upon one pedestal, side by side.

The applause which followed these remarks showed that the right chord had been struck, and every speech thereafter was in favor of the motion as amended, which passed without a dissenting vote.

The planners of the event had economic and political ambitions that were motivating the reunion of the hordes of Coffins. They proposed a railroad line on the island. With the growth of tourism they hoped to get family members to invest in their enterprises.

During their separation Ellen wrote from her family home in Waltham that she "had the house fixed to her liking and felt very much at home, but lonely." On September 4, 1880 Ellen wrote using her pet name for Phebe.

My precious Aunt Winnie,
How I wish you were here tonight to put your dear arms around me, and love me for I am lonely. Every soul in the house is in bed, and I with my faithful little Gypsy in my lap, sit listening to the lovely tick tick of a clock. I am pretty tired, for Annie and Howard have been down the harbor today, and much of the work has come upon me, as dear Lizzie is not able to do much, though she is getting along nicely. I am glad you had a good time at the meeting. I received your letter, or postal, today, and trust that the glimmer of light which it contained may grow into full effulgence. I think some thing will come to us. I feel very much discouraged about Jennie. She is way down in the "Slough of Despond" and I cannot get her out. What a summer I have been put through! Martha and I went up to see her last night and she

entertained us until half past ten, crying, and wishing she was dead. She is no worse than she has been, but she seems determined to make sure we suffer with her. I want to get settled in some way, and I shall be glad to get back home, and plan in quiet for the future. Darling one I try so hard to look with a brave heart the future in the face. If it be separation I must accept it. But thank God, it cannot be a separation from you, though I should carry the burden of a heavy heart to my grave. Then and there I should find rest. Come when you can. You will not find me away for long…. All I want now is to lay my head beside yours on our own pillows, and in our own home. I'm so tired! Now I will go to bed. I do not sleep well for some reason or other. Please look for my Sorosis pin in Mary's cushion. Give love to her. Have you heard from Florence? Now good night, my darling, and love forever, your own Nellie[199]

Weeks wore on with no relief for Ellen's duties in Waltham. Phebe wrote and asked Ellen to meet her in Boston to attend the Association for the Advancement of Women in October. Ellen agreed and the friends had the day together. Their reunion undoubtedly ended with tears when the time came for Ellen to leave. On her return Phebe had a brief note from Florence saying Mr. Warner had taken an assignment in Tonawanda, New York. They would be moving.

In contrast to Florence's brief note, Phebe received a long letter from Mary Hanaford written on October 12 from Nantucket. It appears Howard is again looking for a new position and "he

---

199   Ibid

did not find such a demand for his talent as he had hoped." She wrote that "Lennie is improving <u>morally</u>." She wished the two "grammas" would take a flying visit before winter set in and not wait a year before seeing the darling baby. Again Mary closes with a view of Phebe's family. "I never see or hear from S'conset when you are not here. I think if anyone was dead then we might hear, so as we don't hear I assume they are all alive up to date. Please write as often as possible for your letters are always so welcome."[200]

As if in the fulfillment of Mary's mentioning a death in the Coffin family in Siasconset, Phebe wrote to *My beloved Friend* a short time later of her remaining with the family on Siasconset for eleven days when her stepmother, Emmeline Cartwright Coffin, died in November, 1880. In this undated letter Phebe mentions a difficult Christmas season at the church. She also writes of Florence living in Tonawanda where her husband, Thomas Warner, owned half the *Tonawanda Herald* and was a practical printer as well as editor. Of herself she writes,

I do not want to shirk my duties but I am weary of pastoral care. And also I often sigh for the tender grace of the days that are dead and wonder if I may not know something of them again. Heaven will surely give me all the tender grace tho' it will be in one of the other days, not one of these days.

You can never know how happy you made me last year—how delightful it was to sit once more at your table, to look once more over your books, to feel your dear arms again around me, and to receive again the kiss of a love that has been a blessing to me all these years. Separation and distance had not chilled either

heart I found, and my heart blesses you more than any words can for all you have been and are to me. In the galaxy of my choicest friends you shine as a bright particular star. And your good model husband—I was so glad to meet him again. And again that quiet ride—like olden days—with you to Reading, and join kindness in getting me the pleasure of seeing Emily & Cornelia and Anna! Now I must pause because duties press, and say "God bless you as I love you."
    Ever lovingly your friend P.A.H.[201]

On the front page of the January 31, 1881 edition, *The Evening Journal*, under the heading "SECOND UNIVERSALIST", reported excerpts from Rev. Phebe A. Hanaford's morning sermon on "Predestination to Holiness" and her evening discourse, "Christian's Longings for the Immortal Home," which encouraged the faithful to "cherish them for his encouragement, but not permit the longings to hinder him from performing all his duties on earth."

Now in the eighth year of her labors in Jersey City and her fifth at the Second Universalist Church, Rev. Hanford performed her duties in the face of the strained atmosphere between the two Universalist Societies. The trustees of the Second Universalist Society had failed to raise funds for a church as originally planned. Rev. Hanaford and Ellen Miles lived on the salary received for their services, a sum that may have been reduced due to the financial circumstances in the church. Reduced finances may have led Phebe to write her second biographical dictionary, *Daughters of America*, "to honor women of the second century."

---

201   Nantucket Historical Association

The centenary observance of Tristram Coffin's death brought descendants of Dionis and Tristram from around the country to the docks of Massachusetts seeking passage to Nantucket Island. In August 1881 they filled every hotel, and private homes received the Nantucketers in a great spirit of friendship. The Town welcomed them with a clambake the first day. The second day of celebrations passed with literary exercises and the laying of the cornerstone for the monument. People congratulated Mrs. Hanaford on her idea for the monument to honor Dionis and Tristram. In an atmosphere of relaxation relatives found one another, some folks traveled out to S'conset and Sachacha, and others walked to Brant Point. In the evening of the third day a grand reception with music and dancing also provided time to make plans for the future.

The newly founded Historical and Genealogical Committee included George Howland Folger, John Coffin Brown, Alexander Starbuck and Phebe Hanaford. They met in Boston on September 5, 1881 with the election of George H. Folger as chairman and Phebe A. Hanaford, recording secretary. On the recommendation of S. J. Coffin, Phebe agreed to write a history of the family reunion, "not to exceed forty pages in length." Phebe honored a request from Anna Gardner to write the introduction to her book *Harvest Gleaning in Prose and Verse* to be published by Fowler & Wells of New York. In her twenty-one page introduction, Phebe noted on page nineteen the historic fact that Anna Gardner had called the convention in Nantucket at which Frederick Douglass spoke in 1841.[202]

While the celebrations of the Coffin clan were proceeding, President James Abram Garfield lingered between life and

202   Amherst College Library Archives

death. President Garfield died on September nineteenth, recalling Lincoln's assassination sixteen years earlier. Rev. Hanaford held a memorial service on the day of his funeral. Phebe's *Life of Abraham Lincoln* appeared in a series of biographies entitled *Library of Distinguished Americans.* All of the United States Presidents since Lincoln had served the Union honorably during the Civil War.

Reconstruction included the desegregation of schools in New Jersey while the nation's representatives continued to deny the rights of women. The majority of men and women thought women at the polls would destroy the authority of the head of the family and that women who lectured on the cause of suffrage were destroying the foundation of society. When the woman was a minister, she appeared to be going against her vocation to preserve and protect the family as a God given value.

Ellen, relieved of her Waltham family responsibilities, returned to Jersey City. The two friends had accumulated additional names for a total of nine hundred fifty-seven women of Christian virtue ranging from the wives of presidents to philanthropists for the second biographical dictionary. Phebe included herself in seven chapter headings: Literary Women, Poets, Lecturers, Reformers, Preachers, Journalists and Historians. Phebe labored at her desk during the winter months writing and editing the biographical sketches.

A typhoid epidemic during the winter of 1881-1882 claimed the life of Erminnie's son, Simon Smith. He was buried on January 19, 1882 from his parent's home in Jersey City. Throughout the epidemic, Ellen Miles could be seen visiting the families who lived on the canal. The epidemic ended as mysteriously as it had started. News of recoveries and healthy births brought new hope to the depressed city. Phebe received news from Tonawanda.

OFFICE OF THE
Tonawanda Herald,

CHAPMAN & WARNER,
EDITORS AND PROPRIETORS.

Tonawanda, N. Y. <u>Nov 24, 1881</u>

Dear Mother Hanaford,

I telephoned you this morning of the "interesting event" which has occurred in our family. Florence bore the pains of parturition splendidly and aside from considerable but inevitable suffering from labor pains during the night—had an unexpectedly comfortable time. She is now comfortable (at 9 pm) and has received congratulations of many friends upon her condition.

The young lady who by the way, is howling lustily just now—is pronounced a pretty little baby, who might be six pounds and is an object of great interest to all—to Florence and her fond "papa," especially. Florence has sought to keep her <u>prospects</u> altogether unbeknown to you. I suspect—she has done so completely. The baby lies on her mother's arm now sputtering unintelligibly about something, and Florence talks back to her—How do you like that picture?

Good night,
Yours, Tom E. Warner[203]

The baby was named after the matriarch of the Nantucket Coffin family. "Dionis Coffin Warner, daughter of Florence Hanaford, christened by her grandmother, Rev. Phebe A.

----

203   Nantucket Historical Association

Hanaford on Easter Sunday 1882 in Jersey City at 770 Grand street, the residence of her grandmother."[204] The ceremony added another "first" to Phebe's list as a woman minister. It is not surprising she was the first grandmother among the three earliest Universalist ministers. Married in 1849 at age twenty she was a wife and mother for nineteen years before ordination. Augusta Chapin was ordained in 1863 at age twenty-seven and never married. Olympia Brown married at age thirty-six, ten years after her ordination. Unlike her peers, throughout Phebe's early years as a preacher and ordained minister, she had family responsibilities including their financial support.

Throughout her years in Jersey City, Phebe maintained contact with friends in New Haven who now offered her a position as pastor at the Church of the Holy Spirit. The situation at Library Hall appeared futile and even damaging to Universalism in the state. She had long entertained a hope of returning to New Haven, but with reservations. She wrote on July fourth to "Dear Unforgotten Friend. I shall never live there again, and I should not care to, unless I could be so engaged as to be more independent of a society than before." Regarding Ellen Miles, she assured her friend there was no need for Mrs. Hawkins to "demure" since "Nellie would not interfere with the S. S." The "S. S" meant the Sabbath School where Ellen had always reigned supreme.

Unable to finish the letter due to the heat, Phebe picked up her pen two weeks later to write to her unforgotten friend. In it she acknowledged her friend's current position as Superintendent of the Sabbath school "where you are doing so much good there and you seem to do it without running afoul of anybody."

---

204   1882 Coffin Genealogy

Phebe read from her diary that it seemed to be a question of who should speak to the other first. She closes her letter with news of her granddaughter. "Florence's baby is a new darling for me, and she and Nellie seemed to become reconciled over the sweet child, which was a joy to me." Phebe's unforgotten friend seems to know of earlier trouble between Ellen and Florence. Ellen had been a divisive figure, however well meaning she had been.

The only evidence of Phebe's visit to Tonawanda after Dionis' christening is a poem presented at a Sorosis meeting on March, 5 1883. Their dignified vice-president unabashedly read her poem entitled "My Apology" to an amused audience of friends. In several verses she described in rhyme every feature of her granddaughter's charm. She called Dionis her "Queen." Phebe wrote in the last stanza,

> *Forgive me, Sorosis; forgive me kind friend*
> *Whose paper has waited so long —*
> *How can I write epic or lyre or hymn*
> *"Mid the echoes of nursery song?"*
> *Oh, surely you'll chide not, but joy in my joy —*
> *Be glad in our innocent glee;*
> *Wrap the mantle of charity 'round and forgive*
> *My little granddaughter and me.*[205]

We have no record of Phebe seeing her grandchildren, Lennie and Maria Hanaford and Dionis Warner, during their younger years growing up in New York State. Although not living nearby, they were within traveling distance of their grandmother. Letters show Phebe's gifts to the grandchildren and her keen interest in their talents, particularly writing.

205   Hanaford Family Archives

Finalizing her biographical dictionary of "the many women of the first and second century whose lives were full of usefulness," Phebe wrote a "Prefatory Note."

Having decided to extend the record of noted women, this new edition is revised and improved, and its new title "Daughters of America," permitted to cover not only the names of women who were prominent in the first century of our Republic, but also many others whose birthday may be in the first, but whose labors are now making the second century glorious. The women of the first and second centuries of our nation's life will for ever be acknowledged as the shapers of its lofty destinies and marvelous triumphs in very many directions. The sowers and the reapers shall rejoice together.

P.A.H.

Jersey City, N.J. 1882

True & Company of Augusta, Maine agreed to publish *Daughters of America or Women of the Century,* in 1883. The record of sales of *Women of the Century* suggested a successful sequel. That year, eight years into their separation, Dr. Hanaford published a fourth edition of *Mother and Child,* originally published in 1878 in Reading, Massachusetts. As a writer he possessed the ability to explain medicine and nourishment in understandable language to mothers who bore the responsibility for home remedies. He wrote of his convictions on the origin and importance of the life of the unborn. The publisher appears as J. H. Hanaford.

The sale of her books brought a degree of financial security for Rev. Hanaford when such did not come from the congregation. The finances of the Second Universalist Church continued to show a deficit into 1883. Rev. Hanaford and the members of the finance committee agreed to ask for donations wherever possible. At the May meeting of Sorosis a collection gleaned $274 for which Phebe thanked the members. In responding to mail from friends in New Haven, Phebe enclosed a public letter that the finance committee had published entitled "An Earnest Appeal." In doing so she stated that due to the fact that "prominent members of the parish have died or moved from the City, the rent for the Hall is in arrears and other necessary expenses remain unpaid."

In a note to her friend Phebe identified her concerns for the membership, adding she was not sending a copy of "An Earnest Appeal" looking for donations. She wrote that she hesitated to leave the Second Universalist Church in Jersey City because those who currently attended services in Library Hall would not be likely to go elsewhere. Secondly, the children Miss Miles gathered for the Sunday school would otherwise go without Christian training. Lastly, if they left, the rooms they now occupied would pass into "the hands of those who wish to make it an attractive saloon." Her concerns reflected her passion for temperance and ministry. For Phebe, a return to New Haven offered her only hope of continuing in the ministry.

The Woman's Ministerial Conference began with Julia Ward Howe's circular letter to the Women Preachers of the Country whom she "...addressed with an earnest desire for their membership and co-operation." Regular recordings of conventions of the Women's Ministerial Conferences began in 1883. Officers for the Ministerial Conference for the year ending June 1883 include Mrs. Julia Ward Howe as president with "14 vice-presidents including Mrs. Mary Livermore, Rev. Augusta Chapin, Rev. Olympia Brown and Rev. Phebe Hanaford."

That year Phebe and Ellen's August vacation included Ellen's sister, Jennie Miles, who came along to enjoy the pleasures of Siasconset. Jennie, Ellen and Phebe waited for the River Queen to come into view, and once aboard the women relaxed. As always, Ellen fared better than Phebe in the rough waters, while Jennie enjoyed the strangeness of the fog. When they left Oak Bluffs, the fog lifted. With a view of the lighthouse on Great Point the worst of the sea voyage came to an end.

In Phebe Hanford's novel *Heart of Siasconset,* she records actual events of vacations over the years. From this novel, we learn that in 1883 her brother George stood on the wharf awaiting their arrival. Riding in his carriage Phebe learned that her father seldom left S'conset. His youngest child, Emma, remained as his companion and seldom left the island. Once they had arrived, neighbors came with baked goods. Captain George caught fish for their afternoon meal, and Phebe hunted for a spyglass that she had used all her life at the beach. Talk with friends included plans for a chapel. Natives explained how they had gone for years without a place of worship on S'conset but now that Mr. Horatio Brooks had donated the land, they would have a chapel. There would be a ceremony at 8:30 P.M.

Phebe described the ceremony.

On August 30th by the light of the moon the choir led the singing of "Nearer My God to Thee" accompanied by the small organ brought from the school. Rev. Phebe Hanaford led the group in a prayer of dedication and thanksgiving for the fulfillment thus far of the hopes of the people of S'conset for a place of worship. She also expressed gratitude for the life of the young visitor that was rescued from the sea a few days ago. Members of the assembly expressed words of gratitude. Ellen Miles placed a wreath of fresh flowers.[206]

The young visitor, Miss Garrison, rescued from the ocean after a mighty struggle referred to in the sermon then expressed "publicly her gratitude for her rescue from death: first to God, and then to Rev. Dr. Johnson who went to her rescue...."[207] Natives identified her as a stranger because she did not know the might of the sea and would have drowned except for the young teacher who could have drowned in the rescue. Phebe and her family and friends were part of the crowd on the beach that grew as people left their cottages to offer help. They carried the young girl on a makeshift stretcher to the nearest cottage where she made a full recovery.

In the third story, easily identified as autobiographical, Phebe asks her brother, Robert, to take her to Sachacha Pond, her mother's favorite place. Phebe remembered visiting it only once before and believed there might not be many opportunities to visit it again. Ellen took the seat beside Robert in his new spring wagon. Phebe and Jennie Miles sat in the back. They enjoyed a perfect summer day at Sachacha Pond where the quiet surf scarcely made a sound. Phebe knew her brother had not many hours to spare and suggested they start back mid-afternoon.

Not far down the road a young boy hopped on the back of their wagon for a ride. Suddenly the horse jumped forward and the child grabbed the back seat to save himself from falling. The seat, not fastened, went over backwards with Phebe and Jennie thrown to the ground. The horse charged forward. Ellen, the first to know what had happened, managed to get off the wagon

---

206   Hanaford, Phebe A., 1890, *Heart of Siasconset*, p. 63
207   Ibid, p. 61

and run to Phebe and Jennie. Both women lay on the ground unable to move and appeared to be unconscious for a brief period. Phebe got to her feet but her speech was incoherent. Ellen bent over Jennie to hear her say, "Ellen, I am killed."[208] With Robert's help, Ellen got her sister into the front of the wagon and she then clung to Phebe in the back. The young boy had fled.

Once home, Jennie was gotten to bed while Phebe collapsed on the lounge. Dr. Emily Jones, a visitor to S'conset, examined them and declared them to be sound of body but that the bumps on the head needed to be watched. The doctor believed they would be fine. By morning they were ready to keep to their schedule. Phebe and Ellen returned to Jersey City, and Jennie to Waltham.

With the start of the new season in September 1883, attendance at Library Hall for Sunday services showed a decline. Although no longer a schismatic church, with no plans for an alternate location for a Second Universalist Church, members believed they should return to the Church of the Good Shepherd. No one had expected they would be housed in Library Hall indefinitely. Rev. Hanford had never before failed to bring in sufficient funds to the church. New residents to Jersey City seeking Universalism joined the Church of the Good Shepherd in the early months of 1884.

Easter celebrations saw a small increase in attendance and three young adults received confirmation. The Trustees gave a nod of approval for the ceremony but remained distant from both Rev. Hanaford and Ellen Miles, seemingly forgetting whose idea it was to start a second church. With no talk of a new location for the church and the consequent decline in their membership, it appeared the best option for the Second Universalist Church was to officially dissolve. The place for

---

208   Ibid, p. 85

them to do that would be during the 1884 New Jersey State Convention. Until then Phebe would serve as their pastor.

Because her church remained opened in July, Phebe declined an invitation to attend the July meeting of the History and Genealogy Society on Nantucket Island. The highlight of Phebe and Ellen's Nantucket vacation in August was the dedication of the first chapel in Siasconset. "Bright flowers adorned the pulpit, and music was so in keeping with the high character of the rare occasion that all hearts were wafted heavenward." Rev. Hanaford describes herself as the "woman whose island birth and training gave her more opportunity than the other speakers to know the circumstances which made the erecting of a place of worship at so late a period, so entirely reasonable, though it appeared so strange unto the summer visitors." She spoke from John 4:23-24.[209]

While Nellie and Emma enjoyed the beach, Phebe worked in her room. Before noon cousins Christopher and Alexander Coffin stopped at the cottage and said they wanted to get to Polpis and asked Phebe to go with them. Thrilled at the idea of a geological excursion, she hastily packed a small bag and left Ellen Miles to get to Waltham where she was again summoned home to help with Jennie. Phebe later wrote an apology dated August 18, 1883, signed "Aunt Winnie." Within a week, Ellen's first letter arrived from Waltham. Ellen is sick with a cough and swollen legs and in need of care. Her nervous condition appears aggravated by their separation. She longs to return to her "Aunt Winnie" as she called Phebe, and together, leave Jersey City.

At the Farm
Sunday morn.

---

209   Ibid, p. 110

My loved one,

My first written word shall be to you, my darling, who comes first to my waking thoughts, and last before my eyes close to sleep. Your dear letter came last night with its assurance of your love and thought for me, always so welcome, though often so underserved.... I did not sleep until past midnight and I planned until my brain was weary. I slept alone, and got kind of nervous. How I did long for my dear Aunt Winnie to put her arms about and hear her say, "Nellie, darling."

....I do want to work at something that will pay. Then we will snap our fingers at Jersey and let them demure all they want to. I think we have both of us worked too long and faithfully to be forsaken now. We will try and hang on a bit longer, and I will try, my darling, to be more patient and encouraging. My aching nerves and body have been a great drawback. I'm going to leave my nerves here on the farm, if I can. You did not speak of Mary or little Maria in your letter. You mentioned Howard and Lennie. I do want to see you three females but I don't hanker after the male gender. They are more or less sad fish and disagreeable.... Can't you come out over a night, and we will talk over Nantucket.... Have you heard from Florence and how is our baby? Give love to Mary and dear little Maria.

A big share for my darling with kisses from her own.
Nellie.

This is the first confirmed assertion of Ellen's dislike for men; a trait never evident in Phebe.

While Phebe and Ellen endured their separation, Phebe resolved to settle their situation. Rev. Hanaford met with the trustees to force a decision on the future of the Second Universalist Church. She explained that her situation was unsatisfactory. She believed the need for an alternate parish had long passed and asked them to put their agreement with her on this matter in writing prior to the State Universalist Convention. Nonetheless, because several trustees were absent at this time, no final decision could be made. This allowed time for Phebe to get away from the trouble within the parish and she went to visit Ellen in Waltham. Her reunion with Nellie was brief and full of emotion. Whereas Phebe and Ellen chose not to burden the family with details of the trouble at their church, Jennie felt free to burden Phebe with her need for her sister Ellen to be near her. Though Ellen's family wanted Phebe to stay longer, she returned to the work of her ministry.

During the State Universalist Convention in September 1883, Rev. Hanaford agreed to remain on as pastor of the Second Universalist Church until the end of her contract on April 1, 1884. With this agreement confirmed, Phebe wrote to the women at the Second Universalist Church in New Haven of her decision to leave Jersey City at the termination of her contract and asked if the position of resident pastor was still available. In the meantime Ellen remained in Waltham and wrote from the farm.

Waltham

Thursday

My own darling,

Sitting in the warm sunshine my heart turns to you my precious, and I long to fold you in my arms and hear you say "darling Nellie," the sweetest sound on earth to me. But I will try and be patient, hoping you are having a rest from worry.... My little house is a perfect haven of silk and plaids, and I only wish you were here in the sunshine with me. Darling I love you. When I woke this morning I found myself saying "darling."

...If there is anything in the world that I pray repeatedly and hopefully for, it is that your success in Jersey City may be complete in every respect. Eyes are on you in all directions. I am so willing to work with you and for you.... I love and trust you darling, and I know you do me. I am so hoping for a word from you. I will get home to you just as soon as I can.... Darling I wish you could come and rest awhile. ...my heart's devotion to my darling. Nellie.[210]

These letters offer the reader an entry into the private life of Phebe Hanaford and Ellen Miles and the depth of devotion shared by these two friends. When Ellen was free to leave Waltham, she returned to Jersey City. They needed to be together. Phebe made plans for their trip to Washington DC for the 1883 Universalist General Convention scheduled for October twenty-second. Pages of Phebe's diary have survived this period and offer details of those days such as the reduced rate for the train tickets of $9.80 roundtrip. All in all the events recorded show continuous rain and bad food, which Phebe complains about repeatedly. Ellen was sick, giving Phebe sleepless nights.

Members of the Universalist Society who had met for years in rented quarters now had the new John Murray Universalist Church. Because the Woman's Centenary Association had made major contributions towards the furnishings, they were a part of the General Convention. The only recorded event of the first evening was a visit to Mrs. Soule at Tenth & P Street.

After breakfast Phebe and Ellen walked across the street to see the church. With a brief introduction, the deacon ushered them into the pastor's study where he left them alone. They used the time to "write postals" as the rain poured down. Deciding there was nothing for them to do there, they visited Mr. Ballantyne's bookstore on Seventh Street. He greeted them cordially, encouraged them to browse the store and during tea presented Rev. Hanaford with a nickel-plated inkstand. He reminded them they were invited to his home that evening.

Back in their room Phebe noted in her diary on October twenty-second that she did not understand these Washington meals of "bread and butter, cheese with applesauce." At the meeting of the Woman's Centenary Association, Mrs. Adams nominated Rev. Hanaford for vice president from New Jersey. Phebe urged her to nominate Ellen Miles. "We intended to nominate Mrs. Mary Norton," Mrs. Adams said. "We have a better excuse since she is a minister's wife." Mrs. Thomas invited Rev. Hanaford to conclude the meeting with a prayer.

That night Phebe wrote the following in her diary.

Had supper in a large dining room — bread, butter, chop, peaches, cake, new biscuits. Went to our church. Rev. Dr. Capen, Pres. of Tufts College was talking on education; but it was a poor talk, not worthy of himself. Low voice then screech mentioning men as students only. Will such men ever learn to speak also of advantages for women? ...Nellie, poor child, had a spell of indigestion and it was an hour before we could get to sleep, slept till some one rattled the furnace about 7:00. Expenses, carfare. 10-candy in pretty box 50 —

Phebe and Ellen spent the next morning at the Franklin School. Superintendent Wilson arranged for them to meet Miss Charlotte Garrison, the young woman who had almost drowned at S'conset in 1882. Miss Garrison asked Phebe to speak to her students. Phebe told the children of the days when Superintendent Wilson gathered penny shells on S'conset for his students to count with. All in all it was a pleasant morning. Elections at the General Convention for president and vice-president proved less pleasant. In Phebe's opinion, the choice of Mr. Atwood for vice president carried no hope for the advancement of women in the ministry. Her diary reads, "Mr. Atwood's election as vice-president disheartens me." After another unsatisfactory meal Phebe wrote in her diary, "I don't like Washington lunches."

During the night Ellen woke with indigestion and in the morning showed no interest in attending the meetings. She complained of feeling feverish with a cold. Hannah Tyler Wilcox, a homeopathic physician from St. Louis, gave Phebe medicine for Ellen and Phebe remained with Ellen. Doctor Wilcox stopped to see Ellen before the evening session at the church and found Ellen improved. She encouraged Phebe to come with them to church. Phebe attended meetings and found only a few talks worth hearing.

The morning of the twenty-sixth dawned with the first sunshine since they had arrived in Washington. After a good night's sleep Ellen was in good spirits and they went downstairs for tea, then Ellen returned to her room to rest. Phebe left for the Council Meeting. Worthy of note for the day was her meal, "oyster soup and salad, cream cakes, fruit and ice cream." Record of the events of the day included the day's expenses: "$3.80 for purchases plus 20 cents carfare, total $4.00." In the morning Phebe watched the familiar tempo of Ellen's movements as items of clothing filled the suitcases. She knew Ellen felt well enough to travel. Perhaps the disappointing Convention explains Phebe's preoccupation with food that continued to the end of her visit with the comment, "at breakfast and we both ate heartily."[211]

Once home they resumed their trips to New York for Sorosis meetings. As Chair of the Committee on Education, Ellen Miles designed the December program as a debate on the question, "Does the present system of education in both public and private schools, sufficiently prepare the pupils for self-support?" Phebe presented her paper, "Practical Education." Ellen presented "The Curriculum of our Common School," and Erminnie Smith presented "Half Hour with Webster."[212] The three women traveled home together. The mental stimulation relieved Phebe's mind of the problems at the parish.

Christmas at Library Hall drew only a moderate attendance to the evening recital while Rev. Codington, pastor of the Church of the Good Shepherd, drew a large crowd for Christmas services. The house at 770 Grand Street had few callers. The inappropriateness of the two churches operating directly across the street from each other became more evident in the early months of 1884. Rev. Hanaford worked to maintain harmony within the church while she awaited news from the New Haven Ladies Aid Society regarding her appointment as pastor of the Church of the Holy Spirit.

Phebe had a retreat from the troublesome matters of her ministry when she attended the American Woman Suffrage Association Convention held March 4-7, 1884 at Lincoln Hall in Washington DC. The Convention addressed the question of restoring the right of women's suffrage in New Jersey. Susan B.

---

211   Ibid
212   Sophia Smith Collection

Anthony published the details of the Convention. "The Rev. Phebe A. Hanaford, pastor of the Second Universalist Church of Jersey City, was the next speaker. Her Subject was 'New Jersey as Leader.'" There remained the question of a federal amendment to the Constitution. Members of the convention knew if they failed to have their amendment passed during the current session of Congress, they could not resubmit it for five years. At the end of the convention, Phebe Hanaford traveled to Trenton with Henry Blackwell to the New Jersey State Assembly where, as a representative of the delegates of the American Woman Suffrage Association, she made her last plea for universal suffrage as a resident of New Jersey.

In her address of March 1884 to the Assembly, Phebe Hanaford asked that universal suffrage be restored in New Jersey. The New Jersey colonial charter of 1709 guaranteed universal suffrage. It was reaffirmed in 1790 with the words "he or she" when referring to voters. She reminded them that in 1797 the law read: "Every voter shall openly and in full view deliver his or her ballot which shall be a single ticket containing the names of the person or persons for whom he or she votes." Women and black men and women lost the right to vote in 1797 when John Condict of Essex County proposed, "...after the passage of this act no person shall vote in any state or county election for officers in the government of the United States or of this state unless such a person be a free white male citizen of this state."[213] Once again Universal Suffrage failed to gain the necessary votes in the state of New Jersey. Once again, Phebe was outvoted.

In mid April, Mr. Barber, clerk of the Second Universalist Church in New Haven, invited Rev. Hanaford to preach in the Church of the Holy Spirit in May. He confided in her that his

---

213   McGoldrick & Crocco, p. 5

wife's illness had contributed to his delay in writing. Excerpts from Phebe's response to John Barber, Esq., written on May 2, 1884, read, "I shall take great pleasure in supplying for the Church of the Holy Spirit on May eleventh, and hope that such arrangements will be made, that we shall all labor together successfully in days to come."

Within days Phebe received a second letter from Mr. Barber informing her of his resignation as Clerk of the Second Universalist Church in New Haven to which Phebe responded on May 6, 1884.

John Barber, Esq.

Dear Sir,

Yours of yesterday is before me, and I am pleased with the upright frankness which while honest, is not blunt but kind. We cannot all see alike, and if we cannot agree in all things, there is a Christian way of agreeing to disagree, and that way you seem to understand.

Yet, while I regret that you feel that you had better resign, and am sorry that you do not have entire unity with the proposed methods of establishing our Cause, I cannot but express my sense of the great help you have been to the Second Church, and I feel grateful to you for it. May I not add the hope that circumstances may so shape themselves, by our better acquaintance as that you will still feel able to work with us, and though you prefer to rest for a season now, that you will some day renew your kind and desirable services.

You love our faith, and whether you decide to remain as Clerk or not, I do hope I shall have the pleasure of seeing yourself and wife always in our church, and that the visit which we all remember with satisfaction will prove to be only the first of many equally satisfactory in days to come. I do deeply sympathise with you both. As I am a mother, I know something of the great sorrow you have been called to experience. May the Divine Strength still be granted you, and the Divine consolation ever be afforded!

Please remember me in Christian love and sympathy to your wife, and believe me,

Yours cordially and appreciatively,

Phebe A. Hanaford

P.S. Permit me to say that I think it a beautiful trait in the character of any man or woman when there is pleasure in giving to others a pleasant surprise. May God send many agreeable surprises into your life! Someday we shall be where, as Whittier tells us God's "new surprises" will never fail," and they will all be pleasant and welcome. P.A.H.[214]

Whether Phebe saw Mr. Barber's resignation as "the woman question" rearing its ugly head, we will never know from her kind and subdued reply.

Rev. Hanaford supplied the Second Universalist Church on the eleventh of May. Her sermon was "Be strong and quit yourselves as men, O ye Philistines." She also met with the members of the Ladies Aid Society. Among them were women who had held the community together for decades. One of their project had been the audience room, which was painted with bright frescoes and had crimson carpeting and upholstered pulpit chairs purchased by the Ladies Aid Society.

Rev. Hanaford accepted the unanimous call extended to her by the members of the Second Universalist Church of New

Haven. It was agreed that Rev. Hanaford would preach the following two weekends and be settled as their pastor on June 1st for a term of one year. Her acceptance of a one-year contract appeared in the *New Haven Journal and Courier* the following day.

Mrs. Hanaford Accepts

Mrs. Phebe Hanaford has accepted the call which was so unanimously extended to her by the members of the Second Universalist church last Friday. Mrs. Hanaford will be settled on the first of June for one year. She will occupy the pulpit the next two Sundays. The text of her last evening's discourse was from 1st Samuel, fourth chapter, ninth verse, "Be strong and quit yourself like men, O ye Philistines, that ye be not servants unto the Hebrews, as they have been unto you; quit yourselves like men and fight." In the discourse life was treated as a battle, a continued conflict against superstition and besetting sins. A strong appeal was made to the hearers to "acquit themselves like men, and not be overcome in the battle."

On Rev. Hanaford's return to Jersey City, she informed the former trustees of her call to the Second Universalist Church in New Haven and delivered her request for a Letter of Transfer. Rev. Codington negotiated the return of the parishioners of the Second Universalist Church to the Church of the Good Shepherd. Thus ended Rev. Hanaford's decade of service to the Jersey City Universalists willing to be served by a woman.

CHAPTER SEVEN

CALLED BY WOMEN

In 1884, I came to the Second Universalist Church in New Haven...I am still here, preaching as I have opportunity, and engaged also in literary labors.[215]

The carriage ride to Howard Avenue took passengers away from the noisy area near the railroad tracks and into the residential section of the city. Phebe's study on the second floor of 539 Howard avenue (New Haven City Directory, 1884) overlooked a semi-circle of graceful elms whose limbs blew in the breeze and seemed to bend to welcome her. In time her memorabilia changed an unfriendly room into her familiar office. The "Protection Paper" signed by George Washington and dated 1796 hung on the wall. This Paper given to her grandfather, Captain Henry Barnard, granting passage of his ship into foreign ports symbolized her family roots in the nation's history. Photos of Lucretia Mott and Maria Mitchell and a bust of Benjamin Franklin on the desktop recalled the members of her family tree. The rotating bookcase reclaimed each book that carried its own memory.

Her business card read, "Church of the Holy Spirit (Second Universalist) Rev. Phebe A. Hanaford, Pastor New Haven, Conn. 1884." Rev. Hanaford's May 6 entry in *Voices of Faith*, Rev. J. W. Hanson's birthday book, records her faith.

....

215   Hanaford, Phebe A., 1890, "Twenty Years in the Pulpit"

A Universalist is one who believes thoroughly in "the father-hood of God and the brotherhood of man," and in the ultimate salvation of all souls from sin, through the grace and truth that came by Jesus Christ, and who believing thus, acts accordingly, serving God in serving humanity, seeking to establish justice for all, regardless of class, color, or sex, and prayerfully trusting God for the experience of time and eternity.[216]

The New Haven Daily Morning Journal and Courier featured Rev. Hanaford's first sermon, delivered June 1, 1884.

Inaugural Sermon

...After referring to the facts connected with the origin of the new enterprise and saying that she felt as if re-turning home by coming to New Haven, she went on to speak of appreciation as being the truest praise—and that reward is most welcome when it is most deserved. She referred in the course of the sermon to the appreciation shown for our "boys in blue." ... After enforcing the du-ties of consecration to God, of fidelity in active service for humanity, and of a large and liberal charity towards those who differ from us, she closed with the words,

The gospel which this pulpit is to proclaim, and which these pews are expected to indorse is the gospel of the Lord Jesus Christ. He is our guide, our example, our teacher and Saviour. As a church we hold him to be our ever-living head. His gospel is the gospel of freedom, fellowship and character, the gospel of temperance, helpfulness and good will, the gospel of purity and peace. We are to be hospitable to new truths while yet holding fast to every recognized truth however old. We are to dwell in neighborly kindness with our own household of faith, both far and near, we are to dwell in Christian fear and gospel friendliness. Reverencing "the power not ourselves that makes for righteousness," we are to respect the opinions of those who do not see in that power what we see, an eternal, personal pre-server, our father and our mother God. We are to be faithful over all that God places in our charge, and his promise shall be fulfilled to us and we shall enter into his joy.[217]

The prospects of their return to New Haven faded as the changes that had occurred during their ten years away from New Haven became evident. "It would have been like coming home, except the scythe of Death had been busy and many of the former supporters had passed on." There would be no chaplaincy in the legislative bodies or addresses to these same bodies on the rights of women. The fight for universal suffrage had waned in the wake of Victoria Woodhull's run for the presidency. The trials imposed on Phebe and Nellie during the past decade weighed heavily on them. No longer were they the two women who once walked New Haven streets and entered the brothels to rescue the women.

Women in the ministry remained an issue at Universalist State Conventions of the late nineteenth century. Some states authorized the ordination of candidates regardless of sex. Other states required a committee to study the usefulness of continuing to encourage women ministers in the church. The limited number of women applying for ordination postponed any decision to deny women admission to ordination. As with

217   June 2, 1884, p. 2, col. 2

Rev. Hanaford's Jersey City experience, women's increased voting privileges in the church did not always favor women when debating "the woman issue." The question of Ellen's position in the New Haven Sabbath school run by the Ladies Aid Society appears answered in a Children's Sunday leaflet, dated June 4, 1885, in which she is listed as, "Ellen E. Miles S.S. Supt."

In response to her request to use the library at the Yale Divinity School, still an all-male institution, Rev. Hanaford received a favorable response.

YALE COLLEGE
New Haven, Conn.
Dec 16, 1884

Rev. Mrs. Hanaford,

Yours of the 13th received and you will find that all the privileges which you previously enjoyed will be most cheerfully accorded you on making yourself known at the Library and other offices. Admission to the Lyman Beecher and other public lectures given at the Theological...does not require special action of any kind.

With best wishes,
N. Barber[218]

Mary Hanaford sent word of her plans that would allow Ellen Miles to visit her after their vacation on Siasconset when Howard would be on the mainland for interviews for a new position. After their vacation in S'conset, Phebe and Ellen took a carriage to Howard's home for a visit with Mary before retuning

---

218   Yale Divinity School Library

to New Haven. Phebe learned that her son planned to leave Nantucket with no offer of a pastorate and Mary had no idea where they would live.

Home at her desk, Phebe responded to Susan B. Anthony's request for her photograph for the *History of Woman Suffrage* that she and Elizabeth Cady Stanton were writing at Mrs. Stanton's home in Tenafly, New Jersey.

> *New Haven, Conn.*
> *Aug. 17, 1885*
>
> *Dear Mr. Buttre,*
>
> *Please deliver the plate in your keeping which represents me (i.e. my engraved portrait) to Miss Susan B. Anthony, for her to use in printing such a number of impressions, as she may wish for her "History of Woman Suffrage." The plate belongs to me. Possibly Miss A. may prefer to have you print the pictures for her. If so, she will tell you so, and she will settle with you. I give her use of the plate, for that purpose. B. B. Russell gave me a note to you which I would enclose in this, if I could find it. If you have any doubt as to whether I own the Plate, Mr. R. will inform you.*
>
> *Respectfully yours,*
> *Phebe A. Hanaford*[219]

From Mary Hanaford's hastily written note, Phebe learned that Howard had accepted a position in Bedford, Massachusetts to begin before the end of the year. Howard depended on his ministry as his only work. He wrote very little about the appointment. Left to pack up their possessions with two small children underfoot, Mary had only a few weeks to leave

219   Henry Huntington Library

Nantucket before the freeze. While she considered herself dependent on Howard, however incapably he performed his duties, her responsibilities belied her dependence on him as a wife. Mary failed to understand that emotional dependence grew out of financial dependence.

Mary Weston Landerkin, born in Wellfleet in 1855, was raised a Methodist. The observance of the tenets of John Wesley dominated her childhood just as the steeple of the Methodist church dominated the view of Commercial Street. The Civil War divided the town on the issue of slavery, but not on the preservation of the Union. Citizens of Wellfleet supported the war effort. At war's end, the small boat commercial fishing industry, while still operating, showed signs of waning. When the young Rev. Hanaford arrived at the Wellfleet Universalist church, the young men of Wellfleet were moving to the main-land for economic opportunities. The young minister's proposal of marriage may have looked very promising.

Howard's assignment in Bedford proved less promising than she had hoped. From Middleboro Green Parsonage, Middleboro, Massachusetts, Mary wrote a lengthy letter on May 2, 1886 that this latest transfer would test her husband's ability as pastor. Describing her own feelings, she wrote,

...I think I am learning one lesson as my care freighted years pass by, that is that our truest happiness, depends not upon outward things, but comes from cultivating this little Kingdom of God within us, and making our lives as harmonious as possible with the glories of the Kingdom outward, which is Nature, and the looking forward to the uniting of all these blessed harmonies with the one grand source of them all when we get to our Father's House on high, and behold the King in his beauty.

The people are kind, and seem appreciative of all we do for them. Howard is working more diligently than ever before and he finds it pays to be faithful.[220]

With the Hanafords no longer living in Nantucket, but now living in Middleboro, Phebe's dilemma regarding her vacations with Ellen came to an end. Ellen and Phebe visited her family on S'conset, and friends in town. Many changes had come about to make Nantucket Island a different place. Hotels housed vacationers and some visitors owned summer homes. Robert Coffin moved to Town with his family. The Coffin bungalow on S'conset, where Emma, now past marriageable age, cared for her father, remained a haven for Phebe and Ellen. Each year, nieces and nephews grew to be mature young adults. Their lives bore little resemblance to Phebe's life on the mainland. Deaths and births marked the passing years. While she spoke and wrote of her great affection for her beloved island, she never returned to live there. She remained guided by her Inner Voice of her Quaker childhood while she earned her living as a paid preacher, something the Friends did not condone. Her marked consistency of belief and practice was the dignity of the human person and the equality of women and men. Rev. Hanaford's work for women's rights permeated her contributions in every organization in which she served.

Among her friends, Erminnie Smith had served as the one bright light in those dark years in Jersey City. Erminnie died on June 9, 1886. Her obituary from the *New York Times* dated June 10, 1886 reads,

Mrs. Erminnie Smith, well known among scientific and literary people in this city died yesterday in her home, No. 203 Pacific avenue, Jersey City.... Six weeks ago overwork brought on paralysis of the brain which resulted in her death. The funeral will be held tomorrow at 9 pm at the Reformed Church, Lafayette, Jersey City.

Phebe knew Erminnie to be a member of the New York Historical Society, the London Scientific Society, and the Academy of Science. She was the first woman admitted to the New York Academy of Science and was a member of the American Society for the Advancement of Science. And yet her talents did not give her the right to vote. Her death closed a chapter in Phebe's life, but the struggle for universal suffrage went on.

The first vote in the Senate on a federal amendment for universal suffrage failed two to one in 1887. The defeat heightened radical feminist thinking. Elizabeth Cady Stanton and Lucy Stone blamed the failure on organized religions' interpretation of the Gospel that placed women in a secondary and submissive role. In the face of their reactions, Phebe served as a Universalist minister with unwavering faith. To the frequent references to St. Paul's admonition that women should not speak in church, Phebe noted no such quote began with the words of Jesus; "Amen, Amen, I say to you." The equality that Universalism gave to women never guaranteed full acceptance of women in the ministry or that members of the congregation would agree on women's rights.

In observance of the fortieth anniversary of the first Woman's Rights Convention in Seneca Falls, Susan B. Anthony opened the National Council of Women on March 25, 1888. Women representing fifty-three organizations came from across the country to Albaugh's Opera House in Washington D.C. The conference opened with services conducted by the Revs. Phebe Hanaford, Ada Bowles, Antoinette Blackwell, Amanda Deyo, and included

Rev. Anna H. Shaw's address, "The Heavenly Vision." The generous invitation united temperance advocates, social workers, and
moral and civic reformers with suffragists. Lucy Stone's presence
indicated that the National Council of Women had risen above
the differences between the two suffrage organizations. Suffrage
advocates came believing they would find large support for their
cause. To their disappointment the omission of the word "suffrage"
in the constitution denoted the failure of the National Council of
Women to aid the cause of suffrage. The Constitution read,

> We, women of the United States, sincerely believing that
> the best good of our homes and nations will be advanced
> by our own greater unity of thought, sympathy and pur-
> pose, and that an organized movement of women will
> best conserve the highest good for the family and the
> State, so hereby band ourselves together in a confedera-
> tion of workers committed to the overthrow of all forms
> of ignorance and injustice, and to the application of the
> Golden Rule to society, custom, and law.[221]

During the remaining sessions at which Susan B. Anthony
presided, speakers addressed their issues with little friction.
Jane Croly, however, representing Sorosis, the only literary club
invited to the Council, negatively influenced the atmosphere
of unity. She asserted her club's dominance and reminded her
audience that Sorosis had initiated the founding of the Association for the Advancement of Women. In spite of the claim that
the New England Woman's Club predated Sorosis, they had not
received an invitation. Francis Willard publicly apologized, stating that when any movement comes into existence it develops

221   Harper, p. 636

in more than one place at a time. She assumed Sorosis to be the oldest literary club. Interesting is Phebe Hanaford's membership in Sorosis, which never espoused suffrage, while she remained an outspoken advocate of universal suffrage.

While in Washington, Phebe Hanaford, Julia Ward Howe and Antoinette Brown, with a group of women including Clara Barton, met to form a literary society. They pledged as authors to "believe in pure literature and high standards of literary work, to cooperate as members of a Society to be known as 'The Author's Guild of America.'" The Alma Lutz Collection contains the document signed by eleven women.

> We are convinced that Union is strength, and consultation a source of education; and we hereby pledge ourselves to aid each other in all legitimate channels of work, to exercise our utmost diligence to purify all publications and to insist, that literary work performed by women if worthy of publication is also worthy of just remuneration.[222]

A week before the National Council of Women, Jane Croly hosted the celebration of the fifteenth anniversary of the Association for the Advancement of Women that grew out of Sorosis in 1873 during Charlotte Wilbour's presidency. That year, 1888, also marked the fortieth anniversary of Sorosis. It became evident why Jane Croly planned to organize Sorosis clubs into a Federation. Whether to upstage the National Council of Women or not, Jane Croly planned a celebratory convention for the following year.

Of the ninety-four clubs invited, sixty-one from nineteen states from California to New York sent delegates to the celebra-

---

222   Schlesinger Library

tion in Madison Square Theater in New York March 18–20, 1889. On 18 March, *The New York Times* reported a reception at the home of Mrs. Jane Croly at 148 East 46th Street. Phebe Hanaford is not listed among the reported guests. On Monday the delegates and invited guests gathered at Delmonico's for a reception and anniversary dinner. On Tuesday a hundred delegates gathered at Madison Square Theater. A letter from First Lady, Mrs. Benjamin Harrison was read before the first order of business.

The program allowed a representative to report on their clubs' methods and results. Out of Jane Croly's genius for empowering women grew the Federation of Women's Clubs. At this convention, Charlotte Emerson Brown of New Jersey was elected the first president of the General Federation of Women's Clubs. Ellen Deitz Clymer was elected the sixth president of Sorosis. The Program (p. 30) included Phebe Hanaford's address to the group.

> *I think this an honor, and I am proud to speak for Sorosis to-day.*
>
> *You have heard how clubs have been organized in various parts of our land, but I do not think that any one has mentioned the Isle of the Sea. Today in SOROSIS there are several ladies who are natives of this Isle of the Sea, and it has been a matter of great satisfaction to me as a Nantucketer. As I have always said to Mrs. Mary Livermore, when she is proud of being a Bostonian, it is the next thing to being born in Nantucket.*
>
> *In the year 1872 or 1873 we called together those who were interested. There were Professor Maria Mitchell and Mrs. Morse, leading worker of Sorosis, and myself; and I believe our honorary member, Mrs. Elizabeth Starbuck, who is absent in California.*

I believe Nantucket's sons and daughters are all the world over. You cannot go to a place that you do not find them. We organized a Sorosis in Nantucket years ago among the women, because there were no men. The men were off on the ocean as whalers doing their duty elsewhere, and the women took care of the children, were the leaders in education, and in all the affairs of the island. If there is a spirit that dominates, it is the spirit of love, and this, after all, is the one spirit that rules and governs the world.

*Speed then thy years, Sorosis! Speed
Toward victory for Right;
Toward equilibrium—thus toward peace—
And toward a holy might.
The world shall hail, at last, the time
When this our Club was born
To usher in true Woman's day—
The star of Woman's morn!*

Members of Sorosis were treated to a visit to the Metropolitan Museum of Art for a private viewing of the Cypriote Collection, and A. M. Palmer, Esq. provided a hundred orchestra seats for the evening performance at the Madison Square Theater. During the week, *The Daily World* gave the women a tour of their presses at the *World* building. The celebrations were still a fond memory when the papers carried news of Victoria Woodhull's return to the United States with her English husband. Now Mrs. John Martin, she set up residence at 142 West 70th Street where she announced to the press she intended to run for president of the United States as the candidate of the National Equal Rights Party. Running against Grover Cleveland, she promised to eliminate various evils from society through women voters.

Susan B. Anthony, and most suffrage organizations, chose to ignore her, as did the press.

Phebe Hanaford, never one to ignore an invitation from the press, gave an interview to the *Ladies' Home Journal* that appeared in the February 1888 issue.

Rev. Phoebe (sic) A. Hanaford

A Woman Minister of the Gospel, Pastor of the Church of the Holy Spirit in New Haven, Connecticut: A native of Nantucket and springing from the best families on the Island. A woman's work, as Preacher, Pastor and Author of many successful books

---

Phoebe A. Hanaford is a representative of American woman, not only as standing prominent in the comparatively small company of women preachers in this country, but in her eloquence, fervency of feeling, rare discretion of utterance and earnestness, rivaling favorably the majority of clergymen in the United States.

She is now fifty-eight years of age, an attractive, lovable and magnetized woman of medium height, well-proportioned figure, and a face essentially feminine and full of intellectual sweetness.

She has large dark eyes and dark hair which waves upon her temples and falls behind her ears in one or two curls. The picture shown above was taken some years ago but is an excellent likeness, only lacking the fullness and added benignity of maturer years.

Such is the force of her mind, her prominence in efforts for public reforms, her success as pastor of several churches, and her literary reputation that she becomes an object of interest to all American women, and one whose character and life works it is a pleasure to hold up to the strong light of publication.

In 1866 she began regular ministerial work, (since which time she has been engaged in unremitting gospel labor) and two years later was ordained pastor of the First Universalist church in Hingham, Mass.

In 1870 she was called to New Haven to take charge of the First Universalist church of that city. The congregation at present occupies a new church of attractive appearance and convenience for the various departments of the work.

Mrs. Hanaford's sermons are inspiring, full of hope and encouragement, permeated with confident expectancy of good in the present and future life, tolerant, sympathetic and helpful. Many of them have been published and had a large sale. In this day of interest in the preaching of women, a volume of her sermons would undoubtedly meet with a ready sale. As a preacher Mrs. Hanaford has spoken in most of the New England and Middle States and at Washington and in the West. As a lecturer on literary subjects and speaker at reform gatherings she is well known in scores of cities and towns this side of the Mississippi, and has delivered sermons, orations and poems, at various institutions and colleges. She has assisted at many ordination services, reading her hymns written for the occasions or giving the charge to pastor and people. She offered the ordaining prayer when her own son entered the Christian ministry. When her daughter was married to the present editor of a newspaper, she officiated, and a few years afterward baptized a little grand-daughter.

This woman is remarkable not only as a successful minister of the gospel, but quite as distinctively for her versatility of gifts and the enormous amount of pastoral, reformatory and literary work accomplished in the past twenty years. It should be mentioned that her health is absolutely perfect. The physical vicissitudes of womanhood have passed her lightly by and she attributes her good health to the constant occupation of her mind and the forgetfulness of self and this mortal shell, in the hopeful, helpful work for others, and the persuading of multitudes to her convictions. Besides church, parish, hospital and temperance work in which she is earnestly engaged, she is an influential advocate of woman suffrage, her dignified womanly presence commanding respect from the men most opposed to the ideas.

She "keeps house" with her friend and companion of the past eighteen years, Miss Ellen E. Miles, once a Massachusetts teacher and now a writer of children's books and many popular little volumes, a fine compilation called "Our Home Beyond the Tide and Kindred Poems."

So does this woman preacher combine in her gentle personality the strength, perseverance, intellectual force and rightness, the sympathy broad and deep, the faith, hope and charity which are essential to success in the ministry; the courage and persistence which must be the possession of one who can stand up firmly for issues like suffrage and prohibition; the grace, tact and patience for an executive in a woman's club like Sorosis, and the sweetness and unselfishness forethought for others which is the chief charm of the queen of a household. She is a luminous example of the effective work which may be done by a woman in a sphere rarely occupied by one of her sex, while preserving in their purity the modesty and grace of a religious, unselfish, tactful feminine character.

Florence Thayer McCray

Phebe's enthusiasm for the cause of universal suffrage never wavering, she continued corresponding with those working for the cause.

May 31, 1888
Rev. E. F. Strickland
Rev. and Dear Sir,
I am exceedingly gratified to learn by your letter and poem, that you are in sympathy with those who believe Woman's enfranchisement to be necessary to Human advancement, and I cannot but see in this an evident token of your adaptability to the Gospel ministry, since you comprehend thus fully the Master's teachings, and the Apostolic words concerning the fact that there is no distinction of sex to be made, when considering human rights.
Woman has borne her full share of the World's burdens; she should have equal share in the honors, emoluments and privileges of the State, as well as in the responsibilities, since she is the daughter of the Lord Almighty. He who is no respecter of persons has not given her a subordinate place among His children, nor is there one moral standard for His sons and another for His daughters. The exaltation of Woman to her

proper place will prove the uplifting of humanity, and secure
the victory of righteousness. Yours for equal rights,
Phebe A. Hanaford,
New Haven, Conn.[223]

Emma Coffin's letters brought news of Captain George's limited activity. Phebe traveled to Siasconset and found her father as Emma described. Her brother George lived with his family on S'conset, giving some assistance to Emma. Robert had a home in Town. Lydia and Sarah lived on the mainland. Captain George's long life ended after Phebe had returned home. He left seventeen grandchildren and four great-grandchildren including three of Phebe's grandchildren. His lengthy obituary, framed in the Nantucket Life-Saving Museum, concludes,

He passed peacefully away August 10, 1889, at his home in Siasconset, surrounded by all his surviving children save one, (who had however been with him during his sickness for a time) and the Sunday following, his funeral was attended from the town residence of his son Robert B. Coffin, where the Rev. Louise S. Baker and Rev. Mr. Beal, of the Methodist Church, officiated with words of sympathy and consolation.

It remains an untold part of Phebe's life story why she did not return to participate in her father's funeral.

Within weeks of her father's death Phebe went to Tonawanda to visit Florence and her family and spend time with her granddaughter. Eight-year-old Dionis had inherited her great-grandfather's "droopy" eyes, which had not appeared in the previ-

---

223   Universalist Archives, Andover – Harvard Theological Library

ous generation. With Dionis in school, Phebe failed to interest Florence with news of the Woman Suffrage Movement. Thomas Warner, on the other hand, was a great conversationalist and showed a keen interest in his mother-in-law's activities as evidenced in the memorabilia he saved. He suggested she speak at the Alumnae of North Tonawanda School. Phebe agreed, believing public schools to be the source of a nation's intelligence. In response to the toast, "The Public Schools," she spoke on the origin of the public school and its progress. In conclusion she defended the institution.

While there may be those who would argue that the public school does not make for the fullest individual mental development, it is certain that it has been good for some of us, and I would say that the experience is one I would not willingly forfeit, for I feel that its activity and pleasant associations have been a power for good, and it seems an honor to say "I am a graduate of the Public School."[224]

Back in New York, Phebe resumed her work in the growing Woman's Club Movement headed by Jane Croly. After the death of her husband in May of 1889, Jane Croly returned with renewed energy to the women's rights movement as she perceived it. Jane founded the Woman's Press Club "to provide a center of usefulness and furnish a bureau of information in regard to women's professional work and professional workers." Mrs. Croly assumed the leadership as president. Phebe served as 1st vice president and as a member of the Executive Committee. The group met on the second and fourth Saturdays of the

224   Nantucket Historical Association

month at the Waldorf Astoria. These meetings encouraged social intercourse and the establishment of friendly relations between women of literary pursuits. Phebe Hanaford, a charter member of the group, wore her pin of purple enamel with great pride. The gold lettering of "Woman's Press Club" accompanied the insignia of a gold quill and lighted torch.[225] Jane Croly's sixtieth birthday was celebrated on December 19, 1889.

On one of her regular trips for Sorosis business, Phebe wrote to Rev. Antoinette Brown Blackwell, living in New Jersey.

The Waldorf Astoria

Dear 'Beloved Physician' of the Soul,
Who ought to have been a D.D. years ago—
I have done something for which I wish to be forgiven if I've done wrong. I have ventured to allow your name to be put on our program for next Saturday afternoon—Nov. 25 at Press Club Mtg. in the Waldorf Astoria. Do forgive me know that you forgive me by coming and speaking. Only a word of greeting from our honorary member, Rev. A.B.B.—it will not tax your mind to do that—and if it is an effort, you are equal to it. We want your benediction, dear friend.
Mrs. Wilbour is to speak—also the Consul-General de France and the American President of the Alliances. The program may not reach you in season—but do come 2:30 P.M. as usual.
It will be Installation Day, you remember—some 15 officers or so to be installed.
I write in great haste because I have a friend here helping on a draft for the above occasion, and as I am also a nurse and

225   Columbia University

domestic etc, etc. and often interrupted—I can only say, We
both send love—and I am ever affectionately,
Phebe A. Hanaford[226]

At the October 1889 meeting of the American Woman Suffrage Association, Lucy Stone presented a plan for the merger
of the two suffrage associations. She and Susan B. Anthony
negotiated for a new suffrage organization. On the occasion of
Susan B. Anthony's seventieth birthday, February 15, 1890, the
National Woman Suffrage Association and the American Woman Suffrage Association united to form the National American
Woman Suffrage Association. On Susan's insistence, Elizabeth
Cady Stanton served as president and Lucy Stone became chairman of the Executive Committee. Before the end of the year
Mrs. Stanton sailed for Europe leaving Susan B. Anthony in
charge of the united suffrage organization.

At the start of the 1890 season at the Church of the Holy
Spirit, Rev. Hanaford received a request from the Board of Trustees to continue her services. Ellen Miles' position as the Sabbath
school teacher met with their approval. The Second Universalist
Society had been meeting rent free since 1884 in the Church
of the Holy Spirit owned by Mr. H. H. Olds. With no plans
to acquire ownership of the church, the Second Universalist
Society in New Haven lacked permanence. With the death of
Mr. Olds in 1890 the trustees of the Church of the Holy Spirit
waited for the reading of his will. When it was learned that
Mr. Olds had died without a will, the church was sold. The
Universalist Register of Connecticut Churches 1886-1890 reports that in 1890 "this Second Church of New Haven is marked
dormant...Mrs. Hanford remained in New Haven until 1891."

226   Schlesinger Library

Previously shielded by their mutual commitment to the community, Phebe and Ellen's lifestyle now lay open to scrutiny. In the eyes of the members of the congregation, Rev. Hanaford's ministry no longer justified her separation from her husband who continued his medical practice in Reading, Massachusetts. While it did not demand one type of relationship, society felt most comfortable with male-female relationships within the sphere of marriage. Phebe's marriage, though never dissolved legally, held no constraints on her. Long before Joseph's relationship with Harriett, Phebe had freed herself of the demeaning imbalance of power within traditional marriage. Traditionally, however, the world's acceptance of women's supportive networks outside the home was limited. The two friends separated, with Phebe going to Tonawanda and Ellen to Waltham. The first correspondence dated October 1892 from New York indicates they had reunited and would remain together "til death."

CHAPTER EIGHT

PHEBE AND ELLEN

Ere we leave this spot we will breathe a prayer,
I for thee, and thou, love, for me
That our love may endure when we meet no more
On the shore of the sounding sea...[227]

At a time in history when few women could choose their lifestyle, Phebe Hanaford and Ellen Miles chose to share a common pillow. In a world dominated by men, only financial security allowed women options outside of marriage. Evidence of Phebe and Ellen's financial security may be estimated from the location of their first Manhattan residence at Forty-Seven West Twelfth Street. A plaque erected on that street reads, "Since 1844 houses on this street were the last word in elegance." On the corner of Fifth Avenue and Twelfth Street the beautiful stone structure of the First Presbyterian Church still stands with its spacious gardens, considered a spiritual inspiration in the city. Within walking distance Phebe and Ellen found Grace Church at Broadway and Tenth Street, home to society weddings and funerals. Public transportation enabled them to visit the Universalist Church of the Divine Paternity on Central Park West where Rev. E. H. Capen occasionally preached. Phebe added her name to the mailing list of the Universalist Woman's Alliance of the Metropolitan District. The headquarters of the National

227   Hanaford, Phebe A., 1871, *From Shore to Shore* p. 203

American Suffrage Association located in the Grand Central Terminal Building added to the conveniences the city afforded them.

At fifty-six Ellen Miles exuded confidence, which was confirmed by her ability and her comely stature. Her talents burgeoned in response to Phebe's needs. Ellen defined her role as "coadjutor, intimate personal friend and minister's wife." Phebe referred to her as "Sister Pricilla, the wife of Aquila." Ellen could speak with a sharp tongue when provoked. She had a gift for pantomime that could cool a tense situation or add fuel to the fire. Phebe curtailed Ellen's tendency to sarcasm with a gentle "Now, now, Nellie." With no predetermined role based on gender, neither considered herself superior to the other. Phebe's and Ellen's dependence on each other was mutual and balanced. They lived in each other's presence as Phebe's family remained in the shadow of their relationship. At a cost to her ministry, Phebe had chosen not to sacrifice Ellen's friendship when Ellen caused disunity within the community.

Phebe attended the twenty-fourth annual Woman Suffrage Convention held in the Church of Our Father in Washington D.C. on January 17, 1892. During the three-day gathering, Susan B. Anthony was elected president of the National American Woman Suffrage Association. On the first day of the convention, Elizabeth Cady Stanton appeared before a Judiciary Committee of Congress seeking passage of an amendment granting woman's suffrage. During the remaining days, Elizabeth Cady Stanton and Lucy Stone, who had resigned from their offices, were elected honorary presidents of the now united suffrage association.

In the nationwide plans to celebrate the 400th anniversary of Columbus' discovery of America, Chicago won the bid for the World's Columbian Exposition to be held May through November 1893. Susan B. Anthony, recalling the treatment meted out to women during the Philadelphia celebrations two decades earlier, asked Congress to include women's affairs at the federally funded Exposition. The all-male commission established a Board of Women Managers of the State of New York. They appointed Mrs. Blanche Wilder Bellamy chair of the National Committee on "Women's Work in Literature." Mrs. Bellamy visited the members of Sorosis on October 17, 1892 to ask Sorosis to choose one of the three categories available under "Literature" to contribute to the Exposition. The members chose the category "Literary Clubs and Classes." As 1st vice president under Jeanne de la Lozier, Phebe Hanaford was asked to assume the chair of the committee to prepare the material. Phebe called for a committee of six to assist her. On 8 November the committee met at Sarah Youmans' suite in the Madrid, overlooking Central Park to draft a circular letter enlisting the participation of sixty clubs in Long Island and New York.

SOROSIS

1892

Dear Madam:

The Board of Woman Managers of the State of New York wishes to prepare and present at the Columbian Exposition an exhibit to be entitled "Women's Work in Literature in the State of New York." This work has been divided into three branches, namely Books, Work in Literary Clubs and Classes of at least three years standing, and Work in the Press and Periodicals. Each of these branches has been placed in the hands of a prominent woman's club, which will serve as a committee to prepare one part of the exhibit.

Sorosis has assumed the work in Literary Clubs and Classes, and we write to ask if your club or class will join us in making a practical and beautiful showing of the work of women in the Empire State.

We enclose to you a miniature model of the folios to be prepared. They are to be typewritten upon paper nine inches square in size, and sent to us.

We shall then place them in leather covers of artistic design, bearing a seal with the motto of the State, and below this, the name and date of your organization.

They will then be sent by us to Chicago, and so hung that they will be accessible to everyone interested in this field of woman's work.

The success of your work, and the method of your organization may thus become one of the educational factors, and one of the beautiful and noted features of the Women's Building.

The cost to your club will be only that of having your material typewritten, by yourselves, with the addition of three dollars sent to us to meet the expense of the cover. This cover will correspond to the outside page of the model, and must be made in New York to secure a harmony of design for all the clubs and classes represented. It will be made under the direction of Mrs. Candace Wheeler, of the Associated Artists.

The typewritten folios need not be in our hands until the first of February, but we hope you will kindly favor us with an early reply, that we may reserve a place for you.

In this reply please be sure to give us the full title of your association, with the date of its organization, and the three dollars for the cover, which can then be prepared in season to place at once upon your folio when it arrives.

Very truly.
PHEBE A. HANAFORD,
SARAH E. YOUMANS,
ADA M. BROWN,
HESTER M. POOLE,
CATHERINE SHERMAN,
C. L. FOREST,
Committee of Sorosis

Blanche Wilder Bellamy, Chairman of Committee on "Woman's
Work in Literature" from Board of Women Managers of the
State of New York
Please address your reply to
Rev. Phebe A. Hanaford
47 West 12th Street,
New York, N.Y.[228]

The Sorosis committee met again on the twelfth to discuss ways of presenting the material. Phebe gave a report of the meeting she had with Mrs. Bellamy and the New York Board of Women Managers. Following the laws of Parliamentary Procedure, it was decided that rather than submit papers, Mrs. Poole would prepare a Historical Sketch of Sorosis, Mrs. Sherman would list the "notable occasions" and Mrs. Youmans would prepare a list of Officers and Members for the folio.

When the committee met with Mrs. Bellamy on 21 November, she restated her insistence that papers be submitted. Charlotte Wilbour then offered to write a paper, "The Matron of the Period." Jane Croly contributed "The History of the Club

228   Sophia Smith Collection

Movement." Also, they agreed to include "The Significance of Flora to the Iroquois," a paper previously delivered by Erminnie Smith. The meeting adjourned "sine die" but the work lasted for months. Sixty clubs and classes of New York State each prepared a folio according to a model, and by the accompanying papers and records, constituted the folio of exhibit of Sorosis.

At the January 1893 Sorosis meeting, Mrs. Poole's "History of Sorosis" was accepted. Members agreed she was free to publish her article if she wished. Albany submitted reports from three clubs including the Friday Morning Club, Sesame Reading Club and Semper Fidelis. Brooklyn reported on nineteen clubs, and Elmira reported "The Entre Nous by Mrs. Otis Dockstader of 373 Gray Street." After seven months of committee work and wearying delays on the part of the Clubs and Societies, seventy-one clubs and classes had prepared folios and, together with the records of Sorosis, these constituted the folio for the Centenary Exposition at the Chicago World's Fair.

At a special meeting of the executive board, Phebe announced the final report was completed. She described the soft yellow cover with "Sorosis of New York 1868-1893" embossed in mulberry. On the left side a black seal showing the eagle, with separated letters forming the word "Excelsior" illustrating the motto of New York State. Below was written "State Board of Managers – 1893." As directed by the committee, Phebe had ordered a duplicate copy of the folio for the General Federation of Women's Clubs.[229]

Julia Ward Howe, founder and president of the Woman's Ministerial Conference, presided over the opening ceremony observing their tenth anniversary on June 1, 1892 at the Church

---

229   Ibid

of the Disciples in Boston. The ceremony booklet program includes a hymn by Rev. Phebe Hanaford sung to the tune of "Coronation." Records of the Woman's Ministerial Conference[230] show Rev. Mary Graves as Corresponding Secretary, Rev. Ada Bowles, Recording Secretary and Rev. Anna Shaw as Treasurer. Those gathered looked at the last decade to measure their progress in gaining ecclesiastical equality with men. Rev. Louise Baker, ordained by the deacons of her church after four years of preaching and pastoral labor, had never had her name included in the list of ordained ministers in the church yearbook. Rev. Bowles reported that the refusal of the Congregationalist Church to place the names of women ministers in their yearbook made it impossible to obtain reliable statistics regarding women's ministry in this church.

It was reported in the minutes of the Conference that "of the eight Theological Schools nominally open to women, only Canton Theological School at St. Lawrence University and Ryder Divinity School at Lombard University, all Universalist schools, offered ordination or accommodations or financial assistance to women." Records from 1891 listed the number of women preachers:

Friends, three hundred fifty, ordination not necessary; Universalist women preachers numbered thirty-seven, and were ordained under the same conditions as men as the accepted policy of the church since 1860; Unitarian sixteen, ordained upon the same conditions as men since 1870; Congregationalist ordained ten; Methodist ordained women by exception.

---

230   bMS199/1(3)

The statistics showed little success for women deserving to be recognized as equal partners in the preaching of the Gospel. "In this union of women ministers and preachers, members were too widely separated to hold frequent meetings or unite in practical work."[231]

Rev. Hanaford, recognized as one who encouraged women in their desire to preach as ordained ministers, reminded the members of the great courage it took and still takes to withstand the resistance of the local congregations, regretfully often from women as well as men. She spoke from her personal experiences and of her renewed resolutions, in spite of opposition, to insist on her right to preach as an ordained minister. Referring to the growth of women in the ministry, she mentioned Revs. Lorenza Haynes, Sarah Perkins, Ada Bowles and Anna Shaw as representative of the increasing number of ordained women ministers.[232]

In the midst of these responsibilities, the year 1892 closed with an invitation for Phebe to speak to the Manhattan Liberal Club at the German Masonic Hall on 9 December. The morning issue of the *New York Times* the following day reported the controversies over her talk under a bold heading.

DIDN'T AGREE WITH HER
LECTURER HANAFORD'S SENTIMENTS EXCITE
OPPOSITION.

When the Rev. Phoebe (sic) A. Hanaford had finished her lecture last evening on "Modern Mental Activity" before the Manhattan Liberal Club, at German Masonic

231   Universalist Archives, Andover – Harvard Theological Library
232   Ibid

Hall, 220 East Fifteenth Street, it was very evident that she had considerably antagonized many of the pet notions of the members of the club.

The whole trend of the lecture was that God was nearer now to man than ever before, and that consequently modern thought was much surer and more progressive.

The lecturer even went so far as to say that the civilizing influences of Christianity promised a greater mental activity in the future.

T. B. Wakeman, who followed the lecturer, admitted that her paper was very pretty from a poetic or allegorical standpoint, but as to the basis on which it rested he ridiculed the fact that the Rev. Phoebe A. Hanaford really seemed to believe that there was a God.

"Such an idea," he said "was exploded long ago, and instead of Christ having made Christianity, it was Christianity that made Christ."

The same idea animated the other speakers of the evening. Mrs. Dunleavy, Caleb W. Weeks, Henry Rowley, Moses Oppenheimer, and William Horan—all of whom seemed deeply impressed with the fact that all modern mental activity was confined to those who hold the opinions which the speakers hold.

A large audience was present at the meeting which was presided over by Wilson McDonald, Vice-President of the club.

Preparations for the World's Columbian Exposition scheduled to run from May through October of 1893 included Julia Ward Howe's request for autobiographical sketches and photographs of members of the Ministerial Conference for an album to be displayed in the Woman's Pavilion. Mary Livermore and Francis Willard worked on a biographical dictionary to honor outstanding women for the quadricentennial. They also asked for photographs. Phebe sent a photo of her portrait done by Mrs. Sairman showing a full-figured Phebe in her sixties wearing her Sorosis pin. This painting now hangs in the home of Audrey Johnson, Phebe's great-great-granddaughter.

Phebe and Ellen left for Chicago in May. Phebe carried the folio to be presented at the World's Congress of Representative Women held in conjunction with the Exposition. There, Lucy Stone, in obvious poor health, gave her talk "The Progress of Fifty Years." She appeared weak yet filled the hall with energy when she described how many women had been accused of flying in the face of Providence with their efforts to take women out of her predetermined sphere. Physically spent, she moved away from a grateful audience. The young American women listening to her who then walked through the Woman's Pavilion had little awareness that the hard-won privileges and legal rights that they enjoyed had been denied to women a generation ago.

For weeks women from twenty-seven countries walked through the Woman's Building designed by MIT graduate, Sophia Hayden of Boston. The invention of Harriet Tracy, the "Tracy Gravity Safety Elevator," carried visitors to the rooftop restaurant. The exhibit included Josephine Cochran's dishwashing machine and Margaret Wilcox's combination stove and house heater and other inventions that would ease the burden of housework. Phebe sent a report of the convention to be read at the monthly Sorosis meeting. The minutes of May 15, 1893 included a report on the Columbia Exposition. "The report to be read by Mrs. Jammus as P. Hanaford will be out of town." The

Exposition was an extravaganza amidst the economic depression caused by the Wall Street Collapse in June 1893.

Once back in New York, Phebe picked up her pen in defense of the Exposition. Of the critics who saw the exhibit "as useless objects which have not even the merit of artistic beauty to recommend them," Phebe wrote to *The New York Times,*

The question is sneeringly asked some times, "Can a woman invent?" The Great Centennial Exposition answered the question satisfactorily to believers in women's capabilities; and those who saw and heard the dish-washer and other women who were displaying their own inventions, they will not soon forget them. Some woman with sufficient leisure would do royal service to her sex and the cause of woman, if she would prepare a volume in which, with all detail, it might be shown the help of women in the onward progress of society in regard to household and other conveniences.

Within a week, newspapers published messages of retaliation on Phebe's observations of the Exposition saying, "They hoped no woman had leisure to drive a nail into the women's rights cause."

The Universalist Convention met in Murray Grove, New Jersey the week of August 17, 1893. Phebe attended with a keen interest in news from the Jersey City Universalist Community. The brief report in the *Jersey Courier,* the home newspaper of Ocean County, did not include reports from individual Societies. "Rev. B. B. Russel of Clifton Springs, New York gave the opening talk followed by a dedication of Potter's grave." Hurricane winds repeatedly visited the Jersey Shore that season. The first blew on 24 August, causing floods on the rail lines. Forced to interrupt her trip home, Phebe holed up in Asbury Park some fifty miles north of Murray Grove. The familiar roar of the sea kept her awake and she watched the rescue operations from her hotel room. Her lengthy poem about what she witnessed is filled with memories of her beloved island.

Strong and brave men on the sands
Battled with the sea,
In the gray light of the morning,
While the winds blew free:
And the hungry waves were roaring,
And the foam-decked surges growing
Then libation, Death, to thee!

See! the rescued reach the shore,
Safe-the mystic seven; —
Hush! the others speak no more,
Of that craft's eleven.
Then the sun rose, cloud-surrounded,
And the far horizon bounded
Human Vision, save towards heaven.[233]

When Sorosis meetings resumed in September, Phebe, as 1st vice president under M. Louise Thomas, planned the programs. The topic for discussion at the December meeting read, "Do not Mothers often rest too implicitly in the thought that they have the full confidence of their children? And are home attractions equal in degree to outside influence?" The minutes quote Phebe's insight into the situation that included the presence of grandmothers in the ideal home, and even the old maid aunt,

233   Nantucket Historical Association

"if she is full of human kindness and can see without speaking and hear without repeating."

Over the wire service on October 18, 1893 the world learned of Lucy Stone's death. Her death served as a reminder the original suffragists, now grown old, would not live to see universal suffrage guaranteed by a federal amendment. Phebe, already active in the Women's Rights Movement, had pioneered in Lucy Stone's American Woman Suffrage Association founded in 1869. Her alignment with Lucy Stone's Suffrage Association resulted from her geographical location in New England and her friendship with Caroline Severance and Julia Ward Howe more than any differences in the means used to achieve woman's suffrage. Except for the intrusion of Victoria Woodhull's views on free love and Elizabeth Cady Stanton's demand for the right to divorce into the National Woman Suffrage Association platform, Stanton's belief in universal suffrage by a federal amendment had never clashed with Phebe's views on equal rights for women. Over the years she had worked with both suffrage groups, rising above the tension between her friends, Lucy Stone and Elizabeth Cady Stanton.

When Mrs. Stanton returned from Europe, she took up residence on West Ninety-Fifth Street between Columbus and Amsterdam Avenues in New York. Affirmation of Phebe's continued friendship with Elizabeth Cady Stanton comes from Mrs. Stanton's invitation to Phebe to contribute to the Revising Committee of her *The Woman's Bible*. Over the years Elizabeth had written and lectured on men who falsely interpreted the Bible and then proclaimed their message to be the word of God. In her search for freethinking women, she turned to Transcendentalists, Unitarians, Universalists and other liberal scholars. Phebe knew of Mrs. Stanton's heterodox view of reading the Bible as literature rather than as the divinely inspired word preached in the orthodox churches. Phebe maintained her orthodox faith in the Bible while identifying the patriarchal misinterpretations of the scriptures used to subordinate women in society.

In response to Mrs. Stanton request, Phebe wrote,

Dear Mrs. Stanton: —I believe, as you said in your birthday address, that "women ought to demand that the Canon law, the Mosaic code, the Scriptures, prayer-books and liturgies be purged of all invidious distinctions of sex, of all false teaching as to woman's origin, character and destiny." I believe that the Bible needs explanation and comment on many statements therein which tend to degrade woman. Christ taught the equality of the sexes, and Paul said: "There is neither male nor female; ye are all one in Christ Jesus." Hence I welcome "The Woman's Bible" as a needed commentary in regard to woman's position.

Phebe A. Hanaford[234]

Mrs. Stanton also received letters of acceptance from Universalists, Olympia Brown and Augusta Chapin, the only other ordained ministers on the Revision Committee. The insights of freethinking scholars expressed in their essays on Stanton's "Commentaries on the Old Testament" constituted Part One of *The Woman's Bible*. Rev. Hanaford wrote a commentary on the Book of Numbers, not out of anger at male interpretations but out of her response to the Inner Light.

Phebe also wrote an article on the role of women in the ministry and included a photo of her portrait done by Mrs. Sairman.

---

234   Stanton, 1895

WOMAN AS PREACHER AND PASTOR IS NOW A FACT
By the Rev. Phoebe (sic) Hanaford

During the closing century there has been great advancement for woman in regard to her work in the church. The nineteenth century has opened wide the pulpit doors to those qualified among women in many denominations of Christians, and pastoral duties have been fully and gladly placed in her hands. Many a faithful, energetic woman called to be a pastor's wife has done splendid work in visiting the sick, caring for the poor and leading souls into the sunshine of truth. That church has always been considered specially favored which, in addition to a good minister in the pulpit, could also boast of a pastor's wife who could and would in her own blessed way supplement her husband's work among his people. But the nineteenth century has seen women acting both as preachers and pastors with great success. The Quakers have always sanctioned the preaching of women. Methodists approved Susannah Wesley.

The first woman to be ecclesiastically ordained was Antoinette Brown Blackwell, who now resides in this city. She was a graduate of Oberlin and was ordained in 1853. She is a native of New York State, though of New England ancestry. She was ordained in South Butler, Wayne County, N.Y. by the council called by the First Congregational Church but a Methodist minister preached the ordination sermon. The Rev. Olympia Brown was the next woman ordained. She was ordained at Malone, N.Y. in June 1863. She was the first woman ordained in the Universalist denomination. She was closely followed by Rev. Augusta Chapin who was ordained in December 1863. She is the first woman to receive the title of Doctor of

Divinity. Next came the ordination of the Rev. Phebe A. Hanaford, who was the first woman to be ordained in New England. She was ordained at Hingham, Mass. in 1868. It is a noticeable fact that all these four women were of notable New England descent. Since the ordination of these women there have been more than sixty—perhaps by this time a hundred ordained in various denominations.

The nineteenth century has advanced religious influence in opening wide doors for woman's work in the church. Woman as preacher and pastor is an accomplished fact belonging to the latter half of the closing century.[235]

Amid the flurry of these activities, Phebe and Ellen moved to an apartment at 336 West Fifty-First Street in Manhattan, where as an additional means of support, Phebe listed in the local papers her availability for preaching and lecturing on terms she described as "Expenses and reasonable compensation for time and effort." Later, in a pamphlet announcing she was available in the season 1895 and 1896 for Professional and Literary Lectures upon reasonable terms, she listed thirteen topics for lectures, representing an accumulation of her interests and experiences over the years.

Rev. Mrs. Hanaford is a graduate of the Chautauqua Literary and Scientific Circle (Class of '91), and is prepared to conduct classes in the Chautauqua course or in Parliamentary Law or in the Metaphysics known as the Philosophy of Mental Science. Also prepared to organize Women's Clubs, W.C.T. Unions and any similar organi-

235   New Haven Colony Historical Society

zations. At present Mrs. Hanaford is a Vice-President of Sorosis, (of which she has been a member 23 years); a Vice-President of the Society for Political Study, a member of the Woman's Press Club, and other societies, all of New York City; and is President of "Philitscipoma" of Newark, N.J. She is also one of the officers of the Universal Peace Union, and while residing in Connecticut was the State Superintendent of the W.C.T.U. for peace and Arbitration. She is also a member of various Historical societies.

In addition to organizations listed, Phebe joined the Society of New England Women founded by Mrs. Slade in 1895. The Society encouraged women of New England origin to study American History and to provide "social intercourse as a bond of union and fellowship leading to power and influence." Rev. Hanaford served as chaplain at their meetings held at the Waldorf Astoria. Phebe founded a club she called PHILITSCIPOMA, an anagram, for a study of philosophy, literature, history, poetry, oratory, music and art. They met at their clubhouse at 17 Center Street in Newark. In her active role in the Woman's Club Movement, Phebe gave the Welcome Address on October 24, 1895 at the First Annual Meeting of the New Jersey State Federation of Woman's Clubs.

Several women were invited to give ten-minute lectures including Rev. Antoinette Brown Blackwell who spoke on "Immortality." Phebe spoke on "Evangelical Work Among Women." The New York City Woman Suffrage League met at Sherry's to celebrate Pilgrim Mother's Day. The President, Mrs. Lillie Deveaux Blake, noted that the pilgrims' landing two hundred seventy-five years ago occurred on December 21, although it is traditionally celebrated on the twenty-second. "The only thing that occurred on the twenty-second was the birth of a child, and one of our vice presidents is a lineal descendant of that baby." Mrs. Blake referred to Phebe as that descendant of Degory Priest's daughter, Mary.

Mrs. Blake, as President of the New York State Suffrage Association, led several unsuccessful campaigns for woman suffrage legislation at the State level. She led successful campaigns for legislation requiring women physicians to treat women in mental institutions and women matrons in police stations. Other rights for women in the job market achieved by the New York City Woman Suffrage League demonstrated how broad the interests were of the women who were demanding the vote. They knew suffrage remained the key to political power.

The European Publishing Company of New York published *The Woman's Bible, Part I,* in 1895. It was a commentary on those sections of Genesis, Exodus, Leviticus, Numbers and Deuteronomy that dealt with women or excluded women. The Revising Committee credited with making the selections appeared as follows.

Elizabeth Cady Stanton

Rev. Phebe Hanaford	Lillie Devereaux Blake
Clara Bewick Colby	Matilda Joslyn Gage
Rev. Augusta Chapin	Rev. Olympia Brown
Mrs. Mary Livermore	Mrs. Francis Ellen Burr
Mrs. Mary Seymour Howell	Mrs. Chapman Catt
Mrs. Josephine Henry	Mrs. Helen H. Gardner
Mrs. Robert Ingersoll	Mrs. Charlotte Beebe Wilbour
Mrs. Sarah A. Underwood	Mrs. Lucinda Chandler
Mrs. Catherine F. Stebbins	Mrs. Louise Thomas
Ellen Battelle Dietrick	Mrs. Louise Southworth
Mrs. Cornelia Collins Hussey	Mrs. Martha R. Almy

Note – A complete list of the names of the Revising Committee, including those of foreign members, will be published in Part II.

Newspapers carried reviews of *The Woman's Bible*, calling it audacious and outrageous. At the twenty-eighth annual convention of the National American Woman Suffrage Association held in Washington, DC in January 1896, a resolution stated:

...this Association is non-sectarian, being composed of persons of all shades of religious opinion, and that it has no official connection with the so-called 'Woman's Bible,' or any theological publication.[236]

Phebe Hanaford's name is not listed among the members of the National American Woman Suffrage Association who took part in the debate that followed. Susan B. Anthony failed to have the resolution cancelled, and it passed fifty-three to forty-one. Clara Colby returned to Kansas where she published some of Mrs. Stanton's Commentaries from *The Woman's Bible* in the *Woman's Tribune*. Despite the negative commentaries, *The Woman's Bible, Part I* continued to sell.

In the following months Phebe received an invitation to visit her cousin Louis Coffin and his family, now living in Brooklyn. She and Ellen decided to move to Brooklyn. Directories of 1896-1897 record that Phebe and Ellen were residents of 473 Bedford Avenue. The Brooklyn Bridge provided more reliable passage across the rough East River than the ferries and made affordable suburban living possible while working in the metropolitan city. The neat rows of houses on tree-lined streets provided

---

236   Stanton, 1898

a contrast to city life, and rents proved cheaper in Brooklyn. The Chamber of Commerce described Prospect Park as the finest of several parks in Brooklyn. It was also home to many churches, some with well-known preachers. The Brooklyn Naval Yard provided work for hundreds of men, some of whom were immigrants. Living in Brooklyn, however, proved inconvenient. In the spring Phebe and Ellen took an apartment at 201 West Eighty-Eight Street in Manhattan, a convenient location for their many involvements in women's organizations.

In acknowledgement of the influence of women's clubs, *The New York Times* published an extensive article on the "Woman's Club Movement" on December 5 and 12, 1897. Mrs. "Jennie June" Croly, honorary President of the Federation of Women's Clubs, was featured on the cover of their *Illustrated Weekly Magazine.*

That this is a women's century seems in nothing to be as strongly emphasized as in the women's clubs. Sorosis, named the mother of women's clubs, had under Mrs. Croly's leadership, brought together "women engaged in literary, artistic, scientific, and philanthropic pursuits, with a view of rendering them helpful to each other and useful to society."

The article described Phebe Hanaford as "well known as a member of Sorosis and other large organizations and as an author outside her regular ministerial duties."

As President of the "Society for Political Study," Phebe led classes designed to prepare women for their future role in government. Her goal, "to prepare women to be productive and active citizens," included classes on understanding government in all its forms. The "New Century Political Study Circle," with a membership of 200 women, met at St. Andrew's at 72nd and Broadway to study the New York State Constitution. At role call they responded with quotations from works of an author previously agreed upon. The journalist reported, "Mrs. Hanaford's classes in Parliamentary Law gave her an honorary membership in the Medico-Legal Society." The article gave particular recognition to the popular "Society of New England Women," founded "for the benefit of New England women, not as a charitable body, but to establish a free masonry between all New England women and women of New England descent."

Members of the Revising Committee received notice in 1898 of Mrs. Stanton's plans to publish *The Woman's Bible, Part II Comments on The Old and New Testaments FROM Joshua to Revelation.* Again Mrs. Stanton wrote the major portion of the Commentaries. Contributors on *The Old Testament* included Ellen Battelle Dietrich, Matilda Joslyn Gage, Clara B. Neyman, Louise Southworth, Lucinda Chandler and Phebe Hanaford. In her Commentary on the Book of Judges, Phebe referred to this period in Jewish History as the "colonial days," quoting Dr. Abbot's commentary, "in war they united; in peace they separated again."

Though *The Woman's Bible, Part II* published by the European Publishing Company in 1898, failed to unite women, the volume did fulfill its function of linking the misogyny of the day with woman's secondary position in the Biblical creation story. It was also the first attack on male bias in the Bible, revealing human authorship and human error in translations. Its publication opened the door for future feminist interpretation of the scriptures. Elizabeth Cady Stanton's final work was not acknowledged as a scholarly commentary during her lifetime.

A noted scholar of the day, the Rev. Antoinette Brown Blackwell, author of *The Philosophy of Individuality* (1893), accepted an invitation as an honored guest at the October 13th Philitscipoma meeting that year. Phebe opened the meeting with words of gratitude for Rev. Blackwell's presence and acknowledged her literary accomplishments in the area of science and philosophy. Phebe then began her talk on the topic of Blackwell's book.

The philosophy of all the ages has been tinged with hope. That which holds despair in its composition cannot be accepted as philosophy. Voltaire was a doubter....Ingersoll is an agnostic. Neither of them could be called a philosopher except by that courtesy which regards every thinker as such, and draws no line between negative assertions and positive truths. Intellectual dreaming is not philosophy. Theories are not ideas. An idea has vitality. It advances, and other things move before it. People, races, events, facts, all are affected by ideas, while a theory, "baseless as the fabric of a dream," is but an adumbration of the mind, and will disappear in due season, "like the morning cloud and the early dew."[237]

During the next year, Rev. Phebe Hanaford's life was touched by death many times. Howard's wife, Mary, was ill during the fall of 1898. She died in early December after a long illness. Mary Landerkin Hanaford was buried in Pleasant Hill Cemetery, plot #97 in Cape Cod. Her headstone reads, "Sacred to the Memory of Mary Weston Hanaford – wife of Rev. H. A. Hanaford – daughter of I. N. Landerkin 1851-1898."

In Phebe's letter to Howard of 27 December, the brief reference to Ellen's visit recalls Mary's attachment to "Nellie" and fixes Ellen Miles in the less familiar role of confidant and friend who travels some distance from her family home in Waltham to

237 Nantucket Historical Association

the hospital in Newton to find Mary alone and very ill. Phebe appears less able to show her daughter-in-law the tenderness she feels for her. Evidence of Phebe's concern for Mary during her long illness is apparent when she writes to Howard that she had been

...weary with domestic matters since Nellie has been in Waltham for a fortnight and went to Newton to the hospital before she returned. They told her our dear Mary was unconscious for three days, and she thought they ought to have sent you word sooner; but perhaps they did. As she was unconscious, she did not miss the home faces at the last and she was contented there. She wanted to be there, and you gratified every want, sparing no expense. So you have no need to have any reflections, you tried to do your whole duty by her, and after she gave up and allowed you to take care for her health, you did all that could be done. She would not give up til she was obliged to do so.

Having done her best to console Howard, she turns the light on her own behavior.

But I did not realize—not at all—how feeble she was in body and mind till I saw her and I don't think I fully realized it then. I talked with her of her health, but she did not confide in me, as in Nellie: she did not seem to understand how tenderly I felt for her, especially after she was motherless. And I am sure now, it was her state of health. Evidently she was not able to pass through those trying years, and come out well; and the Heavenly Father has taken her to a better country...[238]

238   Hanford Family Archives

Phebe also writes to her eighteen-year-old granddaughter on December 27, 1898, expressing her sympathy for "the loss in the departure of so dear and good a mother." The letter praises Mary as a daughter, wife, mother and Christian devoted to her church. She encourages Maria to follow her mother's example and do good works for her sake, and writes further:

> *You must be a comfort to your father now. He must lean on you for your sympathy and help. Don't fail him in his hour of need. He may have his faults, as we all have, but he has many virtues; and he tries to be a faithful father and preacher and pastor. Help him.*[239]

Remaining at her desk Phebe continued in her efforts to increase women's awareness of their rightful role in the ministry. Phebe published descriptions of theological schools open to women. In so doing she helped to make a place in America for women in the ministry of all denominations. Phebe wrote, "That women can perform all pastoral duties I can confidently affirm from a personal experience of more than a quarter of a century, the endurance of woman matches that of man as far as pulpit and pastoral work is concerned."[240]

The endurance of woman was never more evident than in the life of Emily Ruggles. News of her unexpected death on November 28, 1899 came to Phebe in a telegram from Mrs. Walden, who wrote that with the news of her death flags flew at half-mast. After the funeral people closed their stores to attend the burial at Laurel Hill Cemetery. Mrs. Walden wrote that "the obituary told the story better than she could."

---

239   Ibid
240   *Public Opinions,* April 13, 1899

OBITUARY
Emily Ruggles

Friends of Emily Ruggles were almost incredulous, Tuesday morning when her death was reported. She had been ill but a few days and at no time had her condition been considered dangerous.

Tuesday morning she rapped at her niece's door as was her custom. She reported having slept nearly all night. A little later, Mrs. Ruggles, on entering the room, found her lying unconscious on the bed, partially dressed. Dr. Parks was immediately summoned but she passed peacefully away a few minutes after his arrival, without regaining consciousness. Her death was due to heart failure.[241]

Emily Ruggles lived her life differently than women of her generation. In Emily, Phebe found a woman who challenged the mores of the day and created her path to success.

Phebe continued to cut her way to success. She challenged Jane Croly, the founder of the Woman's Press Club, in the 1900 elections for the office of president. Phebe felt justified in seeking the office of president because Mrs. Croly spent much of her time away from New York City due to her failing health. The vote favored Jane Croly, forty to thirty-eight. As 1st vice president Phebe served as acting president while Mrs. Croly lived in London.

In the closing months of 1899 correspondence reveals family concerns for Phebe. A letter from Florence's husband, Thomas

---

241   The Reading Daily Times

Warner, told Phebe of his plans to take his wife on a vacation, believing "a change would brighten her spirits." He wrote that their niece, Maria Hanaford, had returned home to Henrietta, New York to begin college, having been with the Warner family in Orleans for much of the summer. In Maria's absence, Mr. Warner arranged for Howard Hanaford to stay at the house with Dionis while they were away. In an October letter to her "Precious Granddaughter Maria," Phebe shows continued concern for her son, Howard. Referring to the Warner home in Orleans, New York, Phebe wrote, "don't you leave your father alone all night in the house." Of Howard she wrote to Maria, "Every dollar he earns will aid him, not alone in money but in self respect. And his health and power will be the stronger. He will find other work. No matter what the work is, if it is honest, he is fortunate."[242] Whatever Howard's state of mind was—grief, depression or loneliness—he appeared unable to hold a job. She closed her letter in haste as she left for a meeting of the Woman's Press Club.

With the turn of the century, more than a quarter of a century had passed since Phebe Hanaford had left her husband. Dr. Joseph Hibbard Hanaford died on July 15, 1900 "at his residence, 19 Spring Street." His obituary goes on to report "he was twice married and leaves two children and two sisters to mourn his departure from earth." After a summary of his medical career, it concludes, "He was a valued and prominent member of the Baptist Church, a friend of Home Missions and a benefactor of his race. He will be sincerely mourned by all who truly knew him and by many who never saw his face." Statistical Records of Reading Deaths identifies him as "married at the time of his death at age eighty-one from cerebral hemorrhage." With no known record of a second marriage and no surviving widow listed in the obituary, it is not known if Harriett was present at his death. The obituary offered no details on the funeral.

A poem written by Dr. Hanaford entitled "My Seventy-Seventh Birthday" speaks of happy memories.

> I still survive the flight of time,
>   And still am blest of gracious Heaven;
> Long since I passed my manhood's prime,
>   And now my years are seventy-seven.
>
> The boyish sports, the childish plays,
>   Long, long since have passed from me;
> Yet, now, I oft recall those days,
>   Their pleasure and their mirthful glee,
>
> My early home, the dearest spot on earth,
>   Its rural views, I love them still;
> O sacred home that gave me birth,
>   Thy much-loved gifts my bosom thrill.
>
> When, now, the hours as moments fly,
>   Like fleecy clouds around, above.
> So fondly merged, in years gone by,
>   My thoughts e'er flow to home in love.
>
> I love those many verdant hills,
>   The mountain grand, with craggy sides,
> The river broad, the sparkling rills,
>   As on each gently, sweetly glides.

Those much-loved homes once more I'd see,
    Their well-filled barns, their flocks and herds,
The farmer home-bred, strong and free,
    And hear again the sportive birds.

Once more those mates in school I'd meet,
    And bid love's fountains freely flow;
Once more the dear ones there would greet
    And kindly deeds in love bestow.

How few the loved of bygone days
    Have reached Life's zenith's lofty brows;
How few could meet my eager gaze, —
    How <u>very</u> few as I am now!

Still Time's full-freighted spacious train,
    With stores of wealth and mental lore,
And fruits of growth ne'er sought in vain,
    Is rushing on, as ne'er before.
            Dr. Joseph Hibbard Hanaford
            b. January 27, 1819[243]

At a later date Phebe wrote to Maria about her grandfather.

Dr. Hanaford wrote excellent hymns, especially for a book to be used at the Sailor's Church in Boston. Dr. H. was an earnest worker in behalf of that noble Boston Church of which his school friend, Rev. Phineas Stowe, was Pastor. Both have passed on and both did noble work in their day.[244]

243   Ibid
244   Ibid

Phebe continued her work in the various clubs when they resumed their meetings in September. Mrs. Ida Trafford Bell chaired the Committee on Journalism and Literature at the Woman's Press Club. Mark Twain addressed the group in the Chapter Room at Carnegie Hall on 27 October 1900. Phebe joined the West End Women's Republican Club. The Club appealed to representative women anxious to be intelligently informed on political conditions. Their monthly meetings held at Delmonico's included former abolitionists who remained loyal to Abraham Lincoln's party over the years.

When Jane Croly returned from England, the October Sorosis program included an account of her travels. Her failing health prevented her from attending meetings of Sorosis or the Woman's Press Club in the following months. Phebe resumed her responsibilities as 1st vice president of Sorosis and acting president of the Woman's Press Club. The minutes of March 1901 read,

In acknowledgment of what our 1st vice-president, Mrs. Hanaford, has done for the Club and its appreciation for her work with and for all women, its members had the pleasure at a business meeting of presenting her with a Life Membership in the Women's Press Club.[245]

Jane Croly died in her home on December 23, 1901. The *New York Times* obituary called her the "best known woman Journalist in America and the originator of women's clubs." After detailing her impressive career as a journalist with its link to women's issues, the article credited Mrs. Croly with founding the Woman's Circle, the New Cycle, Sorosis, the Federation of

245   Columbia University

Women's Clubs and the Woman's Press Club. The obituary concluded, "In 1898 Mrs. Croly met with an accident, which crippled her, and since then she had spent much of her time in England. She was to be buried at the Church of the Transfiguration and interred with her husband in Lakewood, New Jersey." Phebe wrote her personal tribute to Jane Croly.

It was eminently fitting that one who had been stirred in former years by the absence of social recognition in journalism as within woman's province, on the part of the men of the press, and moved to take a prominent part in the formation of Sorosis, should organize a club of women writers – women journalists especially – which should be known everywhere as distinctly a Woman's Press Club.[246]

The minutes of January 1902 reported, "The Press Club acknowledges the faithful and devoted service of our 1st vice-president, Rev. Phebe Hanaford during the long absence and illness of our late and honored president, Mrs. Croly." There was a motion recognizing Mrs. Hanaford as president for the remainder of the club year. In the absence of a vice president, the acting Secretary, Mrs. Staples, took the chair and put the question to the members. Several spoke to the motion resulting in the unanimous vote for Phebe Hanaford as president. The chairman of the Executive Committee insisted in being put on record as opposing the motion from a purely parliamentary point of view. The motion prevailed; the club formally recognized Phebe A. Hanaford, president. The minutes read, "In her own strong and eloquent way—our new leader accepted the trust which came to her."[247]

....

246   Ibid
247   Ibid

On January twenty-eight Phebe chaired a meeting of Sorosis where a committee of eight was asked to prepare a service in memory of Jane Croly. Phebe and Charlotte Wilbour invited members of the Press Club to join them. In her address at the joint service on February 15, 1902, Phebe Hanaford spoke of Jane Croly's motivation in forming the Woman's Press Club. In conclusion, she addressed the members:

> *As members of the club, that she who has now passed into the eternal light founded, may we seek earnestly to walk in the light of Truth, strenuous for that more than royal liberty of conscience, which means liberty under righteous law, and for the Unity which obeys the Golden Rule, and thus binds heart to heart. So shall the Woman's Press Club of New York City truly honor the memory of its founder and first president, Jane Cunningham Croly.*[248]

The summer brought news of Maria Hanaford's upcoming marriage. The wedding announcement indicates Howard has remarried. His mother's hope that he find "someone to look after him" seems fulfilled.

> *Mr. and Mrs. H. A. Hanaford*
> *request your presence at the marriage of*
> *their daughter*
> *Maria*
> *to Fred F. Feasel*
> *Thursday, July tenth, Nineteen Hundred and two*
> *at five o'clock Henrietta, New York*[249]

---

248   Ibid
249   Hanaford Family Archives

A letter of congratulations from her grandmother written on 22 June from Winchester, New Hampshire assures Maria of "a good big loud yes to your proposal to visit us and make our house your home while in this vicinity." Phebe asks, "Are you going to do housekeeping? I want to know."[250]

In the Tonawanda Historical Society, housed in the original railroad station ticket office, is to be found *The Evening News* of August 15, 1902, whose front page reads,

Shot Herself

Mrs. Florence E. Warner of Goundrey Street Cannot Survive—
Temporary Insanity Is said to be the cause—
Has Been in Unusually Good Spirits During the Evening—

Last night about 9:30 o'clock, Mrs. Florence **E. Warner** of 213 Goundrey Street shot herself in the head while temporarily insane. The wound is fatal and death is expected any minute.

Mrs. Warner had been in particularly good spirits during the evening which fact had been remarked upon after supper by members of the family. Shortly before the shooting occurred Mr. Warner went into the house leaving Mrs. Warner on the verandah, where the family had been spending the evening together. Mrs. Warner had expressed the desire to remain there a few minutes longer to enjoy the cool air and moonlight.

---

250   Ibid

A few minutes later, Miss Dionis Warner, who had been out walking, returned and found her mother unconscious beside a table on the back porch. Her head was resting upon the table and her arms extended. A revolver which was lying near her, told the story.

From the nature of the wound it seems Mrs. Warner placed her elbow upon the table to steady her hand with the muzzle of the pistol pressing against the upper part of the forehead pointing downward. The bullet had plowed through the brain and lodged in the lower part of the head near the neck.

The shot was heard by neighbors who thought someone was shooting cats.

Temporary insanity was undoubtedly the cause which prompted Mrs. Warner to commit the deed. She is said to have had slight attacks before, though they were not frequent. It is not improbable that while hunting for something she accidentally came across the revolver and prompted by temporary aberration, did the shooting upon the spur of the moment.

Mrs. Warner's mother, Rev. Phebe A. Hanaford of New York City, was informed of the tragedy by telegram early this morning....

The late edition of the paper carried this headline.

Mrs. Warner died this Morning Without Gaining Consciousness

Mrs. Florence E. Warner, wife of Thomas E. Warner, who shot herself Thursday night, died this morning at the family residence on Goundrey Street.

Mrs. Warner remained unconscious from the time she was found until death came. There was never the least hope of recovery and the bullet passed through the brain and lodged in the back of the skull. The attending physicians say that had the muzzle of the revolver not been held close to the head, death would have been instantaneous. The surviving family is the husband Thomas E. Warner, parents Rev. Howard A. Hanaford (sic) and Rev. Phoebe (sic) A. Hanaford and daughter Dionis Warner.

The funeral will take place Monday afternoon at 4 o'clock at the residence on Goundrey Street. After the ceremony the body will be taken to Orleans, N.Y. and interred at the convenience of the family.

Phebe could not have reached her daughter's bedside in time. Ellen's poor health would have made it impossible for Phebe to accompany the body to Orleans where Florence was laid to rest in the Warner family plot. The train bearing her body left from this station, now the Tonawanda Historical Society. A month later from the Warner family home at 213 Goundry Street in Tonawanda, Phebe wrote to Fred Feasel, her granddaughter Maria's husband,

Sept. 15, 1902

Dear Grandson Fred, I thank you for your kind letter, and I write to explain why I desired greatly to have our dear Maria here for a few days.

Of course we all desired to have her come because she more than any other person on earth, seems to comfort me, by her affectionate, cheery, loving ways. I may never come this way again, and I long to see her once more before I go back.

*We cannot stop to see you all in Henrietta, because Auntie Nell
is worse than when she came, and is longing to get home to her
Doctor and the comfort of being on one floor. It hurts her to go
up and down stairs here, and she can only do it twice a day.
I desire especially to see Maria in reference to my property here
and elsewhere. This is private—dear Fred—for you and Maria
only—and not for dear Maria to mention to anyone here when
she comes, if she comes at all.
My will was made leaving Aunt Florence as executor—and
now I must make another will. And I want to consult Maria
about it.
Also, Uncle Tom thinks of renting this house, and I want to
give Maria some silver spoons, and many other things, if she
wants them. I may as well give them to her now as to wait till
I am in the Father's house.*[251]

No surviving correspondence indicates Maria's response to her
grandmother's request. At seventy-one years of age, burdened
with grief and the care of Ellen, Phebe left Tonawanda for New
York City where death remained her companion in the remaining months.

Elizabeth Cady Stanton died in her home on October 28,
1902 a few weeks before her eighty-seventh birthday.

Miss Anthony went with the family to Woodlawn
Cemetery, where another old friend, the Rev. Phebe
A. Hanaford pronounced the committal to the earth,
which thus ended: "O, Thou Infinite and Eternal Power,
whom so many of Thy children love to call Our Father
and Our Mother, into Thy hands we commit the spirit

---

251   Ibid

of our beloved one, assured that all is right where Thy rule extends.[252]

At the anniversary meeting of the Woman's Press Club in 1903, members unanimously nominated Phebe Hanaford as their president. At the November elections of the Woman's Press Club, members cast forty-nine of the fifty votes for president in favor of Phebe Hanaford. In response, Phebe asked for kindness and support for her future work and spoke of her great desire to serve the club. It was agreed she would ex-officio represent the Woman's Press Club at the State Federation of Women's Clubs in Brooklyn. As president, Phebe initiated the plans to publish a memorial to Jane Croly. The George Putnam Publishing Company published the "Jennie June Memorial Book" in March 1904.

A directory of women's clubs for that year available at the New York Historical Society shows Phebe Hanaford's residence at 230 West Ninety-Fifth Street. Later that year, Phebe Hanaford's literary career received recognition when her *Life of Abraham Lincoln* was included in a series *Library of History and Biographies*. During the winter evenings spent with Ellen at their apartment, Phebe wrote an account of her childhood, *Old-Time School Days*.[253] With the news from Henrietta that Maria Hanaford Feasel had safely delivered a baby girl, Helen Mae, on 1 May 1903, Phebe became a great-grandmother,

In the 1903 elections of the Woman's Press Club, Mary Coffin Johnson joined the officers as 1st vice president under Phebe Hanaford. Meetings continued in the Chapter Room of Carnegie Hall throughout the years 1903-1904. Phebe's atten-

252   Harper, p. 1264
253   Nantucket Historical Association

dance at Sorosis appears irregular in the winter months of Mrs. Charlotte Wilbour's second term as president. On a snowy evening in January 1905, as agreed, a reporter from the *New York Times* rang their doorbell. Once the journalist was settled, the young woman inquired what it was like when Phebe began to preach. On January 22, 1905 *The New York Times* carried the story.

HOW REV. PHOEBE (sic) A. HANAFORD
WAS ORDAINED

A Pleasant room, with quaint and shining crystal-knobbed furniture, with ferns at windows, a shaded lamp on the center table, Ellen E. Miles, the writer of hymns, sewing carpet rugs for charity close to the lamp, big variegated balls near by and filling a basket at her feet, and Phebe A. Hanaford, pastor of the Universalist Church and President of women's clubs, idling hands folded, resting awhile in the evening of her life.

This was the scene upon which The Times reporter entered. She put some questions relative to the life of the woman pastor.

"I'm afraid I am too tired to talk tonight," smiled Mrs. Hanaford.

The writer of hymns looked up from her carpet rags.

"Talk," she urged. "She has come all the way in the cold. If you don't talk, I will," she threatened.

"What happened when you first began to preach?" asked the Times reporter, encouraged somewhat. "Did they persecute you in the name of God? Did they throw things at you?"

"Tell her," said the writer of hymns, "how they bore you up in their arms, like the precious thing you are, and always have been," Ellen reproached Mrs. Hanaford. Then I see," she added, "if this is to be told correctly, I must do it myself."

Then she began to tell how she had come from a Quaker family, where all her life she had heard the women talk in the congregation, where more women talked than men. How Lucretia Mott, whose sweet old fashioned picture hung above the mantel in the pleasant room, was her ancestress. How she was descended, too, from Degory Priest, one of the twenty-nine signers of the Mayflower Compact, the first expression of true republican principles in the world, and had thus come naturally by her tendency to preach right living and the Gospel.

"Tell how you are the fourth woman in the world to be ordained," prompted the writer of hymns, "and the first from New England."

"Antoinette Brown Blackwell," began Mrs. Hanaford, "was the first woman in the world to be ordained. She was ordained in New York. The second was Rev. Olympia Brown, also from New York State. The third was the Rev. Augusta J. Chapin, New York. She is the only woman in the world who has received the degree of Doctor of Divinity. The fourth to be ordained was myself, in New England, at Hingham, Mass., in the year '68. Eight men and one woman ordained me. That woman was the Rev. Olympia Brown. At my ordination services, the hymns were written for me by women. One was written for me by Julia Ward Howe, who is one of my dearest friends, the other—"

Here she waved her hand toward Ellen E. Miles, who looked up again from her carpet rags.

"I wrote the other," she nodded.

"She wrote the other," said Mrs. Hanaford.

"Tell how you ordained your own son," once more prompted Ellen E. Miles, "and afterward exchanged pulpits with him. Tell how you assisted at the marriage service of your daughter. Tell how for fifteen years you preached, rain or shine, without missing a sermon, without taking a vacation, without going to England, Italy or France, as men preachers do. Tell how you were one of the first women Chaplains in the Legislature of Connecticut."

"It was before the Capitol was moved from New Haven," resumed Mrs. Hanaford. "I served as Chaplain in the Legislature in 1870, then again in 1872. I was paid just as men Chaplains were, (this proudly). My check was sent to me. I am the only woman minister also who ever gave the charge at the ordination of a man minister, the occasion being the ordination of the Rev. W.G. Haskell, in Marblehead, Mass."

"Was there no objection to you among the men?" questioned the reporter. "Was there no feeling against this usurpation of their territory?"

"Some little," replied Mrs. Hanaford quietly. "I was sent one summer to occupy the pulpit of a minister who was away on his vacation. He complained bitterly. Since then, however, his views have broadened. He is now President of a theological school in which women are received and ordained, Tufts College, Boston.

"Yes, I had considerable opposition to overcome, now that I recollect, I remember once I was sent to the garden of Maine to take charge of a pulpit over Sunday. I was to spend the day and night with some parishioners at a private house. When I arrived I was put into a cab and driven to a hotel.

"It suited me very well. If I had gone to the house I should have been obliged to talk, to entertain, to make myself agreeable. As it was I had my time to myself and my work before I preached my sermon.

"When I entered the church and walked to the pulpit I saw a couple sitting not far away.

"One could see by their dress and manner that they were well-to-do—that that they were wealthy, in fact. You may say what you please, but it is wealth that gives the advantage of education and culture, of refinement. All these constitute leadership in Church and State. Wealth is not to be despised, since it gives such advantages.

"They looked earnestly at me, these two, throughout my sermon. When it was finished, they came up to me and congratulated me upon it. Then they asked me to go with them to their house. They insisted, taking me with them in their carriage, going to great pains to make me comfortable, lighting a cheerful fire in my room when I got there, and making much of me.

"They were the couple who refused to receive me, who had had me sent to the hotel. The husband particularly was deeply opposed to a woman preacher. Still, he felt it to be his duty to go to the church, to hear me preach, to see what I looked like, and how I conducted myself. When he had seen and heard his opposition to me was ended."

The writer of hymns glanced at her proudly, then at the reporter as if to say:

"And do you wonder?"

"The decree of St. Paul that women should keep still tongues in the congregation," mused Mrs. Hanaford, "retarded the progress of woman for centuries, but not for all time. She has risen now to take her place in the world and the Church. In the world you know yourself what excellent work of every description the women are doing. You know their clubs, their charities. In the Church, well, in the Universalist Church alone there are sixty women pastors. In other churches I do not know their number, but there are quite as many, if not more. The world is not hurt by the preaching of women," she finished, "nor ever will be."

"On the contrary," softly said Ellen E. Miles, "it is purified."

Within weeks of the news article a note requesting Rev. Hanaford to conduct a memorial service the following day announced the death of Mrs. Ida Trafford Bell. On Tuesday at four o'clock Rev. Hanaford conducted a service in the Bell home at 141 West 84th Street. She arranged for a memorial service at the meeting of the Woman's Press Club for the untimely death of the forty-four-year-old friend and chair of the Committee on Journalism and Literature. From the Trafford family we have the letter Phebe wrote to Ida's mother. Her reference, "my son is pastor," confirms Howard's continued ministry.

Feb. 7, 1905

My dear Mrs. Trafford,

My heart is with you in the sorrow that must come to your heart, with the departure of your dear daughter Ida, and I write to express my sympathy. *I well know how a mother suffers when her children depart before her to the better land, for it is but little over two years since my own daughter went to the Father's house. She and I loved Ida, and I have always been glad to feel that Ida loved us. Now you and I have each a dear child in the other life, who knew us and knew each other. I have faith to believe that they will meet and enjoy talking with each other about us who are still here in the midst of the earthly activities, trials and sorrows. And we must not forget that many blessings are still left to us. You have your sons and at least one daughter left, and your grandchildren. I have grandchildren, and one son. My son is pastor of the Presbyterian church in La Fayette, New York, and I have just written to him to tell him of dear Ida's departure, for he had met her, and she was very kind to him, cheering him in his hour of illness, one winter when he was with me. It was a joy to our dear Ida to do good, and I can truthfully say as I said this afternoon, that I never knew her to be uncharitable in speech or unkind in action....But you know her better than I could know her, and I do not need to tell you of her virtues. She will be greatly missed.*

The clubs sent flowers to express their love for her, and their sympathy with those who were near and dear to her....

No goodnight dear sorrowing mother. A bereaved mother reaches her hand out in sympathy to you. God comfort you as He alone can....

Yours in loving sympathy
Phebe A. Hanaford

Miss Miles wrote with me in love and sympathy. A telegram told her of the death of her only sister.

Ellen's poor health ended their trips to Nantucket Island. Phebe's sister, Emma, remained in Siasconset surrounded by nieces and nephews following the deaths of her brothers, George and Robert. At eighty-six years of age, Phebe's family consisted of the younger generations. She wrote to her two-year-old great-granddaughter, Helen Feasel.

May 1, 1905

My dear <u>little</u> Great Grand daughter, Helen,

I do long to see you but cannot yet, as I have no spyglass that will reach Henrietta from New York.

I congratulate you, and all of us who love you & that you have reached your second birthday, and are so well, and so sweet and so pretty. The Lord help you to be not only sweet and healthy and handsome, but also always good.

Tell your dear mother that I long to see her also, and I want to see your dear papa, and your Grandma Feasel, and all the good friends in your native town, where my revered and beloved friend, Rev. Antoinette Brown Blackwell was born. I think your dear grandpa Hanaford is very likely at your house tonight, celebrating your second birthday. I wish I could look upon you all.

Tell your mother that I am well, but Auntie Nell is not as well as usual. She slept poorly last night—for she sat too far forward on her rolling chair, and it rolled away from her and she fell to the floor. She screamed, and I ran in to the parlor, and Miss Williams (Aunt Peggy) ran and Miss Ella Ward, the artist was there already—and all three lifted her up. She has been weak today—from nervous shock—but not much worse in lameness.

It is late and I must say "Goodnight." Your granduncle
Tom is going to visit the West on business and Mrs. Tiler and
her niece are going to stay with Dio.

Tell your mother that I will write her a better letter than
this one sometime, but I can do no more tonight as I am very
tired, not having slept last night very much.

With love to all—
You're loving Great Grandmother,
Phebe A. Hanaford[254]

The *New York Times* reported the indictment of Berthe
Claiche for murder on July 18, 1905. "Seven of the jurors declaring
that Emile Gerdron had come to his death as the result of a bullet wound inflicted by Berthe Claiche while five declared to the
same effect but added the words in self-defense.… She pleaded
not guilty and the case was set for trial. Berthe Claiche was committed to the Tombs without bail." Phebe attended the trial.

The Courthouse on Chambers Street held the depressing
truth that the maximum sentence called for was twenty years
imprisonment. In spite of or because of that power, anyone entering the Courthouse felt a sense of pride in the judicial system
represented by the beautiful building. Judge Jerome accepted a
plea of guilty of manslaughter in the first degree on March 6,
1906. He dismissed the jury with these words, "When the final
result is reached and sentence passed by the court, it will undoubtedly be seen that the best interests of the people have been
served." The Court clerk asked the defendant, "Do you withdraw the plea of 'not guilty'?" Berthe replied yes and collapsed
and was carried away by the Deputy Sheriff. Phebe wrote an
article for *The New York American* with her photo enclosed.

254   Hanaford Family Archives

PITY FOR WRECKED LIFE OF A GIRL IS
INSEPARABLE FROM CLAICHE TRIAL
By Phebe A. Hanaford

The law recognizes the sacredness of human life, at the same time making a distinction between what is sometimes termed "judicial murder" and the taking of human life wantonness or in revenge. A motive or incentive must be proven beyond a doubt or there can be no legal condemnation."

In the case of Berthe Claiche there is no doubt to the fact that she ended the life of Emile Gerdron by shooting, and of the motive there is still less doubt, because she frankly states the reason for her illegal action.

She was weary of slavery, she sought freedom. She was tired of being beaten and she brought the castigations to an end. She did not wait for a lawful, chivalrous defender, but took the matter of securing a cessation of persecutions into her own hands. In this she was at fault. It was a grievous mistake. It was an error which rendered her liable to legal restraint, to long imprisonment, or to electrocution, as an unbiased jury might decide. Death made the vicious man let go his hold on her, but the act which caused his death, placed her at once in the clutches of a law designed to keep the public peace and protect the life of every individual. Her life according to testimony was in jeopardy.

Jury made of Earnest Men

As far as I could perceive, the jurors were intelligent, thoughtful, earnest men. Phrenologists would describe them each and all as having fine mental endowment, for they were men of large and finely developed brain, judging from the wide and high foreheads which were plainly in evidence. We can but expect from such men a fair and honest verdict. I saw that they paid strict attention to the witnesses, and not once did I notice any sign of levity or carelessness, indeed, the whole atmosphere of that courtroom was tinged with the seriousness of the situation. The sunlight came in upon the mural pictures, but it did not seem to enliven the occasion.

For there sat the pale, thin, slender object of that assembly, herself not only an object of curiosity to visitors but an object of sympathy.

I agree with Judge Davis (as reported in the press) that there should be no maudlin sympathy for a murderer such as is too often shown, but no tender heart of a parent could look upon that young, pale face and not grieve in spirit that her life should have proved so sad a failure. Her presence saddened the hearts of all who have learned to count mortal life a blessing only as it conduces to moral growth and spiritual advancement. To have been born with limited moral sense, educated without reference to moral obligations and surrounded by the most immoral and degrading influences seems to have been the lot of this young woman.

The Judge spoke of a desire to know all the truth and in that knowledge to maintain the majesty of the law.

I was gratified to notice the impartial ruling of Judge Davis. He seemed the embodiment of judicial dignity and power, whether he overruled or sustained an objection of the opposing counsel. No doubt he pitied the poor, pale defendant in the case, but he was there to see that the legal rights of prosecutor and defendant were secured; and whatever may be the result I shall be satisfied that a fair hearing has been given to the case.

Opposed as I have been to capital punishment, I should regret exceedingly that any woman or man should find the gallows or the electric chair at the end of an impartial trial before a conscientious and intelligent jury, and, therefore, I cannot but hope that the result of this trial of Berthe Claiche may be for her an opportunity for repentance and an upright life, even though it should be found only within the walls of a reformatory.

The trials in our city seem to be almost in the presence of the whole people since the newspapers give such complete reports and vivid pen pictures. I looked at the long table where sat the patient, plodding, faithful reporters, doing their best to hear and record; I watched the messenger boys as they came for "copy" and bore it away, from time to time, that a million and more hearts in this great city—and far and wide over our land might read the judicial decision to safeguard the rights of human beings and the overwhelming testimony to the fact that the young need moral restraints and I thank God for the power of the press and the influence of the pen.

Many Noble Men on "the Force"

I am glad to add that in later years I have learned to recognize many noble and honorable men upon the force, and can but believe that the city's youth are better cared for by the police than in olden days, notwithstanding the testimony given in connection with the trial of Berthe Claiche.

The time has surely come for reform in respect to the morals of every large city. And if such trials bring to light iniquity, even among those whose duty it is to guard the homes of our land and the peace of the community, we may also hope that the light may thus be let into the dark places and our hearts be able to hail the dawning of a better day.

Meanwhile let society throw the arms of its philanthropy around the girls and boys of our cities till there shall be no such sad lives as that of Berthe Claiche and no more heart ache over the injustice which condemns one sex while allowing the other that liberty which is license and can only lead to sad results. Sin is slavery, and the only true freedom is that which comports with righteousness.

Newspapers reported on March 9, 1906 that Miss Claiche had given incriminating evidence regarding police corruption. She named "four policemen to each of whom she had been paying $2 a week for a long time in order to insure herself against arrest." Those men, it was said, collected similar tribute from scores of other women. "The prisoner gave the names of nearly fifty women who have made similar payments." Newspapers sold very well the next day when reporters linked the arrest of a "BAND OF SLAVE DEALERS" to the Berthe Claiche case. "It became evident that information from Miss Claiche enabled the police to break the case." The charge was reduced to manslaughter. Miss Claiche would later receive a light sentence on June 5 for the murder of Emile Gerdron.

Miss Claiche faded from print and within the week newspapers carried word of the death of Susan B. Anthony. Miss Anthony died at her home in Rochester, New York on March 13, 1906 at age eighty-six. Fifty-eight years had passed since Susan B. Anthony, Lucy Stone and Elizabeth Cady Stanton, the three earliest champions, had begun their work for women's rights. Phebe Hanaford had joined them in making speeches before legislative bodies seeking the passage of the sixteenth amendment to the United States Constitution. Now known as the Susan B. Anthony amendment, it still awaited passage by Congress. The memories of six decades belonged to the pioneers. The funeral ceremony belonged to the officers of the National American Woman Suffrage Association.

Twenty-five hundred mourners passed in front of the simple Quaker casket in the Central Presbyterian Church. Much of what drove both Susan B. Anthony and Phebe Hanaford stemmed from their Quaker roots. Abolition and temperance had led them both into their lifelong fight against injustice. The program for the memorial service does not include the name of Rev. Phebe Hanaford. The hour belonged to the new generation.

In these years marked by the loss of friends, Phebe served as vice president of Sorosis and president of the Woman's Press Club. Her activities gave her hope for the future as evidenced in her poem.

SOROSIS

Now count we not our club by years
Nor count ourselves as old;
There is no age where Life abounds,
No dross where all is gold,
We mourn not then o'er any Past
Nor with the Present pause.
We claim the Future in its strength
By growth's eternal laws.[255]

With little surviving correspondence from Howard Hanaford, the family archives recall that Rev. Howard Hanaford became a pastor in Westerville, New York in 1906. While on vacation in Rochester, New York Howard died on September 1, 1907. Phebe received a telegram explaining Howard's sudden death. "Cause of death organic heart trouble...STOP. Details of funeral to follow."[256] News arrived that Howard's body would be taken to Weedsport, New York for graveside services on 5 September. Rochester newspapers carried no news of Howard's death. Mrs. Charlotte Wilbour wrote.

255   Sophia Smith Collection
256   Hanaford Family Archives

40 Central Park South
September 14, 1907

My dear Miss Miles,

Your letter of sad news reached me in due time but I could not reply because I was unfortunate & burst a blood vessel in my left eye & it was suffused with blood & aside from its repulsive appearance, I could not use it to read or write. I am in town for the moment to attend to business & shall return to Bernardsville this afternoon. I deeply feel the sorrow & anxiety of dear Mrs. Hanaford but there are times when death is our best & kindest friend, & this I count the affliction of our friend. We cannot ask for life when the body cannot serve the spirit. But one cannot read the lessons that come to us clearly, or accept them unquestionably. There is always the feeling that there is something wrong when our children pass out before us. Enclosed please find one hundred dollars, $100, which I send wishing that it were a larger sum. My love & good wishes must not be measured by little gifts. With the love & sympathy of yours always,

Charlotte B. Wilbour[257]

The buoyant spirit that had enabled Phebe to lead meetings and invigorate groups appears to have failed her following Howard's death.. Sorosis records of 1909 only list Phebe Hanaford and Ellen Miles as members. Phebe sent regrets that she would not be at a meeting of the Press Club. In March of that year the First Universalist Church in Jersey City was sold to the Lafayette Colored Presbyterian Church, closing yet another

257   Hanaford Family Archives

chapter in her active life. The Press Club sent a check to their Honorary President for her eightieth birthday in May. The 1910 Press Club minutes record "in the absence of our Beloved President...." The Church of the Divine Paternity took up a collection for Rev. Phebe Hanaford and is on record for a gift of $25 with a note stating that it matches the sum given to the Young People's Christian Union.

The death of Julia Ward Howe in her home in Newport, Rhode Island in October 1910 marked the loss of another friend. Even as her health continued to fail, Ellen remained Phebe's only comfort as friends were taken from her. Phebe resumed her correspondence with Dionis, now married and living in her parents' home in Tonawanda. She wrote to Maria in Henrietta, New York to congratulate her on the birth of her son, William Hanaford in 1910. The injury to her arm from a fall on the ice months earlier made writing difficult. Phebe also continued her correspondence with her great-granddaughter Helen Feasel.

230 W. 95 New York City

My dear Great Granddaughter,

I was delighted to get that nice letter from you, and very thankful to our Heavenly Father that you were able to send me the good news of the departure of the measles and the consequent quarantine. Your dear father's welcome letter eased my mind in respect to your dear mother's health, and now I feel quite easy in respect to the health of all my dear ones in Henrietta.

I trust you are enjoying Cousin Mary Ewer Maynard's book, and I mean to get you the other Little Pitcher as fast as they publish it.

And now I want to know what newspapers you see in your own home, for some times I could send you some that are

interesting, but fear to do so, as you may have them already.
And what magazines do you see at home? Please be sure to
answer my questions. I am looking every mail for a letter from
Tonawanda, as I am anxious to know how your Cousin Dionis
is. I've had one letter since she got home from the Hospital and
she said she lay about the house, is at all meals except breakfast.
I feel very thankful that she can do as much as that.

Tell your dear mother that as soon as I get rested a little,
and do not have so many callers, I shall get a box ready to send
some things to you and to her—some things that will please
dear little Billy, and some books that I hope your father and all
his dear little family will enjoy.

Dear Auntie Nell's nephew was here on Thursday eve-
ning (Howard Barnes) and went back to his family at West
Medford, Mass. yesterday. He thinks of going to Guatemala
next week, and coming back in June to take his wife to see her
dear mother who lives in Texas. He hopes to come back in the
fall to buy a house near this city, and live here in future. I
hope he will.

Your cousin Emma Fraser is here, and is a great comfort
and help to me. Pardon my poor letter. My hand is lame today
and I can only write in a scrawly way. Good morning dear,
Helen. Love to all, including Grandma Feasel— from your
Great Grandmother, Phebe A. Hanaford[258]

In Waltham, Massachusetts, the parish celebrated their
seventy-fifth anniversary in October. The 1913 program noted,
"A letter received from former pastor Rev. Phebe Hanaford
and a letter from an old member, Miss Ellen Miles." *Who's Who*
1912-1913 and 1914-15 listed Rev. Phebe Hanaford's biography.

---

258   Ibid

On receipt of a request from Alberta Stimson Philips, Phebe read the questions "Why did you enter the ministry? What has been your experience as a minister? Do you believe in women as ministers? What can you say in their favor to help them in the future?" Phebe, who had encouraged women to join the ministry with her words and example, never answered the request. She who enjoyed extraordinary health, who never made use of the health resorts popular in her day or resorted to medicine for any chronic ailment, spent her energy on the care of Ellen. A silence fell over the private lives of these two women as they lived out their days in the apartment on West 59th Street. Ellen's health failed visibly. "Sister Pricilla," her beloved friend of forty-four years, would be taken from her.

Ellen Miles died in their apartment on March 20, 1914; cause of death, "Chronic Myocarditis." Phebe rode on the train with Ellen's coffin for burial in the Miles' family plot in Mt. Feake Cemetery. The obituary that appeared in the Waltham *Daily Free Press-Tribune* on March 23, 1914, most probably written by Phebe, reads in part,

MISS ELLEN E. MILES

Miss Ellen E. Miles, who will be remembered by many of our people passed away at her home in New York City on Friday, last, aged 80 years. Miss Miles was for a time a teacher in the public schools. Her sister, Miss M. Jennie Miles was for a long period similarly engaged and there were few of the public school pupils of two generations ago who did not come under her instructions. Soon after Rev. Phebe Hanaford was settled as pastor of the Universalist Church in Waltham, nearly 50 years ago, she and Miss Miles formed a very intimate personal friendship which continued without interruption so long as Miss Miles lived; their companionship was like that of David and Jonathan. She was a woman of exceedingly kind nature, conscientious in her life, strong in her friendships and inflexible in her sense of duty. The remains have been brought to Waltham for internment and funeral services will be held from the residence of her nephew, Frank J. Barnes of Main Street. The date will be given later.

Phebe remained a few days in Waltham and then returned to her empty apartment. Ellen's family notified her that the headstone on Ellen's grave (Lot No. 2167) would read, in addition to her span of life, "Face to Face With Those Who Love Us."

Of those who loved Phebe, Antoinette Brown Blackwell with failing eyesight wrote of her concern for her.

June 15, 1914

My dear friend, Phebe A. Hanaford,

Very much do I sympathize with you in this great loss. Many of us will feel it for you and for ourselves, and we feel how hard it will be for you when you are so far from strong or well yourself. But the heavenly winds are tempered to all need. I believe that they are adapted in the very Constitution of things and are tenderly, faithfully sustained.

If I had been in Elizabeth, I should at once have gone to see you—alone if no one could accompany me. They are all almost overburdened with unusual cares and dates this year or I should have seen you and the dear one who has gone forward not so very long now for either of us. I have passed through the 90th year, strong as I am, the end never can hardly be very remote.

In many ways this has been to me a hopeful cheerful, but in others a trying year. Work has gone on successfully with good cheer but all of my several homes are either celebrating centennials or ambitiously improving their neighborhoods.

I have transplanted and planted many little trees in the place here as well as that in Elmore. Taxes increase even as the roads widen and water and sewer appear.

Now dear, I tell you this that you may realize we all have our own trials. Probably trials and strength all help in the even balance.

I hope to return about early September. If you are still in NY I will see you very soon.

Let me know of your movements if only by a postal or by proxy. Whatever comes, you will be brave but be restful and take the best possible care of your self. Our working contemporaries are few and we are almost the "last leaves" on the tree of pleasant fellowship. God bless and console you.

Ever old friend, A. B. Blackwell[259]

---

259   Ibid

CHAPTER NINE

PHEBE A. HANAFORD, ROBBED

I do not like living on a farm—
I do not like being out of the world in the bushes.
I am too far away from civilization and refinement,
and I have no companionship at all.[260]

Death robbed Phebe of Ellen's companionship and fate robbed her of years of usefulness in the women's rights movements. Records preserved by the Hanaford family describe Phebe's final years spent in the home of her granddaughter Dionis, now married to Edward "Herbert" Santee.

Phebe traveled to Tonawanda after Ellen's death to visit her granddaughter, Dionis Warner Santee, who was living in the Warner family home. The few remaining pages from an undated letter from her cousin Mrs. Cartwright describe how Phebe Hanaford was robbed of her rightful place in women's history.

2390 Amsterdam Avenue

My dear Kinswoman Mrs. Hanaford,

I am always so glad to hear from you! (It always stirs up my fighting blood however. I want to rush out there and literally "wipe the ground" with that brutish and bullying grandson-in-law of yours. (I heard the whole story of his language and his conduct from Mrs. Larry.)

I may as well tell you now—Truth is always the best, it seems to me, even when it hurts, although there are times, circumstances, etc. when it is better to say nothing. It is your right to know that your grandson-in-law sent for the Salvation Army and a junk-man, and what one did not take the other did, excepting the few things I spoke of that Mrs. Whaley and Mrs. Larry rescued. They tried to get more but couldn't. I have been to the Salvation Army places, and seen the men and women "highest up." They have <u>promised</u> to try to find as many books as they can. I spent some hours in their book store going over books, but found nothing. I told the head and manager of the store how shamefully you had been robbed of these things, and he said he would do all that he could to get them back. I shall go there from time to time....[261]

What Mrs. Cartwright shipped to Phebe constituted the surviving records of Phebe's life, and the loss of her diaries and correspondence leaves a void never to be filled. The breakup of her apartment without her permission meant she would be forced to live with Edward Santee, the person who had robbed her of her possessions. If he gained access to her funds, he could make his home her prison. In her farewell sermon to the First Universalist Church of Jersey City in 1877, Rev. Phebe Hanaford had proclaimed, *"I trust strength will be given me to preach Christ as long as I live..."* She was not able to spend her last years preaching. She lost her freedom as well as most of her possessions. She lost her lifelong battle for independence.

261   Hanaford Family Archives

During Ellen Miles' illness Phebe had remained informed about, if no longer actively involved in, the suffrage movement, now energized by Alice Paul. Alice Paul started the National Woman's Party in 1916, separating from the National American Woman Suffrage Association headed by Carrie Chapman Catt. With no one with whom to share her views on issues that were of great interest to her, Phebe wrote letters to associates in New York. Friends from Sorosis wrote that the Federation of Woman's Clubs had endorsed woman's suffrage for the first time.

Suffering from the pain in her arm resulting from a fall on the ice in Manhattan, she frequently wrote to Helen Feasel, Maria Hanaford's daughter.

> *213 Goundry St.*
> *North Tonawanda New York*
> *Oct. 1, 1914*
>
> *My dear Great-Granddaughter,*
> *I enclose with this a little volume which I hope you will enjoy, and find it a spiritual benefit to you. If your father and mother are willing, I very much desire that you would everyday read the text for that day at the table just before or just after your dear little brother says "Grace." I very much enjoyed hearing him, and I should doubly enjoy (if I were there) when both of you took part in that reverential remembrance of Our Father in Heaven, whose blessing we all desire should rest upon the family.*
>
> *With much love to your father and mother, and to you and Willie, I remain*
> > *Your Great-Grandmother*
> > *Phebe. A. Hanaford*[262]

---

262   Ibid

The heavy silence in the childless Santee home created a morbid atmosphere. How much this affected Phebe's health cannot be determined but within the year Mrs. Leach, a widow, and her young daughter, Ruby, became Phebe's companions. On November, 27, 1914 Phebe penned a letter to her granddaughter, Maria Feasel, from Tonawanda.

Never think Grandma forgets you or ceases to love you and yours very dearly because you do not hear from a Grandma who misses your loving words, and kindness, such as I seldom or never hear in this house. Your postal speaking of "enclosure," and the next letter enclosing Miss Whaley's were neither of them shown to any one here.

We have had various matters keeping us busy. So that my letters have not been sent even when I have had hands warm enough to hold open and write them, for I have been unwilling to trust them to Thomas because he is not always wide awake, and might forget to mail them, and I never trust Herbert willingly. While he was ill in his room, I wrote little. When he went to St. Louis, I had a chance to get Dio to take them, when she went every night to mail letters to him. Now he is in Buffalo Hospital, and every day she goes over in the morn (at 10 am) and stays most of the day. His appendix was removed last Wednesday—and he is doing well. I think he sleeps a good deal—eats little. We had Thanksgiving chicken yesterday. (Mrs. Leach cooked nicely) but Dio was not here at noon. Mrs. Leach went over to Buffalo after her and Ruby and Tom stayed with me awhile. Then Tom went off and was not here at supper time; but Dio came with Mrs. Leach, and so we had supper with Dio at last. Now about Miss Whaley. I sent the letter to her as I thought you wished me to, and I enclosed a note. She wrote me today; I enclose her letter in this. Keep it, dear. And let me know what you have to pay for freight. She has not yet told me what she paid for my clock. (Emily Ruggles of Reading gave it to me. When I get to you again, I'll have it repaired.) I long to be with somebody who loves me, and will say so—I am lonely, and sad, nights especially. I miss my own daughter, and miss my faithful, untiring friend. She loved me. I will try to write to you oftener, but I am lame again, and it has been hard to get my letters safely mailed.

He never told me that Miss Whaley bought my clock. Fred would scorn to treat me so. I trust and love Fred but how can I the other? Do you hear from Lennie? I mean to write him more. (But I have hated to tell him how I have been robbed.) I send him and you papers often.

Love to you my dear, Maria and yours, all of them,

Grandma

Thanks for the Thanksgiving card. Dio got hers also.[263]

Phebe wrote again to Maria on December 26, 1914.

My beloved Granddaughter,

My Maria did not forget us at Christmas time. The box you sent waited in my room until Christmas morning and when I went down to breakfast I took it down, and we opened it and bestowed the contents on the fortunate ones. All are thankful, all were pleased. But I think I had the most and best whether I deserved it or not. The apron and the bag are beautiful and use-ful, and I hope to have both in use when I make my appearance

---

263   Ibid

in Henrietta again, with our dear Dionis. She will probably write to you, and thank you for herself. I thank you all for mine, Fred & Maria & Helen & Willie. Dear little fellow, that Willie! How sweet it was for him to say "grace"! I enclose a card I rec'd today, because it made me think of him, the moment I saw it, and I thought he would enjoy possessing it and show- ing it to his little comrades. The lady who sent it to me is the daughter of Lucy Stone and Henry B. Blackwell. Did I tell you, Maria, that I had a letter from Antoinette Brown Blackwell enclosing a ten dollar check, and a letter from Cornelia Post both in New Jersey now, enclosing another check of the same amount. How kind my far off friends are! I wonder if Auntie Nell whispered to them to thus remember one she never forgot! I believe she and my son and daughter have been near me at this Xmas time, for I have thought of them and your dear mother and my sisters and brothers and nieces, and oh! So many other relatives and friends who are on the other side! When shall we all keep Xmas together again?

Do let me know, Maria, if you got the box! While I was gone to the Club Dio and H. nailed up the box. And put in some dishes, I think. I hope they did not disturb anything I put in. I have more that I want you to have—books also. Oh I do wish you could come with a big trunk! I have so many letters to write, I must close. I will write soon again.

Love to Fred and the children and Mother Feasel and all your loving friends. Grandma[264]

Before the end of her first year in Tonawanda, Phebe received a letter from Booker T. Washington.

---

264   Ibid

The Tuskegee
Normal and Industrial Institute
For the training of
COLORED YOUNG MEN AND WOMEN
TUSKEGEE INSTITUTE, ALABAMA

December 11, 1914
Rev. Phebe A. Hanaford
President, New Century Study Circle,
230 W. 95th Street
New York City

My dear Madam:
I hope you will excuse me for the liberty I am taking in asking you, if you think it wise, to place the following matter before the members of your Woman's Club.

We have found by experience that we can use good pictures, either new or old, framed or unframed, to the best advantage in the education of our students. If the pictures are unframed they can be framed in our shops by the students. We can also, where necessary, pay the express charges.

I thought that there might be not a few of your members who would like to help us in this way.

Yours very truly,
Booker T. Washington
Principal[265]

In further correspondence from her friends in Manhattan, Phebe learned they had recovered her picture of Charlotte

---

265   Ibid

Cushman. She directed them to make a gift of it to the Professional Woman's League and wrote a letter to accompany her gift. In mail forwarded from New York, Phebe received a typewritten letter from the President of the Professional Woman's League dated 13 January, 1915.

Dear Madam:
I have read with deepest interest your letter which accompanied your generous gift of the picture of Charlotte Cushman to the Professional Woman's League, and I shall have great pleasure in displaying a copy of it along with the picture as it hangs upon our walls, knowing that it will have equally great interest for every member of our Club.
We are most grateful to you for this thoughtful gift, and beg you to accept our sincere assurance that your own noble life spent so largely in behalf of Womankind, is as great an inspiration and moral uplift to us all as that of your distinguished friend the famous actress whose memory we so lovingly and reverently cherish.
Very sincerely yours,
Maida Craigen[266]

These letters call to mind the work Phebe would never again be allowed to continue. Santee's move to Genesee County brought Phebe away from the limited civilization available in Tonawanda. They moved to Basom where Phebe would live "on a farm." Once settled in Basom, Phebe wrote letters to friends, notifying them of her new location. She received a response from Mrs. Haryot Holt Dey, President of the Woman's Press

---

266   Ibid

Club, addressing her "Honorary President" and expressing an interest in visiting her.

Phebe also received a letter from the National Society of New England Women.

My dear very much loved friend,
Something in your letter brought to my mind the little poem which I enclose—Perhaps it may say to you all that I would gladly write of comfort and hope—We miss you dear, very, very much, and as you know no New England meeting passes without our singing the sweet words you wrote for us when I was President of the National Society. You see I cling to the thought that I was not a Colony President only! I hope that by this time you are settled in your new home, and that the light may be shining through the clouds! It seems now that so many moves have been necessary. Why has it been so? There must be a purpose—and there may be a mission for you in the new neighborhood—and I <u>know</u> you will find and fulfill it. I am enclosing the check and remember that every penny means love and sisterhood! I have not seen Belle Lehman lately—should have been to see her but have not been very well lately and have not been out a great deal.

If there is any one you particularly wish to hear about just ask me when you write again, and I'll tell you "all I know." Don't work too hard—save your strength for we want you with us many years yet.

With heartiest love—yours
Sara A. Palma
July 1st [267]

---

267   Ibid

A notation added to this letter years later, reputed to be written by Phebe's great-granddaughter, Helen Feasel Maxwell, reads, "After this (soon after) that despicable Santee with Dio's consent wrote to Mrs. Scudder (an old rival & enemy of P.A.H's) and got all checks sent to them saying she did not pay for her board."[268] On July 5, 1916 Phebe wrote to her granddaughter Maria Feasel in Henrietta that she had received Nantucket flowers from her grandniece, Marion Coffin on the occasion of her eighty-seventh birthday. Bemoaning her fate, Phebe wrote to Maria of her unhappy life on a farm far from civilization.

> *Basom, Genesee Co. N.Y.*
> *July 26, 1916*

My precious Maria,

I am quite put out with an individual called "P. A. H." because after you had yourself corrected her notion that Lennie's birthday came before yours (because he really is older) I never sent you one thing for a birthday present—and, til your letter came did not realize my mistake.

Well, I'm not as young as I was before your dear father was born, and I am now so old and often so forlorn and lonely that I wonder that I write to anybody or remember anything. I do <u>not</u> like living on a farm—I do not like being out of the world in the bushes. I am too far away from civilization and refinement, and I have <u>no</u> companionship at all. Each one here has his and her own mate—or cares not for anybody. I will not say anymore, but I do think I would rather live in Henrietta a 100 times sooner than here. I would like to help Henrietta to a gift from Carnegie and a public library and museum, thereafter such as I do feel might be accomplished. What I need first is a

---

268   Ibid

talk with you, and I feel as if Fred would unite with you and me in regard to it.

But first, I want to send you a token of remembrance and love for your birthday. No matter if it is late. I think I will enclose a V. in this, and if you think best to give one dollar to the fund for the Cousins, do so with my love — and one to that blessed little Helen for her music — do so. And ask dear Maria to spend the rest for herself. If it brings her to me "some glad day" after Fred gets back, and visitors are gone, I shall be glad. There will be more for Maria "some glad day." Give my love to your husband, Fred. He has treated me like a gentleman, and there are men who have not even the instincts of a gentleman. I long for Henrietta, Nantucket, or Heaven. I am lonely here. Yet I feel that the dear Lord would let me go to Maria. When I can talk with you, I will say more. But I love Dio, and wish I could be happy in this forlorn place. She may be happier than I, with such companionship. I am lonely and alone, I am happier with you and yours.

The desk that I had in Tonawanda (which you saw) was given to dear Nellie by our Sunday School, and when I no longer need it, I want dear Helen to have it — but I want to be sure that it goes to her. Nellie long ago gave it to me, because she could not use it, and my desk was not with us. I hope to write my three books on it, but I want to write them in Henrietta, I can get them published in Rochester. But I think New York had better have "Sorosis Memories." (The Nantucket publishers have expressed interest in publishing my poems, and some here. It seems to me Boston is the place for my "Reminiscences of the First Woman Ordained in New England.")

I am delighted to know "all are recovering," as you wrote. Do they go to school yet? P. A. H.[269]

---

269   Ibid

The Hanaford Family Archives do not contain correspondence from Helen, Maria or Dio. With no mail from Henrietta we are left without any understanding of why Phebe's repeated requests to live in Henrietta were not acknowledged. Phebe's letters show her love for Helen's grandmother, Mary Landerkin Hanaford and her love for her grandchildren. Her letter to thirteen year old Helen on July 5, 1916 included a picture of Sancoty Head, north of Siasconset on Nantucket Island. Phebe wrote: "I think the children love me—I know I love them, and it will be a joy to me to do for them, and for all."[270] She was keen on Helen's writing ability, reminding her "rhyming ability runs in the Coffin Family." Phebe let Helen know that she was proud of her ability to compose in prose or verse and would be glad to read any of the stories, or other compositions, that she might write. She wanted the children to know the history of the Coffin family.

The removal of her possessions from her New York apartment by her grandson-in-law, Mr. Santee, with whom she was forced to live, added to Phebe's distress. As expressed in her correspondence, her desire was to live with the family in Henrietta, a place where they "could share so many things." In April she wrote to Helen, "I wish I was near enough to you to run in and see you every day."[271] An invitation to visit Henrietta never came. Springtime brought some sign of acceptance of life on the farm when Phebe wrote to Maria of "the lovely flocks of chickens and 8 kittens, they are all new along with a lovely Collie dog and puppies, horses, cows, pigs, plenty and nice."

New York, long a bulwark of resistance to woman's suffrage, approved legislation allowing women to vote in the elec-

---

270   Ibid
271   Ibid

tions for the governor of New York State. Who but themselves understood how the suffragists who lived to see this day felt as they voted in the gubernatorial elections across the country? A note from Alice Stone Blackwell to Mrs. Hanaford written in November 1920 referring to her "privilege since 1917" indicates that Phebe Hanaford had voted in 1918.

Phebe's sadness over America's entrance into the war in Europe is evidenced in her letter written March 2, 1918.

To Rev. Antoinette Brown Blackwell
Dear Sister in the Gospel Ministry,
I have been intending to write you a long letter, but the days go by and I accomplish little with my pen. Yet I ought not to complain of having a lame arm, when that is so little compared with the trouble you have with your eyes. If I were near you, I would gladly read to you and often write for you, and I have had proof, as you know, that dear Lucy Stone's splendid daughter could and does write sometimes for you. I have been wanting to write a letter of thanks to her for some very highly praised verses which she has sent me on Christmas and Valentine's cards. But I do not know her address. Can you tell me? Yesterday I received a letter from a lady who is Ninety one years old (Mrs. Fanny C. Pratt now living in Winthrop, Mass.). She used to know dear Nellie Miles in Randolph, Mass. long years ago. It was dear Nellie's birthday yesterday. She was born March 1ˢᵗ, 1835. I was born May 6, 1829. So there were some years between us. Mrs. Pratt wrote very lovingly of Nellie, and I always heard Nellie speak in praise of Mrs. Pratt. They corresponded frequently to the last of Nellie's sojourn on earth. I have not got accustomed to her absence yet, she was like a wise and loving Sister to me for the long period of forty-four years.

I often wonder what she would say if she was with us now in these War days.

My Quaker birth and early training make me averse to human bloodshed, but I mean to be patriotic as I did in the Civil War when I longed for the freedom of every slave. Now women are also free. Of course I am glad the ballot is given at last to New York women, and I wonder that Massachusetts delays. As a descendent of a Pilgrim, I long for Right to prevail over Might in every State. As a Nantucketer, I rejoice that the ballot was given to women for school committee voting, but I do hope Mass. will imitate New York, and soon secure the vote to women as well as to men.

You and Lucy Stone were faithful to the Cause of Woman, and have a right to a place in the success of all labours for human rights. And Alice is gifted with the ability and is following nobly in the footsteps of her lovely mother. The first time I ever heard dear Lucy Stone was on Nantucket over sixty years ago. I was passing the Unitarian Church, and was told she was there speaking. I went in to the door, and stayed only a few moments, for I was then married to a Baptist who did not feel in harmony with Lucy Stone's ideas. But I lived to understand and accept the views which that dear pioneer held, and long years afterward, I preached the Gospel from that same pulpit. If I had known when her birthday was celebrated, I would gladly have written a rhythmic contribution for the occasion.

Pardon this poor writing, dear Antoinette, for my arm is aching from that fall in 1910. I do not expect a reply, but I shall keep on loving you, and remain your grateful friend,

  Phebe A. Hanaford[272]

272 Schlesinger Library

In preparation for her eighty-ninth birthday Phebe sent eighty-five announcements. She added the responses to her collection of correspondence. In an interview for *The Daily News, Batavia* the reporter asked Phebe about living on Pleasant Hill Farm, and Phebe revealed something of her humor. "Pleasant Hill Farm is a place where I am reminded of the saying, 'God made the country, and man made the town.'" She went on to detail the beauty of the country, never referring to how isolated she felt. Extracts from the lengthy article copyrighted by J.G. McJury are quoted here.

THE REV. PHEBE A. HANAFORD, 89 TODAY, MINISTER, LECTURER, AUTHOR AND POET, OBSERVING BIRTH ANNIVERSARY AT BASOM

The Rev. Phebe A. Hanaford, the distinguished Universalist minister, the first woman ordained in the New England States, just fifty years ago, and who is now a resident of Genesee county, observed the 89th anniversary of her birth today at the home of her granddaughter, Mrs. E. H. Santee, at Pleasant Hill Farm near Basom, in the town of Alabama, about seven miles northwest of Oakfield. Mrs. Hanaford is known throughout the United States as a minister of the gospel and as a writer of prose and poetry. Some of her books have reached a sale of 20,000 copies. Her "Women of the Century" and lives of George Peabody and Abraham Lincoln are among her best known works. Mr. and Mrs. Santee entertained in honor of Mrs. Hanaford this afternoon. Many friends attended the reception.

Mrs. Hanaford's Career

On December 2, 1849, she was married to Dr. Joseph H. Hanaford of Cape Cod who was a teacher in Nantucket schools. Dr. Hanaford was a writer as well as a physician, having written several books for his profession and contributed articles to numerous medical journals. Mrs. Hanaford taught school early in life and studied for the ministry (Universalist). She was the first woman ordained in New England States, her ordination taking place at Hingham, Mass. and preached in the united parish of Waltham and Hingham Mass.

Working now on three New Books

Mrs. Hanaford's health is remarkably good. She is very particular as to what food she eats and does not believe in medicine, "which," her companion says, "is probably one of the main reasons for her good health and long life."...

Member of Many Clubs

Mrs. Hanaford belongs to a number of clubs, including Sorosis, which she and her daughter, Mrs. Warner, joined together in 1872. Mrs. Hanaford was elected vice-president of Sorosis and was acting president the entire year in the absence of Mrs. Charlotte Wilbour, the president. She is an honorary president of the Women's Press Club of New York City, and a member of the Society of New England Women...[273]

---

273   May 6, 1918

The party proved a pleasant occasion and pictures show Maria and Helen Feasel attended with other invited guests. When Santee fell behind on the mortgage for the farm, Phebe, in spite of her distaste for farm life and Santee's personal treatment of her, tried to get him financial help. In January 1919 she wrote to Rev. Marshall asking him for a loan of three hundred dollars.

Basom, Genesee Co.
RFD 5 Box 53
Jan. 7, 1919
To Rev. Harold Marshall,
Dear Brother in the ministry,
I little thought when I resided in Beverly, Mass. and my children went to school there, and your dear parents, and many other kind and dear friends resided there that the time would ever come when I should write you such a letter as it is my duty to write today.
I have already written a letter to you congratulating our Publishing House upon being favored. In other words, I need just now the sum of three hundred dollars, and if the Committee in charge of the Pub. House can let me borrow that sum, and save our home, I will gladly repay it in future. Please do help me in this time of need. We have men and women in our Churches who have the means, but I do not wish to make public the matter. I trust you, and hope for a speedy and comforting reply. Please confer with the right persons, and help me as far as possible. With love to your dear mother and all friends, yours in Christian hope and love,
Phebe A. Hanaford

P.S. My books have all brought more money than $300, but I am not at all sorry to have our Publishing House receive a larger sum than that.

The "Rhythmic Utterances" are poems I wrote for and delivered at Buchnell College and Westbrook Seminary, and others are numerous enough (with those longer poems) to make a good-sized volume. The little book which I wrote for the Methodist Publishing House years ago ("The Captive Boy of Tierra del Fuego") brought me a large sum, and all my books have well paid me for my efforts.

I am working now on one book to be called "Sorosis Memories" which I feel sure Sorosis will buy to my satisfaction, and another book of "Reminiscences" which may sell.

I received the "Leader" today and was delighted once more to see Mary Livermore and myself, side by side. So it will be when we get to the Father's House with its many mansions, of which our dear Lord spoke.

Cordially yours, P. A. H.[274]

His response to her request:

January 29, 1919

My dear Mrs. Hanaford,

I am sorry indeed to learn of your difficulties and wish I were personally so situated that I could render you greatly deserved assistance.

So far as the Publishing House is concerned, a matter of this kind would require official action by the Board of Directors. Such has been the stress of war times and other difficulties that I have tried vainly since September to get a quorum at one of our regular or special meetings, and I am quite sure it would be hopeless to try to bring men from all over New England to consider a specific proposal of this character.

Nor could I give you much assurance of a favorable reply in any event.

Yours truly, your friend,

H. Marshall[275]

Happier news came for the New Year with greetings from Lucy Stone's daughter. She refers to Phebe as a "shining light among women ministers in the days when they were few. Alice Stone Blackwell." Her postcard written from St. Louis on March 27, 1919 again pays tribute to Phebe. "Dear Mrs. Hanaford, While attending the National Suffrage Convention, I think of the pioneers who have been lighted towers in the darkness, like yourself. Yours with grateful remembrance, Alice Stone Blackwell." An undated postcard reads, "These bright lanterns, many hued shedding each a cheerful ray, show the many kinds of light you have cast upon life's way. May they throw a rainbow sheen— round your path on Halloween. Alice Stone Blackwell."

Phebe wrote a lengthy letter on the first of May to her dear granddaughter, Maria. "My ninety years will be summed up on the 6th of May." She described the plans for the day to be shared with her companion, Mrs. Leach, and Dionis at the home of Ruby's music teacher. Mailing packages with gifts such as she wanted to send to Maria and Lennie always proved difficult. "I can hardly write today for the pain in my right arm. Dio types

---

275   Ibid

my poems which I intend to publish. Two books of poems are nearly finished."

The birthday celebration rejuvenated Phebe and she answered her birthday greetings. She delighted in answering letters asking her for family history. Although the Nantucket Athenium could not confirm this ancestry, nonetheless, Phebe passed it on to the children. On September 5, 1919 she wrote from "her bright sunny room in Basom."

You are probably aware of the fact that the great Dr. Franklin of Revolutionary days was your relative, for his mother was born on Nantucket, and you and I are descendents from two of Peter Folger's children. Grandmother Love Barnard was from his son Eleaser and Henry Barnard from a daughter, Dorcas.[276]

With the postwar economic conditions, Mr. Santee found work in Kodak Park. In 1919. the family moved into a duplex at 380 Pullman Avenue in Rochester, New York. Mrs. Leach and Ruby came with them. The move freed Phebe from the isolation of the farm and placed her close to Maria and Helen in Henrietta. Along with presents she had received at her birthday party, Phebe brought her travel bag containing the collie skin given to her when her favorite pet and constant companion had died in Basom. With Ellen's picture and the few remaining tokens of better days, Phebe established her domain, however small.

Members of the press recognized the name Phebe Hanaford, who had recently moved to Rochester. When *The Rochester Herald* phoned, Phebe agreed to an interview. Taken by Phebe's pleasant appearance and manner, the reporter noted "her lavender scarf worn about her shoulders, an exquisite bit of black lace

276   Ibid

creeping from her sleeve and a scrap of a dainty black lace cap from which silver curls escaped on all sides and a black velvet gown, the waist of which was beaded in silver." This was the way Phebe wished the world to remember her. In her press interviews, Phebe concealed the grief and privation Mr. Santee's robbery had inflicted on her during her retirement years.

Was First Woman to Be Ordained, and First Legislative Chaplain

She has always been active in women's clubs and literary circles, and was the first woman to be ordained in the New England States, as well as the first woman chaplain of a Legislature, serving in that capacity in New Haven, Connecticut about 1870. "I am proud of the fact that I was the first woman preacher from New England and I also regret the fact. There should have been women preachers before my time." She rode nine miles over rough country roads last year to cast her first vote.

Having voted in the 1918 gubernatorial elections, Phebe told the reporter that she looked now with confidence on the future of women in the ministry and said she would still be willing to preach. As always she named her friends, Antoinette Brown Blackwell, Mary Livermore and Julia Ward Howe. She told of the night she had spent with Susan B. Anthony years ago in Rochester. She also told a story, not found elsewhere, of refusing to shake hands with Governor Theodore Roosevelt because of a difference in opinion, only to have him grasp both of her hands and shake them.

At ninety-one years of age Phebe still kept a diary. In her entry of May 18, 1920, she described her birthday.

My 91st birthday was very kindly remembered with flowers from Marion Coffin Folger,—my grand niece (my brother George's granddaughter), and the trailing Arbutus—
I was glad to see Nantucket May Flowers. Flowers in a pretty basket also came from the Rochester florist, sent from the Universalist Ladies.
My granddaughter Maria sent a book and Dionis and her family here all did a great many kind things for me on that day.[277]

In June Phebe attended the Lake Baptist Church. It proved to be her last public appearance. Within weeks of her birthday the Susan B. Anthony Amendment passed both houses of Congress. It now remained for thirty-six states to ratify it. In August 1920 the Susan B. Anthony Amendment became law with Tennessee becoming the thirty-sixth state to adopt the nineteenth amendment. Of the earliest pioneers still living, Antoinette Brown Blackwell, Olympia Brown and Phebe Hanaford, all three were ministers.

In contrast to Antoinette Brown Blackwell who went to the polls escorted by her daughter on November 2, 1920, there is no evidence in the Rochester voting records that Phebe Hanaford voted in the first federal election open to women. There is also no record of Dionis or Edward Santee voting. Voting would have represented the culmination of her life's work since the founding of the Equal Rights Association. Phebe Hanaford's mind remained clear and, with reasonable physical assistance, she might have cast her ballot, recording her name for future students of women's history. It is impossible to describe her feelings, sitting in her room on that memorable day.

Phebe received a letter from Lucy Stone's daughter, Alice Stone Blackwell, written from Boston on November 2, 1920.

---

277   Ibid

Dear Mrs. Hanaford:
It gives me real pleasure today to think that you will be voting—although you have had that privilege since 1917, while I exercise it today for the first time. But in thinking of the women to whom we owe it, you come to my mind & my grateful thoughts go out to you.
Cordially,
Alice Stone Blackwell[278]

It is interesting to note that in her biography of her mother, *Lucy Stone, Pioneer of Woman's Rights* (1930), Alice Stone Blackwell does not mention Phebe Hanaford.

Before the Thanksgiving holiday, Phebe received a visit from Mrs. Haryot Holt Dey, the President of the Woman's Press Club. Dismayed at Phebe's living conditions, on her return to New York she discussed Phebe's situation with the Executive Committee of the Woman's Press Club. They agreed to have a fundraiser for their honorary president. Phebe's financial situation became public information when the newspapers announced the benefit. This proud and independent woman who had supported herself and her children for years, now, through no fault of her own, became the object of charity. The news article in the *New York Tribune*, December 19, 1920 disheartened her. With a shaky hand Phebe wrote next to the print "Did you see this?"

Phoebe (sic) Hanaford, Pioneer Suffragist, Is Penniless
Women's Press Club to Give a Benefit for Her
At the Waldorf on December 28
The Rev. Phoebe Hanaford, pioneer woman minister and comrade of Lucretia Mott and Susan B. Anthony in the

278   Ibid

early days of the suffrage movement, is penniless at the age of ninety-three (sic).

The Woman's Press Club has undertaken to raise a fund to supply the aged woman with physical comforts for the winter, and for this purpose will hold a benefit at the Waldorf Astoria on December 28.

Mrs. Harriet (sic) Holt Dey, its president, revealed the facts of Mrs. Hanaford's needs to members of the club.

After a lifetime spent in working for the woman's movement, in writing and lecturing on subjects then far from popular or remunerative, Mrs. Hanaford is now entirely dependent upon the charity of her granddaughter and her husband in Rochester, N.Y. The young couple are said to be devoted to Mrs. Hanaford, but they have five children, and a very small income.

The Rev. Phoebe Hanaford was born on the Island of Nantucket on May 6, 1829. She taught school there until the inspiration of the woman's movement stirred her and she began to study for the ministry. She was ordained in the Universalist Church in Hingham, Mass., the first woman minister in New England.

The following day *The Jersey Journal* picked up on the news.

PHEBE HANAFORD, ONCE PREACHER HERE IN WANT

Old-time friends in this city of Rev. Phebe Hanaford were surprised and grieved to read that she is in want. Mrs. Hanaford, who was a pioneer in suffrage work and one of the first women preachers in this country, was pastor of the Universalist Church in this city for some years, and there are living here today many of her former parishioners and also many men and women who used often to hear her preach. Mrs. Hanaford left this city a good many years ago, and only a few of the many who were of her congregations were aware she was still alive. She is in her 93rd year and according to the Woman's Press Club is in want. So much so that the Press Club has arranged a benefit for her at the Waldorf Dec. 28.

Mrs. Hanaford is dependent on a granddaughter, whose home is in Rochester, N.Y., and although this relative, according to the Press Club's president, is willing to do all in her power for Mrs. Hanaford, her resources are limited, as she and her husband are young, have a small income and five children.

She was identified with the first Universalist Society in Jersey City from 1874-1877 when she resigned from that society to identify herself as preacher to the second Universalist Society, which she served until 1884. The rupture from the first Society occurred because of serious differences in opinion on the subject of woman's suffrage and other subjects. Mrs. Hanaford had more advanced views than most women of her time and stood with the foremost of the day, a thing more difficult to do then than it is today. Everybody is a Lincoln man now!

The article contained much misinformation gleaned from *The New York Times*. It remains a mystery how the childless Santees could have given the impression of being a young couple with five children.

The benefit held at the Waldorf Astoria Hotel on December 28, 1920 for the Woman's Press Club's Philanthropic Fund remained under the management of Lettie D'Angelo Bergh. The funds raised in 1920 were shared with Ruth B. Chamberlain, a graduate of the University of Rochester. Miss Chamberlain was the beneficiary of the first Woman's Press Club scholarship in the Pulitzer School of Journalism. Phebe Hanaford received $50 each month for the remaining days of her life. Later described, "of all of our activities philanthropically, our contribution to the comfort of our Honorary President in her last days has given us more pleasure and satisfaction than anything."[279]

The Rochester Herald published a lengthy article under the headline,

MRS. PHEBE ANN HANAFORD

A Mighty Social Force in the Civil War Times and the First Woman Minister Ordained in New England, Now Approaching Her Ninety-second Birthday

A year ago last November there came to Rochester a woman who as an American minister, clubwoman and writer is known to women the world over, Rev. Phebe Ann Coffin Hanaford. Since her arrival here, Mrs. Hanaford has been living with relatives at 380 Pullman avenue. Only once before she came here to live, had she visited this city, and that was to spend the night with Susan B. Anthony, a friend whose memory is exceedingly dear to Mrs. Hanaford, who calls her "a very delightful woman, who lived, perhaps a little before her time." Because she was one of those women who dared to blaze the trail for

279   Columbia University

the self-reliant, independent woman of to-day, the gracious, charming-mannered woman whose many years have brought only grace and dignity—she will be 92 years old next month—watches eagerly the affairs of women all over the country, and through them lives again the full years of her early life, when she preached and wrote.

When Mrs. Hanaford was interviewed by a reporter from the Herald, one was impressed chiefly by the fact that she is not one of those persons who having arrived at a ripe old age, is content to live in the past. She is eager to know all the news, is interested in all that is taking place in Rochester, and looks forward to the happenings of each new day. Hers is a young heart, and young people have a peculiar attraction for her.

She chatted in a voice sweetened with age like a fine old Stradivarius, telling of her youth and pleasant incidents of her life that marked off the 91 years.

What is considered by literary critics to be one of the most appealing and appreciated biographies of Lincoln, was written by Mrs. Hanaford and published in Boston in 1865.[280]

The article accurately listed twelve of her books with publication dates. In the interview Phebe told the reporter one of her warmest friends was Julia Ward Howe, and she also spoke of Rev. Olympia Brown, her mentor in the ministry. The article concluded with the biographical text of Phebe Hanaford from *Appleton's Cyclopedia of American Biography* (1888).

With the usual rain of spring, the doctor confirmed that Mrs. Hanaford suffered from severe congestion of the lungs.

---

280   April 17, 1921, p. 35

She recovered well enough to enjoy a quiet celebration of her ninety-second birthday on 6 May where she made it known she wanted to live to be a hundred years old. The weakness that resulted from her recent illness lasted through the month of May, and her heart proved unable to maintain the life she wished to prolong.

Phebe Hanaford died on June 2, 1921, one month after her ninety-second birthday. The register of death identifies her as "housewife" and the chief cause of death "Senility and arteriosclerosis and chronic endocarditis." The cause of death on the death certificate from the New York State Department of Health reads, "chronic endocarditis."

The Rochester Democrat and Chronicle wrote on 3 June, 1921:

Phebe Hanaford
DIES AFTER LIFE OF ACTIVE WORK
Minister, Suffragist and Writer Many Years
EDITED TWO PUBLICATIONS

Nationally known in days following Civil War— Descendant of Pilot of Mayflower—Related to Prominent Women—Funeral

Rev. Phebe A. Hanaford, Universalist minister, writer, a pioneer in the movement for equal rights and a contemporary of Susan B. Anthony and early woman suffrage leaders died yesterday morning at 8 o'clock at the home of her granddaughter, Mrs. E. H. Santee, No. 380 Pullman avenue. Up to a few months ago Mrs. Hanaford had been in unusually good health and her mind bright and active. She had apparently recovered from an attack of congestion of the lungs. The funeral will take place at

1 o'clock tomorrow afternoon from the home of her grand-daughter in Pullman avenue, and burial will be made in the Orleans cemetery. Rev. William Wallace Rose, D.D., minister of the First Universalist Church, of Rochester, will officiate at the services.

Following an extensive biographical sketch, the obituary continued.

NATIONALLY KNOWN SUFFRAGIST

...Mrs. Hanaford was best known nationally for her association with all of the leading suffragists of the period when the movement was being pushed forward slowly from one outpost to another at a time when the dawn of equal rights was obscure. Among her acquaintances then were Susan B. Anthony, Elizabeth Cady Stanton, Lucretia Mott, Mary A. Livermore, Julia Ward Howe, Francis Willard, Isabel Beecher Hooker, Anna Herbert Shaw, and Lucy Stone...[281]

The Rochester Herald under the heading "WAS PIONEER IN WOMAN'S MOVEMENT" described her as one of the last pioneers of the woman's movement and one of the last of the pioneer women ministers in the country. Repeating much of her life story, they concluded with a list of survivors.

Besides Mrs. Santee, Mrs. Hanaford leaves one other granddaughter, Mrs. Fred Feasel of Henrietta, and a grandson, Charles L. Hanaford of Gardner, Mass., her only son and only daughter having died some years

---

281   June 3, 1921, p. 15

ago. She leaves a niece, Phebe Ann Small, of Nantucket and two great grandchildren, Helen Feasel and William Feasel. There is also surviving, her son-in-law, Thomas Warner, of Canandaigua.[282]

The New York Times obituary:

Rev. Phebe A. Hanaford
Suffragist Was the First Woman Minister Ordained in New England

Rochester, N.Y. June 2—The Rev. Phebe A. Hanaford, the first woman minister ordained in New England, the second in the United States and the fourth in the world, died here today at the home of her granddaughter at the age of 92... All forms of feminine advancement she supported. "I was born a suffragist." She had been President of the Woman's Press Club and Vice President of Sorosis.[283]

The *Clifton Springs Press* added a detail not recorded in the Rochester papers. "Members of the family heard the noise of a fall upstairs about 7:30 o'clock, but thought the noise was in another room and did not investigate. Later they went upstairs and found Mrs. Hanaford dead in her room."[284]

---

282   June 3, 1921
283   June 3, 1921, p. 15, col. 3
284   June 3, 1921

AFTERWORD

I know that I must die.
Like withered leaf by chill autumn blast,
Swept from parent-stem, I too must lie
Where all shall lie at last.[285]

Funeral arrangements for Phebe Hanaford included her burial in the Warner family plot in Orleans, New York. Phebe was laid to rest next to her daughter, Florence, whose marker reads,

FLORENCE. E.
DAUGHTER OF
REV. PHEBE HANAFORD
WIFE OF
THOMAS E. WARNER
1854 – 1902

This gesture on the part of Thomas Warner was coupled with his desire for an appropriate marker for her grave. A letter written to Thomas Warner on June 15, 1923 suggests that Mr. Warner had approached the Universalist Church in Rochester requesting a marker for Rev. Phebe Hanaford's grave.

....

285   Hanaford, Phebe A., 1871, *From Shore to Shore*, p. 239

First Universalist Church

Clifton Avenue and Court Street
Rochester, New York
William Wallace Rose - *Minister*

June 15, 1923
Mr. T.E. Warner
236 Fulton Avenue
Rochester, NY

Dear Mr. Warner:
I am very grateful for your communication received to-day concerning Mrs. Hanaford. There is no state meeting in Rochester, but I will at once take the matter up with denominational leaders and believe that something will be done in the autumn if not sooner to mark the grave of so famous and valuable a woman.

Yours sincerely,
Wm. Wallace Rose[286]

Fifteen years later in April 1938 the Ontario Association of Universalists held their 106th annual meeting in the Macedon Church in Orleans, New York. Perhaps the proximity to the cemetery elicited the recommendation for the formation of a committee to consider a marker on the grave of Rev. Phebe A. Hanaford, "first woman to be ordained into the Universalist ministry in New England." The committee included Rev. Max

---

286   First Universalist Church of Rochester, New York – Archives

Kapp, then pastor of the Universalist Church in Rochester, and Rev. Dr. Fred Leining of Syracuse, then the state superintendent. The grave remained "unrecognized" awaiting the report of the committee to be reviewed at the 1940 meeting of the Associated Universalists in Syracuse. A letter from B. Butler of Seneca Castle, New York dated September 18, 1940 addressed to Phebe's granddaughter Dionis, reports,

My dear Mrs. Santee,
The New York State Convention of Universalists is responding to the request of many and is desirous of placing a modest marker on the grave of Rev. Phebe Hanaford....If the suggestion of placing a marker on Mrs. Hanaford's grave is acceptable to you and your sister would you please affirm as much.[287]

The marker for the grave remained unfinished business until 1995 when Phebe's great-great-granddaughters, Audrey Johnson and Diane Dobbertson, the author of this biography and the Rev. Sarah Barber-Braun, UU minister, met with Elizabeth "Betsy" Straw, treasurer of Orleans Cemetery. Her linen diagram of the plots identified the unmarked grave adjacent to the grave of Florence Hanaford Warner as that of Phebe Hanaford. It was here the Rev. Sarah Barber-Braun made her promise to Phebe to erect a marker. Through Sarah's efforts as a founding member of the UU Women's Heritage Society, the Heritage Society received a grant from the New York State Convention of Universalists for the dedicatory marker.

The graveside ceremony conducted by the Rev. Sarah Barber-Braun took place on June 30, 1998 following the UUA

287   Hanaford Family Archives

General Assembly in Rochester, New York. "Friends of Phebe" at the dedication included members of the Heritage Society, the Hanaford descendents and spouses, and this author with her husband, Jim Cody. The marker, designed by Audrey Johnson and her sisters, reads,

THE REVEREND
PHEBE ANN COFFIN HANAFORD
1829-1921
ORDAINED MINISTER FEBRUARY 19, 1868
UNIVERSALIST CHURCH, HINGHAM, MASSACHUSETTS
AUTHOR, PREACHER, LECTURER
LIFELONG WORKER FOR REFORM

In recognition of the grant, the reverse side bears a plaque, which reads,

THE UNITARIAN UNIVERSALIST
WOMEN'S HERITAGE SOCIETY
ACKNOWLEDGES WITH GRATITUDE
THE GIFT OF THE MARKER FROM
THE NEW YORK STATE CONVENTION OF UNIVERSALISTS
DEDICATED JUNE 30, 1998

Loretta Cody

BIBLIOGRAPHY

BOOKS AND ARTICLES

Alcott, William A. (1972). *The young wife: or duties of woman in the marriage relation.* New York: Arno Press & The New York Times. (Published originally in 1837: Boston: George W. Light).

-----. (1972). *The physiology of marriage.* New York: Arno Press & The New York Times. (Originally published anonymously in 1855 and under the author's name in 1866).

Bacon, Margaret Hope. (1986). *Mothers of feminism: The story of Quaker women in America.* San Francisco: Harper and Row.

Bisbee, Frederick Adelbert. (1920). *1770-1920, From good luck to Gloucester: The book of the pilgrimage.* Whitefish, MT: Kessinger Publishing.

Blair, Karen J., & Baxter, Annette K. (1980). *The clubwoman as feminist: True womanhood redefined, 1868-1914.* New York: Holmes & Meier Publishers.

Bordin, Ruth Birgitta Anderson. (1981). *Woman and temperance: The quest for power and liberty, 1873-1900.* Philadelphia: Temple University Press.

Brown, Olympia. (1911). *Acquaintances, old and new, among reformers.* Milwaukee: S. E. Tate.

Burstyn, Joan N. (Ed.). (1990). *Past and promise: Lives of New Jersey women.* Compiled by the Women's Project of New Jersey. Metuchen: Scarecrow Press. (Phebe Hanaford's entry by Marta Morris Flanagan).

Cazden, Elizabeth. (1983). *Antoinette Brown Blackwell: A biography.* Old Westbury, New York: The Feminist Press.

Coffin, Louis. (1962). *The Coffin family.* Nantucket Historical Association.

Cote, Charlotte. (1988). *The battle for equality: The life of Olympia Brown.* Illinois: Mother Courage Press.

Cott, Nancy, & Peck, Elizabeth H. (1979). *A history of her own.* New York: Simon and Schuster.

Croly, Jane. (1890). *The history of the women's club movement.* New York: Henry A. Allen and Company.

Dexter, Elizabeth Anthony. (1950). *Career women of America 1776-1840.* New Hampshire: Marshall Jones Company.

Evans, Sara M. (1989). *Born for liberty: A history of women in America.* New York: The Free Press.

Faderman, Lillian. (1991). *Odd girls and twilight lovers.* New York: Columbia University Press.

-----. (Ed.). (1994). *Chloe plus Olivia: An anthology of lesbian literature from the seventeenth century to the present.* New York: Penguin.

-----. (1999). *To believe in women: What lesbians have done for America — a history.* Boston: Houghton Mifflin Company.

Forman, Henry C. (1966). *Early Nantucket and its whaling houses.* New York: Hastings House Publishers.

Fuller, Paul. E. (1975). *Laura Clay and the woman's rights movement.* Lexington, Kentucky: University of Kentucky Press.

Gilbrath, Frank. (1956). *Of whales and women.* New York: Thomas Y. Crowill and Co.

Glazier, Capt. Willard. (1886). *Peculiarities of American cities.* Philadelphia: Hubbard Brothers.

Goldsmith, Barbara. (1998). *Other powers: The age of suffrage, spiritualism, and the scandalous Victoria Woodhull.* New York: Alfred A. Knopf.

Griffith, Elisabeth. (1959). *In her own right.* New York: Oxford Press.

Hanaford, Elizabeth Neal. (1915). *Family records.* Rockford, Illinois: New England Historical and Genealogical Society.

Hanaford, Joseph. (n.d.). Alcoholic stimulation. Boston: Massachusetts Total Abstinence Society.

-----. (1883). *Mother and child*. Reading, Mass.: J. H. Hanaford, Publisher.

Hanaford, Phebe A. (n.d.). *Anti slavery reminiscences* (Handwritten notes). Unpublished. Nantucket Historical Association.

Hanaford, Phebe A. (1853). *Lucretia, the Quakeress or principle triumphant*. Boston: J. Buffum.

-----. (1857). *Diary*. (Handwritten). Unpublished. Nantucket Historical Association.

-----. (1857). *Leonette, a Sunday school book*. Unpublished.

-----. (1860). *The best of books and its history*. Philadelphia: American-Baptist Publication society.

-----. (1862). *My brother*. Cambridge, MA: John Ford and E. Robbins Publishing Company.

Hanaford, Phebe A. & Webber, Mary Trask. (1861). *Chimes of peace and union*. (No publisher information.)

Hanaford, Phebe A. (1865). *Abraham Lincoln: His life and public services*. Boston: B. B. Russell & Co.

-----. (1867). *Reciprocal duties of pastor and people*. Boston: Printed by S. O. Thayer.

-----. (1867). *The captive boy in Tierra del Fuego*. New York: Carlton & Porter.

-----. (1870). *The life of George Peabody.* Boston: D. Lothrop Company.

-----. (1870, June 5). Honor to whom honor (a sermon).

-----. (1870, December 23). Gospel peace (a sermon). Yale Divinity School Library.

-----. (1870, October 1). Connecticut Woman Suffrage Association - the annual meeting. *The Woman's Journal.*

-----. (1871). *From shore to shore and other poems.* Boston: B. B. Russell.

-----. (1871). *Life and writings of Charles Dickens.* Boston: B. B. Russell.

-----. (1871, January 8). Belshazzar's feast (a sermon). Boston: B. B. Russell.

-----. (1871, February 18). Letter from Connecticut. *The woman's journal,* p. 49, col. 4.

-----. (1871, October 15). Yesterday for the first time in the world, Wyoming put into practice the theory of female suffrage.... Ninety-three ladies voted at the polls in this city...The first being Louisa Swain. *The woman's journal.*

-----. (1874). A biographical sketch of Joanna Quiner. *Essex Institute's historical collections, vol. XII,* pp. 35-42.

-----. (1875, July 3). Mrs. Hanaford's sermon. *Woman's Journal,* p. 211.

-----. (1877). *Women of the century.* Boston: B. B. Russell.

-----. (1877). The Common People, A Sermon. Jersey City: E. R. Pollard.

-----. (1880). *The Sabbath journal* (Handwritten notes). Unpublished. Nantucket Historical Association.

-----. (1881). *Daughters of America.* Maine: True and Co.

-----. (1882). Coffin family genealogy (Handwritten). Unpublished. Nantucket Historical Association.

-----. (1884, June 2). Inaugural sermon. *The New Haven Daily Morning Journal and Courier,* p. 2, col. 2.

-----. (1890, December 27). Twenty years in the pulpit. *The woman's journal,* 414-416.

-----. (1890). *Heart of Siasconset.* New Haven: Hoggson & Robinson.

-----. (1902). Old-time school days in Nantucket or a few personal reminiscences of school days. (Handwritten notes). Unpublished. Nantucket Historical Association.

Hanson D. D., & Hanson, J. W. (1885). *Voices of Faith: A birthday book.* Boston: Universalist Publishing House.

Hanson, Eliza Rice. (1882). *Our women workers*. Chicago: The Star and Covenant Office.

Harper, Ida Husted. (1898. Reprint, 1983). *The life and work of Susan B. Anthony*. Salem, NH: Ayer Co.

Haynes, Lorenza. (1864, January 22). *Waltham Sentinel*.

Hart, Lorena, & Hart, Francis. (1867, September 20). Not all is changed: A life history of Hingham. *The Hingham Journal*, pp. 157, 184-185.

Heaton, Vernon. (1980). *The Mayflower*. New York: Webb and Bower.

Hedrick, Joan. (1994). *Harriett Beecher Stowe: A life*. New York: Oxford University Press.

Hichings, Catherine F. (1985). *Universalist and Unitarian women ministers*. The Unitarian Universalist Historical Society.

Hopkins, Barbara R. (1981). A woman of the century: the life of Phebe Ann Hanaford. (Paper written 1981 at the University of Massachusetts). Unpublished. Nantucket Historical Association.

Hoyt, Edwin P. (1978). *Nantucket, the life of an island*. Brattleboro, Vermont: Stephen Green Press.

Hyde, Lewis. (1998). *Trickster makes this world: Mischief, myth and art*. New York: Farrar, Straus and Giroux.

James, Edward T. (Ed). (1971). *Notable American women 1660-1950: A biographical dictionary, vol. 2.* Cambridge: Belknap Press of Harvard University Press.

Johnson, Allen, & Dumas, Malone (Eds.) (1980). *Dictionary of American biography, vol. 4.* New York: Charles Scribner's Sons.

Joslyn, Clyde. (n.d.). Universalism in Waltham, Mass.; 1836-1858. Unpublished.

Kerr, Andrea Moore. (1992). *Lucy Stone: Speaking out for equality.* New Brunswick, NJ: Rutgers University Press.

Kimmel, Michael S. (1992). *Against the tide: Pro-feminist men in the United States, 1776-1990.* Boston: Beacon Press.

Landmark in Nantucket's Black History Restored. (1997, January 12). *New York Times*, p. 23.

Leach, Robert J. (n.d.) Nantucket Quaker History (audio recording, recorded sometime between 1975 and 1979). Cornell University Library.

Leonard, John William (Ed.). (1914). *Who's who of America 1912-1913.* American Commonwealth Co.

Lerner, Gerda. (1979). *The majority finds its past: Placing women in history.* New York: Oxford University Press.

-----. (1993). *The creation of feminist consciousness: From the middle ages to 1870.* New York: Oxford University Press.

Livermore, Mary Ashton Rice. (1978 reprint of 1887 edition). *My story of the war: A woman's narrative of four years personal experience as nurse in the union army: and in relief work at Ho.* Williamstown, Mass.: Corner House Publishers.

Lockie, Andrew, & Geddes, Nicola. (1995). *The Complete Guide to Homeopathy.* London: Dorling Kindersley.

McCalley, John W. (1981). *Nantucket yesterday and today.* New York: Dover.

McCleary, Helen Cartwright. (1929). Phebe Ann (Coffin) Hanaford, The 100th anniversary of her birth. (Memorial Pamphlet).

McFeely, William S. (1991). *Frederick Douglass.* New York: W.W. Norton & Company.

McGoldrick, Neale & Crocco, Margaret. (1993). *Reclaiming lost ground: The struggle for woman suffrage in New Jersey,* 2nd edition. New Jersey Historical Commission (NJHC).

Miller, Russell E. (1979). *The larger hope: The first century of the universalist church in America 1770-1870.* (Vol. 1). Boston: Unitarian Universalist Association.

-----. (1985). *The larger hope: The second century of the universalist church in America 1870-1970.* (Vol. 2). Boston: Unitarian Universalist Association.

The New York Times. (1897, December 5 and 12). "Woman's Club Movement." (Illustrated Weekly Magazine).

Osterweiss, Rollin G. (1953). *Three centuries of New Haven, 1638-1938.* New Haven: Yale University Press.

Ruggles, Emily. (1866-1874). *Diary.* Unpublished. Reading Library, Reading, Massachusetts.

Rzepka, Rev. Jane. (1993). Our most sanguine expectations. (Sermon given at The Universalist Unitarian Church of Reading). Yale Divinity School Library.

Scherr, Lynn, & Kazickas, Jurate. (1994). *Susan B. Anthony slept here: A guide to American women's landmarks.* New York: Times Books/Random House.

Shaw, William H. (1884). *History of Essex and Hudson counties, New Jersey, vol. 2.* Philadelphia: Everts and Peck.

Sklar, Kathryn Kish. (1973). *Catharine Beecher: A study in American domesticity.* New York: W.W. Norton & Company.

Stanton, Elizabeth Cady. (1895). *The Woman's Bible, Part I.* New York: European Publishing Company.

-----. (1898). *The Woman's Bible, Part II.* New York: European Publishing Company.

Stanton, Elizabeth Cady, Anthony, Susan B., Gage, Matilda Joslyn, Harper, Ida Husted (Eds). (1969). *History of woman suffrage* (6 vols.). New York: Arno Press, Inc. & New York Times.

Steere, Douglass Van, & Vining, Elizabeth Gray (Eds.). (1984). *Quaker spirituality: Selected writings (Classics of Western spirituality).* New York: Paulist Press.

Tedesco, Rachel. (1998). Phebe Ann Hanaford: The years in Hingham, 1866–1869 (Term paper for course on Universalist Unitarian History at Andover Newton).

Trueblood, D. Elton. (1966). *The people called Quakers.* New York: Harper and Row.

Turner, Merle E. (1929). Nantucket Streets and Lanes. *Proceedings, Historic Nantucket,* 48-53. Nantucket Historical Association.

Van Winkle, Daniel (Ed.). (1924). *Story of municipalities of Hudson County, New Jersey 1630 - 1923 vol. 1.*

Ward, Susan Hayes (Ed.). (1894). *The Rushlight.* Boston: George H. Ellis, Printer. (Special Number in memory of Lucy Larcom)

Winefield, Charles H. (1874). *History of Hudson, New Jersey.* New York: Kennard and Hay Stationery, Manufacturer and Printing Co.

Whipple, A. B. C. (1978). *Vintage Nantucket.* New York: Dodd, Mead & Co.

Willis, Gwendolyn Brown (Ed.). (1960). Olympia Brown, An autobiography. (Reprinted in *Annual journal of the universalist historical society, vol. iv, 1963.*)

NEWSPAPERS AND PERIODICALS

Clifton Springs Press

Ladies' Home Journal

Massachusetts Total Abstinence Society

New Haven Daily Morning Journal and Courier

The American Standard (Jersey City)

The Argus (Jersey City)

The Beverly Citizen

The Boston Journal

The Daily Free Press – Tribune (Waltham, Mass.)

The Daily News (Batavia)

The Evening Journal (Jersey City)

The Evening Register

The Hingham Journal

The Jersey City Journal

The Ladies' Repository

The Leader

The Lever

The Inquirer and Mirror (Nantucket)

The New Haven Journal and Courier

The New York American

The New York Times

The New York Tribune

The Reading Daily Times (Massachusetts)

The Rochester Democrat and Chronicle

The Rochester Herald

The Sunday Press

The Woman's Journal (Boston and Chicago)

Universalist

Waltham Sentinel

ARCHIVES

Amherst College Library

Beverly Historical Society and Museum

Coffin, David. Coffin Family Database

First Universalist Church of Rochester (Rochester, New York) – Archives

Hanaford Family Archives, Pittsford, New York

Henry Huntington Library, San Marino, California

Nantucket Historical Association Research Library, MS 38 – Phebe Ann Coffin Hanaford Papers, 1848-1929

New Haven Colony Historical Society, New Haven, Connecticut

Schlesinger Library, Radcliffe College for Advanced Study, Harvard University

Sophia Smith Collection, Smith College, Northampton, Massachusetts

Stowe-Day Library, Hartford, Connecticut, Isabella Hooker Collection

Universalist Archives, Andover – Harvard Theological Library, Cambridge, Massachusetts

Unitarian Universalist Church of Reading, Massachusetts Membership Records 1857–1983

Unitarian Universalist Church of Reading, Reading Archives, 1993

Woman's Press Club of New York City Papers, Rare Books and Manuscript Library, Columbia University

Yale Divinity School Library, New Haven, Connecticut Record Group No 48, New England Church Records

INDEX OF NAMES

teacher 7, 8, 10, 19, 48, 92,
94, 95, 124, 134
temperance 25, 31, 41, 67,
100, 103, 114, 119, 185,
197, 214, 226, 279, 296,
303, 309, 364
Tonawanda, New York
270, 271, 274, 275, 277,
311, 312, 315, 348, 350,
351, 367, 368, 373, 375,
376, 378, 380, 383
Tufts School of Divinity
Ch. 5, 174
Universalism 90, 91, 93,
94, 97, 99, 122, 124, 134,
147, 150, 151, 167, 211,
212, 242, 249, 251, 255,
276, 282, 302
Universalist Convention
99, 196, 217, 218, 225,
240, 243, 285, 32
Universalist Examining
Ecclesiastical Council
115
Universalist Publishing
House 96, 113
Universalist Society 89, 95,
102, 104, 113, 125, 133,
142, 148, 150, 166, 167,
197, 202, 206, 209, 211,

212, 219, 240, 244, 249,
252, 254, 272, 286, 314,
397
University of Rochester
398
Voices of Faith 295
Waldorf Astoria 313, 333,
396, 398
Waltham, Massachusetts
98, 109, 123-25, 133,
134, 136, 137, 143, 144,
146, 147, 148, 153, 165,
195, 210, 267, 269, 270,
274, 282, 283, 285, 286,
315, 338, 339, 368-70,
388
Waterbury, Connecticut
197
Weymouth, Massachusetts
98, 112, 113, 117, 136
White Mountain 120, 137
Woman's Bible, The 329,
330, 334, 335, 337
Woman's Centenary As-
sociation 286, 287
Woman's Congress 200-
202
Woman's Journal, The 92,
143, 154, 161, 166, 171,